THE SECRET TRAIN ROBBER

The Real Great Train Robbery
Mastermind Revealed

LEE STURLEY

EBURY
PRESS

1 3 5 7 9 10 8 6 4 2

Ebury Press, an imprint of Ebury Publishing
20 Vauxhall Bridge Road
London SW1V 2SA

Ebury Press is part of the Penguin Random House group of companies
whose addresses can be found at global.penguinrandomhouse.com

Excerpt from 'Night Mail' by W.H. Auden, first written for *Night Mail* (1936)
and published in *Collected Poems* by W.H. Auden. Reproduced with kind
permission of Curtis Brown, Ltd.

Photo credits: Page 3 (top) ©Daily Herald Archive/Contributor; (middle)
©Popperfoto/Contributor; (bottom) ©Associated Newspapers/REX. Page 4
(top and bottom left) ©Keystone/Stringer; (bottom right) ©Stuart Clarke/REX.
Page 5 (top) ©Mirrorpix; (bottom left) ©PA/PA Archive/Press Association
Images; (bottom right) ©Bentley Archive/Popperfoto. Page 6 (top) ©Central
Press/Stringer; (middle) ©Harry Thompson; (bottom) ©Ian Nicholson/PA
Archive/Press Association Images. Page 7 (top) ©Associated Newspapers/REX;
(middle) ©Keystone/Staff; (bottom) ©Beverley Goodway/Daily Mail/REX.
Page 8 ©Hulton-Deutsch Collection/CORBIS

All other photos from author's collection.

First published by Ebury Press in 2015

www.eburypublishing.co.uk

A CIP catalogue record for this book is available
from the British Library

HB ISBN 9781785030123
TPB ISBN 9781785030130

Printed and bound in Great Britain by Clays Ltd, St Ives PLC

Penguin Random House is committed to a sustainable
future for our business, our readers and our planet.
This book is made from Forest Stewardship Council®
certified paper.

CONTENTS

THE UP SPECIAL NIGHT

'This is the Night Mail, crossing the border / Bringing the cheque and the postal order.' I was never much of a one for poetry but W. H. Auden's lines, to the rhythm of a steam train rattling over the points, do stick in my mind for obvious reasons. Sod the cheque and the postal order, because on the night of 7–8 August 1963 it brought £2.6 million in used notes. They weighed – ask the experts and the blokes who took them – one and a half tons.

You can read the details of the story in any one of half a dozen recent books. Except that every one of those books has missed some pretty vital details out. The removal of £2.6 million from the second coach of the English Electric Class 40 Locomotive – known as an 'Up Special' because of the direction it was travelling and what it was carrying – has come to be known as the Great Train Robbery and the Crime of the Century. You can trust a journalist to come out with headlines like that; it's their bread and butter and it sells newspapers. But in this case they were right. There had been train robberies before – and I'm not talking about Jesse

James and Butch Cassidy here – but never, *ever* had there been a heist as big as this in British history.

By the time the British Transport Commission Police drew up their report, the various pieces of evidence had been put together. You know those American cop shows on the telly where the officers of the law are all falling over each other, squabbling about jurisdiction? Is it NYPD? Is it the State Troopers? Is it the FBI? Well, it wasn't quite like that in the UK in 1963 but there was an element of it. The Transport Police were involved because it was one of their trains that was done over. The Post Office were there because it was their mailbags that had gone walkabout. The Buckinghamshire Constabulary came in because it happened on their turf. And Scotland Yard and the Met turned up because of the sheer scale of the crime that had been committed.

The Transport Police summed up the Crime of the Century in just three sentences. The train had been stopped at an unauthorised signal which had been faked with the help of a glove to cover the green light and four 6-volt Eveready dry cell batteries to keep the red signal glowing. The driver and co-driver had been attacked and the locomotive and two coaches had been uncoupled. The driver had been forced to drive the train to about a mile beyond Sears Crossing when raiders attacked Royal Mail Coach K30204M and helped themselves to 120 mailbags.

On the night in question, a gang of near-hysterical train robbers were turning up the lane that led to their hideout, almost due west of Bridego Bridge in Ledburn where the heist had happened. It wasn't what their leader would have wanted, but it's not every night a handful of blokes net £2.6 million so he cut them a bit of slack. It was probably only the cows of Buckinghamshire who heard them belting out Tony Bennett's 'The Good Life' from their assorted army vehicles. They were the choir invisible, at that moment, but they would not stay that way. The world has known for years who most of them were, but, for the record, let's have a look at them.

The bloke in charge was Bruce Reynolds. He was thirty-one and described himself as an antiques and car dealer. He was a fantasist, seeing himself as some kind of Raffles, the gentleman cracksman, and claiming to have been the youngest major in the British Army (actually he ran away on the second day of his military service as a humble private). A London lad, he was evacuated during the war by which time his mother was already dead. He never got on with his dad and stepmother. He got into petty crime via a mate, 'Cobby', while working for a bicycle company in Clapham. He was a burglar and jewel-thief who always hankered after the good life and saw himself as a cut above. He'd gone down for a few things and his rap sheet followed a dismally familiar pattern. He was fined for riding a bike without lights and resisting arrest in September 1948 and was sent to Borstal eighteen months later for shop-breaking. His first taste of stir was eighteen months for shop, garage and office-breaking in October 1950. For all that he didn't approve of violence, Reynolds was imprisoned at the Old Bailey in January 1958 for two and a half years for wounding with intent. Two coppers had got in his way.

By the time of the train robbery, Reynolds was down on his luck. He'd been fined £10 at Ongar Magistrates' Court for poaching, a crime that takes us all back to Victorian times. He also owed a few people a few favours; one man in particular, as we'll see.

There was no specific pecking order below Reynolds. Because he saw himself as a general and used military uniforms and vehicles as part of the make-believe of the train robbery, a lot of people equate this gang with Jack Hawkins and his team of disgruntled ex-army men in the film *The League of Gentlemen*. It was nothing like that, but the subsequent notoriety of one member of the team, Ronnie Biggs, made a hero out of him, totally out of proportion with his performance both on the night in question and later.

Ronald Arthur Biggs was thirty-four in August 1963. Calling himself a carpenter and builder, he came from Lambeth in south London and first appeared in the dock there in February 1945, accused of stealing pencils from a shop. He denied it (just like he denied being involved in the train robbery) and the case was thrown out. He gravitated to burglary, car theft and robbery and his most recent case had been the theft of a bike and some paint. After that, Biggs had tried to go straight. He married Charmian Powell, a headteacher's daughter, in 1960 and he set up in business in Redhill, Surrey with Raymond Stripp. It didn't do too well, however, because by the summer of '63 he was short of 500 readies. Who did he ask to help him out? Bruce Reynolds.

'Paddy' Daly – you'd never guess it – was an Irishman, at least by descent. Just as well he was, or people might have called him by his real name, John Thomas. He was a giant, 17 stone and 5ft 11ins with a scar on his head. He was born in New Ross, Eire but by August 1948 he was bound over for stealing £1 from a shop in Woking. Car theft, larceny, shop-breaking, that was Paddy. He was thirty-two at the time of the train robbery and almost a natural to be included. He was Reynolds' brother-in-law and Reynolds believed that Paddy was a lucky charm, which made him useful. Officially, like Reynolds, an antique dealer, his last session before the beak took place at Northampton in March 1960 when he got a year's stir for attempted shop-breaking. Difficult to see where Reynolds was coming from, really.

'Buster' Edwards has metamorphosed into Phil Collins thanks to the feature film in 1988. Which is a shame, because it would be difficult to find two men more different. Then aged thirty-two, he was short and stocky. As a wartime kid he had been evacuated to Devon, then he had left school at fourteen and done the usual number of dead-end jobs before joining the RAF for his National Service. Fifty-six days of that two years he spent inside for stealing fags from the sergeants' Mess. He kept out of bother in the Fifties, perhaps for the sake of June Rothery, who he married in Lambeth. Theirs was a sad marriage because their first child, Perry, died at six weeks old and June subsequently had two miscarriages.

Out of court Buster may have been, but not out of crime. He met fellow train robber Tommy Wisbey while working for Freddie Foreman's firm in the late Fifties. He opened a night-club with the Price brothers in August 1959 and, like a lot of nightclub owners, became a bit too fond of the sauce. Inevitably he began to attract the attention of the law. Over a one-year period he appeared no less than four times in various courts, even though the sentences were small fines and short imprisonments. By that time he had met Reynolds and at least two other train robbers. His occupation is listed as 'florist'.

Gordon Goody was a year older than Edwards with previous convictions stretching back to June 1945. He was a hard man who didn't like poofs back in those unenlightened days and he went to jug for the first time after beating up and robbing a gay man he claimed had made advances to him. He was a hairdresser, which sends out all sorts of mixed messages (to the extent that, today, he claims he never was one), and was very much a ladies' man with a great deal of natural charm. In fact one of the first books written on the train robbery was by Peta Fordham, the wife of one of the Defence briefs, and she certainly seemed to like Goody, even visiting him in jug later. Living modestly with his mum in Putney, south-west London, he got involved with Reynolds, Edwards and three other train robbers in an attempt to rob an armoured van.

Two years before the Up Special night he had been fined for illegal ownership of a gun, which was confiscated.

'Big Jim' Hussey was a painter and decorator when he wasn't robbing trains. Living with his dear old mum and dad in a flat in Dog Kennel Hill – not the most attractive of London addresses – his thieving career gravitated to GBH in May 1950 when he was nineteen. Eight years later he was beating up policemen and had a hard man reputation. I've got to quote from the statement he made to the police on one job because it's such a classic piece of underworld cant. 'I'll be honest with you,' he told the arresting officer, 'I was on the unders the other night with a team of dippers and the line bogeys surprised us and we all had it away on our dancers. I got away and I thought you were nailing me for that.' Well, I couldn't have put it better myself. Hussey's life of crime was by no means limited to London and its environs. He broke into a warehouse in Manchester in December 1958 and helped himself to £10,820-worth of fags and tobacco. Three years later, he was picking pockets (unsuccessfully, as it turned out) in Munich. The Germans kicked him out.

Roy James was the littlest of the men driving across the Buckingham countryside that August night. At 5ft 4ins, he was known as the Weasel, according to Scotland Yard, anyway. He was one of those sad cases of a man with real talent who somehow squandered it. He was a silversmith and could have been the next Formula One legend, rivalling people like Schumacher and Lewis Hamilton today. He didn't smoke or drink, which made him unique among the train robbers, and he kept himself rigorously fit. He was a friend of Graham Hill, the world motor-racing champion in 1962 and put his extraordinary driving skills to use as a getaway driver in the BOAC London Airport robbery in November of that year. With his legendary 180-degree turns and his Jaguar Mk II 3.4 litre, the police couldn't catch him. They *had* caught him a few times previously, of course. He had stolen a vacuum cleaner and a cine projector in May 1956 and got a year's probation. His latest brush with the law was, ironically, for dangerous driving, just two months before the train robbery. He was fined £15.

Jimmy White, at forty-three, was the granddad of the gang. He was a café proprietor in Aldersgate Street at the time of the robbery but he was also a war veteran. He'd volunteered and saw service with the Artillery and the Army Air Corps in Africa and Italy. On 7 June 1944 he was invalided out of the army with a duodenal ulcer, so missed D-Day and the drive into Germany. He was typical in many ways of blokes trying to make a go of things after the war, trying his hand at various straight jobs, most of which came to nothing. In the Age of Austerity, a time of rationing, prefabs and utility furniture, White's pension was slashed from 18s. a week to nine and then stopped altogether. All he had to show for his service was a nasty demob suit and a North Africa and Italy star, medals that were ten-a-penny at the time. He had served eighteen months at the end of the Fifties for stealing photographic equipment.

Charlie Wilson called himself a greengrocer. He was thirty-one, famous for his sense of humour and, like all the others, had left school at fourteen. He was that not-at-all-uncommon type you find in any underworld anywhere in the world, a loving husband and father (of three girls) with a reputation as a heavy. He had been a childhood friend of Bruce Reynolds and knew Roy James well. His underworld contacts were wide and useful and it was rumoured that he was the brains behind the BOAC London Airport robbery. His own rap sheet was very modest – four court appearances over five years, but only the last, in May 1959, leading to serious prison time (thirty months for conspiracy to steal).

Roger Cordrey has never got the star treatment dealt out to some of the other train robbers, which is odd because he was a smart cookie. At forty-two he was nearly as old as Jimmy White and listed his occupation as florist and antique dealer. He was leader of the so-called South Coast Raiders and had already robbed six trains by 1963. Cordrey was a keen fisherman, a compulsive gambler and what he didn't know about Grand National winners wasn't worth knowing. Maybe it was a measure of his talent that before the train robbery he had only one conviction. That was back in December 1941 when he was sent to Borstal on two counts of embezzlement and six of falsifying accounts. It may be that he wasn't singing as lustily as the others that Up Special night – his wife had left him a few days before.

Tommy Wisbey was probably doing most of the singing. A 33-year-old bookmaker, he was a Tony Bennett and Frank Sinatra fan and used to entertain everybody using a vacuum cleaner pipe as a mic. He had worked as an errand boy on the *Star and News Chronicle* and as a porter in Covent Garden before becoming a driver with the Army Service Corps for his National Service. After that he worked for his dad in the wholesale bottle business, although his occupation at the time of the robbery was bookmaker. Wisbey's three convictions – for shop-breaking, receiving and an assault on the police – were relatively light given his criminal associations. He had worked with Buster Edwards for Freddie Foreman since the mid 1950s and his father-in-law was a cousin of Billy Hill, the notorious criminal godfather.

Bob Welch was a gambler. It sort of went hand-in-hand with his official occupation – betting-shop owner. He was thirty-five and had run the New Crown Club at the Elephant and Castle, south London until the Old Bill closed him down for selling alcohol after hours. He was one of Cordrey's firm, the South Coast Raiders, and divided his time more or less equally between his wife and long-standing girlfriend. He had only been sent to prison once – in October 1958, for receiving stolen coffee, tea and custard powder.

Everybody says, don't they, that they remember where they were on 22 November 1963, the day they killed Kennedy. Well, I remember 9 August of that year, the day my dad, Arthur

Sturley, came into our living room at 122 Ramuz Drive, Southend, waving the *Evening Standard*. He was laughing. 'Well, son,' he said. 'Your uncle George has just had it off.'

'What do you mean?' I asked him. He showed me the banner headlines – 'Train Robbery: The Total Could Be £160,000'.

'Your uncle George organised that one, son,' Dad said.

I don't suppose, at twelve, I realised exactly what that meant and, of course, nobody at the time could foresee how iconic the Great Train Robbery would become.

'Does that mean we're rich, Dad?' I asked.

There was a strange look on my father's face, one I'd seen before and I'd see again. 'Not rich,' he said, knowing his brother better than I did, 'but we'll get a few quid out of it.'

That was sort of confirmed later that night on the telly when a grey-faced and grainy Richard Baker from the BBC told the country's television viewers that the haul could be as high as £2 million. And even then, they hadn't counted properly.

How's your maths? The eyewitnesses on the Up Special could not agree how many robbers there were. Today, using all sources, the smart money is sixteen. Now, you've only just read about twelve. The thirteenth man is the substitute train driver brought in to move the locomotive. He was useless on the night, but he got away with it – and was lucky to escape without a severe knee-capping from some of the others. The writers Nick Russell-Pavier and Stewart Richards describe the remaining three gang members as Mr One, Mr Two and Mr Three. Bruce Reynolds in his *Autobiography of a Thief* calls one of them Alf Thomas and another Bill 'Flossy' Jennings. I'll introduce them to you later, by their real names, because that's more helpful, isn't it? It's also more accurate. And it's one of the things that makes this book so important. No more speculation. No more guesswork. Just the facts.

Criminal masterminds are the stuff of legend. Conan Doyle's Professor Moriarty, the Napoleon of Crime, was unusual because he was high profile. The real ones aren't. A bit like serial killers, really; they're anonymous; you'd pass them in the street without a second glance. My uncle George was like that. There aren't even any photos of him, anywhere.

For years, most people accepted that Bruce Reynolds was the mastermind for the train robbery, but doubts had already begun to creep in early on. Nick Russell-Pavier and Stewart Richards got it right in their 2012 book: 'If Reynolds was the brains behind the 1963 mail-train robbery he demonstrably lacked the ability to conceive of a plan that would have brought about its overall success.' Too true. He kept away from the law for five years but he was always on the run, always looking over his shoulder. I knew Bruce Reynolds. I'd met him when I was a kid and he was calling himself John Palmer, running Mac's Antiques in the Portobello Road. He was a nice bloke, but a genius he was not. A lot of the pseudo-military organisation was just in his head. He got twenty-five years when he went down but only served ten. And by the time he got out, his money had mysteriously disappeared.

Russell-Pavier and Richards turn their attention to another of the robbers, Gordon Goody, and say that he was 'the only member of the mail-train gang to have got long-term benefit out of it'.

Not quite. Because the man who enjoyed most of the long-term benefit, the man who *really* organised the Great Train Robbery, was George Albert Stanley, a shadowy figure you'll probably never have heard of. Recently, I asked a bloke I met who he thought had organised the Great Train Robbery. Without engaging his brain, he said, 'Ronnie Biggs'. Immediately, he realised the futility of that and corrected it to 'Bruce Reynolds'. 'Getting warmer,' I told him. But of course, he was still wide of the mark. I didn't enlighten him further.

The train robber Gordon Goody has recently outed the mysterious Ulsterman, the go-between and provider of key information, as the inside man. His name was Patrick McKenna and he met Goody on four occasions. The assumption made by many people now is that McKenna was the brains behind the robbery. We know it all now, right? Bruce Reynolds hired the muscle, working on information supplied by Patrick McKenna. And they all lived unhappily ever after. Case closed.

But of course, it isn't. Because behind them all is the master puppeteer, pulling strings in carefully constructed shadows, and he has eluded the authorities and researchers for fifty years. He was Mr Big, Mr Untouchable, and he got away with millions in an entire life devoted to crime.

He was not completely anonymous, however, as a Post Office Investigation Branch (IB) report, released to the public in 2002, makes clear. It makes interesting reading:

Mr George Stanley is the Managing Clerk for Messrs Lesser & Co, Solicitors, London E15 and came to notice very early in the inquiries. Stanley is a shrewd man and the Police know him as an able advocate for the criminal classes. The actual part he was called upon to play is not known.

Until now. Now I can tell you exactly what part he played. All he didn't do was put on a balaclava and bash a train driver over the head at Sears Crossing. But everything else in the train robbery and much more, from start to finish, was pure George Albert Stanley. Some men wear their hearts on their sleeves; George kept his heart and everything else well hidden up his. He was a dark horse to his own brother, my dad. His wife never knew the inside story of his double dealing.

I think perhaps there were only two people in the world who knew how George Stanley ticked. One was his mistress, Edith Simons, who aided and abetted his life of crime. The other was me. Over the years, I picked up the family gossip – 'Your uncle George is a genius, Lee', 'best conman the East End ever produced'. I met the men he worked with, the men he conned, the men he hand-picked for robberies great and small. And I remember like yesterday the time he sat me down in his law office along the Broadway, Stratford and crossed all the tees and dotted the 'i's' of his shady life. It gave me enough information to send George down for a long, long time…

So, I'd like you to meet my uncle George, the mastermind behind the Great Train Robbery and the greatest criminal mind of the twentieth century.

CHAPTER 1

THE EARLY STURLEY DAYS: JACK SPOT, BILLY HILL AND GRANDDAD

C riminal masterminds don't grow on trees. And they don't spring fully formed, ready to plan, organise and carry out their capers. It takes years of attention to detail, a certain mindset and a manipulative personality for it all to work. And to understand how the Great Train Robbery came to be and how George Stanley came to plan it, we have to go back in time.

It's next to impossible to imagine the world my uncle George and my dad, Arthur, were born into. For George Stanley – né Sturley – the time was July 1911. There were riots in Wales, London and Liverpool and some people said we were on the verge of revolution. Everybody seemed to be striking, from dockers to coal miners. Cozzers on strike duty in Liverpool had to be protected by the bloody army and the mood got uglier as the temperatures soared in August. George's London was the second most unhealthy city in the world, with a mortality rate of nineteen per 1,000 people living, several percentage points above the national average;

382 kids died in the city in George's third week of life. At the same time uncaring MPs had voted themselves a pay rise to 400 quid a year (a small bloody fortune by anybody's reckoning). The Labour leader, James Keir Hardie, spoke to an angry crowd on Tower Hill – maybe my granddad was there. 'The masters show you no mercy,' he shouted under a boiling sun. 'They starve you, they sweat you, they oppress you. Pay them back in their own coin.' Granddad, known as John Pedlar, was doing that already.

My dad's time was 8 August 1914, a Saturday. We had been at war for four days. It was all flags and cheering and blokes with no sense running to their local recruitment offices to join up. It would all be over by Christmas and we'd kick the Kaiser's arse. How did we know? General Sir John French said so and he should know. That miserable bastard Kitchener had his doubts, warning that the war could be a long one, but what did he know? We had an army and a navy second to none. Not that you'd find John Pedlar signing on for his khaki and his puttees; he was in a Reserved Occupation. He was a professional criminal.

If the Sturley brothers saw the light of day for the first time in 1911 and 1914 respectively, the place of their birth was common to both. It was a three-bedroomed terraced house in Perth Road, Plaistow, in the heart of the East End. Nobody was born in hospital in those days. Hospitals were places where you went to die, like the workhouses that were still going strong then. My grandma gave birth to those terrible 'twins', as well as to five others – Katherine, Grace, William, Edna and Clifford – gripping the brass headrail of the horse-hair stuffed bed, surrounded by towels, hot water and a couple of women who were neighbours and who had been through this themselves.

If John Pedlar was at home when they were born – and he probably wasn't – he wouldn't be allowed in the bedroom. That was women's business. He'd be along to wet the babies' heads when the time was right.

Perth Road hasn't actually changed all that much despite the bombs the Nazis dropped on it during the war. It's nose-to-tail cars now, of course, but in John Pedlar's day it would be horses, wagons, rag and bone and cat's meat men. A lorry was an event and would attract an admiring crowd made up of every kid in the neighbourhood trying to nick the tyres. Beyond the Thirties stucco and the UPVC windows today, you can still make out the arched porches and the bay windows of the Victorian parlours. What's gone now are the privies at the back, little evil-smelling sheds with wooden-seated water-closets emptied every now and then by the new County Council.

When George and Arthur were born, John Pedlar was just that – a pedlar. He dealt in the street, on shop corners, any place where a gullible public went about their business. The stuff was hooky, straight off the back of a cart at knock-down prices and no questions asked. We all laughed like drains at Del Boy and Rodney in *Only Fools and Horses*, set in Peckham in the Eighties. But the Trotters weren't a million miles removed from the Sturleys, following a risky way of life that adapted to change only as circumstances dictated. John Pedlar could patter for England. He had that affable easy-going banter that could sell snow to Eskimos and sounded like he was doing you a favour as he robbed you blind. George and Arthur learned at the knee of a master – 'bullshit baffles brains every time,' as my dad and my uncle constantly reminded me as I was growing up.

Some of John Pedlar's gear came from the docks. London's riverscape has transformed itself over half a century into a different animal these days, with Canary Wharf, gastro-pubs and bloody expensive flats gentrified beyond recognition. All very lovely, all very twenty-first century. But the disappearance of the docks – finalised by the same Luftwaffe that flattened Plaistow – was one of those changing circumstances I mentioned above.

There's a romance about Dockland now. In my granddad's day it was a different planet. The docks themselves – then the biggest in the world – were almost invisible behind high walls and for half a century by the time George was born, men had queued every day by the huge gates, hoping to be taken on for a day's labour. Those who weren't hired had to find their tommy where they could – usually the grey gruel of the workhouses. Geographically the nearest stretch of wharves and warehouses to Plaistow ran along the bend of the river that skirted Millwall and the Isle of Dogs. Huge works were going on to modernise the East India Dock when George and Arthur were kids, to accommodate ever-bigger cargo ships. Morton's Sufferance Wharf handled preserved goods and oil, the produce being loaded onto lighters that ferried the stuff up and down the brown waters of the Thames before some of it found its way into my granddad's hands. They made and sold wire rope, 600 tons of the stuff per month in John Pedlar's youth, at the London and Stronghold Wharf. He couldn't do much with the grain that came into Millwall Central Granary at the rate of 300 tons an hour, but some of Levy Brothers' sacks and bags from their Empire Works came in handy shifting gear that John would rather the local constabulary didn't clap eyes on. Pigments, paints, distempers and varnishes were available from Burrells Wharf and, via John, there was a market for it all. And don't get me started on the lead industry in the Isle of Dogs. More than a few bags came Granddad's way from McDougall's Flour Mill. Finally, of course, a little downstream the Greenwich and Isle of Dogs foot tunnel made ferry trips obsolete and gave Granddad *carte blanche* to try his hand south of the river, too, pausing to wet his whistle maybe in the Island Garden, laid out so tastefully by the London County Council that it came to be known as Scrap Iron Park.

John Pedlar was operating before the end of Empire, when Britain was still just about the workshop of the world before being crowded out by the Germans and the Americans. Every conceivable sort of produce came into the Port of London and my granddad was quick to see the advantage of it all. There was nothing new in all this. Pirates and smugglers had been operating along the Thames for centuries. In some cases, half of the cargo disappeared before it was officially unloaded and found its way to illicit warehouses, pubs and cellars where men like my granddad would get into the usual horse trading to satisfy the customers. In theory all that should have changed with the creation of the River Police back in the 1790s, but they couldn't be everywhere. Every man has his price and bungs were frequent. Blind eyes were turned, questions weren't asked and of course with the outbreak of the Second World War later, it was party time for the spivs and black marketeers.

But the docks weren't Granddad Pedlar's only source of hooky gear. Some of it he got from the gangs. I've always found a certain poetry in the fact that Dick Turpin carried out his first crime in Plaistow, robbing his boss, Mr Giles, before going on – as legend has it – to set up a smuggling gang between Plaistow and Southend. The problem with criminals is that some of them become heroes; the public can't get enough of them. We'll see this in the context of the train robbers later – they made a movie about Buster Edwards, and Ronnie Biggs became some sort of god as he dodged extradition for all those years. It was like that with Turpin, too. He was actually a pock-marked psychopath who once threatened to put an old lady's bare arse onto an open fire if she didn't tell him where her valuables were hidden. But we'd much rather he was the gallant 'gentleman of the road' who only robbed from the rich and rode his horse Black Bess from London to York while the kettle was boiling.

So, in a way, Plaistow and crime went hand-in-hand for ever. And the place boasted plenty of those pubs that were so crucial to the Sturleys, generation after generation. The Black Lion still has those dark, scruffy interiors, snugs where deals are struck in whispers and where vital snippets of information are picked up. The Boleyn Tavern, on its imposing corner site, became *the* home of West Ham FC supporters from the day they laid the first brick. I often wonder whether Uncle George decided on a new surname having spent so much time in the Lord Stanley along St Mary's Road. William Simmons was the landlord when John Pedlar drank there and by the time George and Arthur joined him his son, also William, ran the place.

I don't know exactly when John Pedlar got involved with Jack Spot, but it set the pattern among the Sturleys that would last until only a few years ago. Organised crime came to the East End out of Eastern Europe when my granddad was a kid. Driven out of Russia and Poland by state-sponsored pogroms, Jews in their thousands reached the Port of London and spread into the neighbouring parishes of Whitechapel and Spitalfields, driving out the Irish who were already there. Some of those new arrivals were honest, hard-working and desperately poor, having spent their last few bob to get to Britain in the first place. Others were gangsters, wary of the police because of their experience back home, and they set up protection rackets in the spielers (gambling dens), coffee shops, pubs and street-market stalls. An old-time copper called Ben Leeson likened Whitechapel in the 1890s to Chicago in the Prohibition era under Al Capone.

Gangs like these, sometimes forty strong, threatened the locals and terrorised them with knives, coshes and razors. Their targets were nearly as dodgy as they were and that was in part why they got away with what they did. If you run a spieler, you know gambling is illegal and you can't go to the law. Similarly, if you keep a brothel – 'bawdy house' was still the legal term – you can't approach your friendly local magistrate for help. You've just got to pay up – or be prepared to spend the rest of your life tooled up, surrounded by your own gang of heavies.

There's been a lot of sociological and psychological research done over the last thirty years into gang mentality and gang culture, but at that time it was partly influenced by the cult of leadership that dominated politics between the wars. What are Hitler, Stalin and Mussolini if they're not gang leaders, using every trick in and out of the book to stay in power? London's gang leaders, of the type my granddad knew, were colourful, larger than life. There was the Jew Isaac Bogard, Darky the Coon (try calling somebody *that* today!), Long Hymie, Monkey Bennyworth, Tinker Jim and Wooden George. They each had their following and even earned the respect of some policemen.

Some of the tension was racial. The Cortesi brothers were known, confusingly, as the Frenchies. There was a Jewish gang called the Yiddishers; the Bessarabians were Russian and so it went on. They clashed with each other, over turf, over who exactly gave protection to which coffee stall. Who ran the street girls in such and such an area. And woe betide you if you found yourself having a quiet friendly drink in the wrong boozer.

For the first twenty years of the twentieth century, during which both George and Arthur Sturley were born, *the* underworld gang were the Sabinis. Their leader, Darby, had been born in Saffron Hill in Farringdon (Fagin's old haunt) in 1889, the same year as Adolf Hitler, funnily enough. This was Little Italy at the time. Darby Sabini ran the West End and the racecourses. Because gambling was illegal, the only betting that could take place was at the races. So at Epsom, Goodwood, even Ascot, the race gangs would turn up and terrify the bookies into coughing up a massive share of their takings. You want some chalk to mark up the runners and odds on your blackboard? You got to pay Darby for that. Lists of runners? They cost 1d. to print, but you got to pay Darby half a crown. You'll need a stool to stand on, of course, so you can be seen and do all that tic-tac nonsense. Stools don't come cheap – ask Darby. Oh, and by the way, have you heard about poor old Nutter? He got a five-year stretch the other day. How about a little something for his wife and six kids, eh? Darby's asking.

Running fights were frequent in the racecourse wars of the Twenties and Thirties when rival gangs met up or the police intervened. Detective Chief Superintendent Ted

Greeno, later one of Scotland Yard's 'big five', cut his teeth in bloody battles during those years.

The racecourse wars and the Sabini years were coming to an end by the mid Thirties. A Sunday paper referred to Darby as 'king of the underworld'. Stung by what was patently the truth, he sued and lost. He was probably earning up to £30,000 a year by that time, an unbelievable sum. But his gang, a mix of Italians and Jews, was falling apart because of external politics. Mussolini's fascists were making life difficult for Italian Jews and some of that spilled over into the less-than-brotherly fraternities of the London underworld. It could never be the same again.

Enter Jack Spot. He was born Jacob Comacho, the son of a poor tailor from Lodz in Poland and he was a year younger than Uncle George. Some Jewish immigrants kept their own names, but the Comachos first became Colmores, then Comers. Home was Fieldgate Mansions in Whitechapel, a Jewish ghetto, and by the time he was seven Jack was already in a gang, fighting Irish boys from across the street. There are various theories for the origins of the nickname, but 'Spot' probably came from the prominent mole on his left cheek.

He gravitated to housebreaking, hustling and the protection racket. Most people saw him as a thug, pure and simple. He certainly had a reputation for violence, unlike my granddad, who was mixing in his circles by the outbreak of the war. By that time Spot had done time, six months for beating up one of Oswald Mosley's Blackshirts. Mosley was a former army officer and MP who had close links to both Mussolini and Hitler and in October 1936 he led a march of 7,000 blackshirted *fascisti* through the East End, jeering at the Jews. An estimated 100,000-strong group of locals faced them and the police were caught in the middle. The battle of Cable Street resulted in eighty injuries, eighty-four arrests and a Public Order Bill being rushed through parliament. Spot's role on that day, according to him, was knocking Mosley's bodyguard, a wrestler called Roughneck, into the middle of next week with a chair leg lined with lead.

The war led to Spot's call-up, but he made such a pest of himself in khaki that he was discharged in 1943 on the grounds of mental instability. It almost went hand-in-hand with being a gang leader. As the war ended, the Americans went home and the Age of Austerity began, Spot opened a spieler – the Botolph Club in Aldgate. He called it the Fruit Exchange, an apparently legitimate front for an illegal business. I'm pretty sure that Granddad was involved in that. Spot made £3,000 a week from faro and chemin de fer, hooking the mugs (and there were plenty of them) with incurable gambling addictions. He described them in his book years later; there were big businessmen, bookmakers brimming with cash, spivs and screwsmen transferring money from dodgy deals. And of course the black marketeers.

The money involved was jaw-dropping. Gin rummy was played for £1 (£37 today) a point. The kitty in most card games was up to £250 (£9,400) a hand. A chemmy party could produce a turnover of £20,000 (three quarters of a million). Huge chunks of all this went to Spot, but he had a team to pay – 'geezers with respectable ties and tea-shop manners'. Men like John Pedlar, in fact.

With Spot rising fast to become *the* leader of the underworld or, as he liked to style himself, the Robin Hood of the East End, it was inevitable that Granddad should prosper too. There was a saying during the war that my granddad thrived in and conned his way through; it was 'loose lips sink ships'. And while the much-feared Fifth Column of spies operating for the Nazis was largely a figment of the Churchill government's paranoid imagination, a great deal of useful information was picked up by John Pedlar and, in their time, by his sons George and Arthur. Buy a mug a drink – make that two. You're on halves and he's hitting the Scotch or the gin and tonic. He loosens up, relaxes, whether it's in the Lord Stanley or the Black Lion or the Grave Maurice or the Fruit Exchange. He talks, he blabs. He's an insurance agent. He's a Post Office worker. He's middle management in a bank. He's in charge of security in a factory. Or a warehouse. An hour or two with John Pedlar and he's telling him all his woes, how his kids are little shits and his wife doesn't understand him. He's also telling him dates, times, places, codes and the kind of inside information that's worth its weight in gold. And all the time the Pedlar is smiling, nodding, keeping the amber nectar topped up.

Granddad had a memory like an elephant. He forgot nothing. He remembered everybody. And in time, he passed it all on to his eldest boys. Their siblings went on to lead decent, honest lives, but not George and Arthur. They were special and Granddad knew it. He taught them the knack, how to pick a mark across a crowded bar, how to break the ice, strike that precise balance of conversation that's going to have him eating out of your hand. Out of this knack, coupled with meticulous planning, came Eastcastle Street, the Great Train Robbery, Mountnessing and even Brinks-Mat – crimes of the century that, in different ways, were the brainchild of Uncle George.

Word got around. John Pedlar was with Jack Spot but he wasn't a slavish gang member; he had too much savvy for that. For the right inducement – lots of it – Granddad could be trusted to pass on certain relevant information to certain interested parties. Jack usually got first pickings, but it wasn't unknown for Alf White's Islington mob to come calling or the Shepherd's Bush boys. Then there were the group from Kilburn and Paddington and even that mad bastard Fido the Gipsy from the Essex marshes.

As far as Spot was concerned, John Pedlar was running the spielers. He raked in cash like it was going out of fashion, often earning in today's terms thousands a week. Did the taxman see any of this? Don't be silly. My grandmother didn't either and I have no idea what he did with it all. He would come home pissed after a day's business, his pockets full of £5 notes, those big white ones the size of school exercise books. He would solemnly fish out £3 every Friday, the day honest blokes usually got paid. That was my grandmother's housekeeping. Out of that she had to pay the rent and feed and clothe seven kids and two adults.

It was the Sturley way and it kept us out of prison over the years. As Uncle George said to Bruce Reynolds when he visited him as his solicitor after the train robbery, 'It's the easiest thing in the world to steal somebody else's money, Bruce. The hard part is keeping it.' I would have loved to have been a fly on the wall for that little exchange, just to see the look on Brucie's face. Act Jack-the-Lad with wads of cash in the pockets of your handmade suits; drive flash cars; buy a mansion in the country; put your kids' names down for Eton (which Reynolds thought was a bit common); get a villa in the Bahamas ... and the Filth will be on you like flies on shit. This was the message that John Pedlar passed on to his sons. They in turn passed it on to me.

But there was a limit. After Granddad had had a meal and an hour or two's kip in front of the fire in the house in Perth Road, he'd usually stagger out to the crapper in the back yard. Still pissed, he'd usually wipe his arse with fivers (one of the most tasteless forms of money laundering I've ever come across). My dad had slipped a local plumber a few bob to rig the bog so that it wouldn't flush properly. He also blocked the pipe under the manhole cover in the garden. When Granddad had gone, dad would fish out the fivers and take them to the shed, where he'd wipe and dry them and give them to his mum. At various times over the years when I've called my dad every sort of bastard under the sun,

I remember this incident and think, maybe he had a heart somewhere after all.

Throughout the war, it was the Whites who ran Soho and the West End. Nobody could set up a club or a spieler without their say-so and that would mean 25 per cent of the takings. The return of Jack Spot from the armed forces led to a show-down. In January 1947 there was a nasty punch-up in the Stork Club in Sackville Street with one of the White gang, Big Bill Goller, left for dead. He pulled through, but Spot lay low in Southend until the heat died down, then calmly returned to the capital and took over the racetracks. For the next few years, Spot played the ganglord to perfection, swanning around places like the Bear Garden at the Cumberland Hotel in expensive suits and camel-hair coats. He smoked a huge cigar, was teetotal in an age of hard drinking and loved the limelight. He had a mansion in Hyde Park and had met Rita, an Irish girl, at Haydock Park racecourse in the summer of 1951.

Whether it was Rita's influence or Spot could read the writing on the wall, in October he walked into the offices of the *People* newspaper and told crime reporter Arthur Helliwell that he was going into legit business. 'No one knows who the next Big Shot will be,' Helliwell wrote, but my granddad and half of London did. It was Billy Hill.

Hill, later referred to as Britain's Humphrey Bogart because of his looks and his calling, was exactly the same age as Uncle George. He was one of twenty-one kids born in Seven Dials to the Hill family. The Dials today are very upmarket, just off Leicester Square, full of theatres, trendy wine bars and offices with plate glass. It wasn't like that then. The place was a rookery, a sort of thieves' kitchen where you carried a cosh or a chiv just to go shopping. Punch-ups were ten-a-penny and the cozzers patrolled in fours.

The Hills had form. Billy's dad had done bird for assaulting a police officer. His mum was a fence. His brother Jim picked pockets for England and his sister Maggie, called Baby Face or the Queen of the Forty Elephants, was the brains behind a gang of shoplifters. When she died, they were that fond of her in Holloway where she'd spent years of her life, they planted a tree in her memory. With a pedigree like that, it wasn't likely that Billy would go into the Church, was it? Unless it was to nick the silver, of course.

Hill was one of the first big-time villains to write his memoirs – *Boss of Britain's Underworld* – in 1955, by which time he knew both John Pedlar's boys very well. By the start of the war, the former grocer's delivery boy, rattling around the streets on a bone-shaker looking for likely burglary targets, had become the leader of a smash-and-grab team. Photos of the gang show arrogant Jack-the-Lads, wearing ties and three-piece suits, the inevitable trilby or fedora worn at a rakish angle on their heads. According to Hill, he was perfectly happy to accept the call-up, rather fancying the RAF with its swagger and Brylcreem ethos. As things turned out, his two prison stretches in five years meant that the government never quite got round to him before it was all over.

The war was a blessing to the street criminal. Blackout regulations provided murky corners for shady business to be transacted. Rationing and deprivation created a market desperate to obtain goods by any means – hence the rise of the black market and the spiv. The Met were stretched to breaking point trying to cope with a crime wave itself caused by a whole raft of new regulations. Hill was making £3,000 a week.

He bought a Tudor manor house (as you do) in Bovington in Hertfordshire, an Aladdin's cave of hooky gear transported daily in and out of London. His gang members sound like the cast of a spoof movie like the Lavender Hill Mob. There was Franny the Spaniel, Taters Mutton, Horrible Harry, Strong Arms, Wide Gaiters Alf and Long Stan. John Pedlar knew most or all of these blokes because, although there may be petty squabbles or even outright hatred between them, the criminal fraternity was just that – a brotherhood of the bent, a family of felons. They had their own code and morality which might strike most people as bizarre, but it was unshakeable. A man who broke it and squealed to the police was beneath contempt and not likely to live out his days with all his senses and limbs.

Billy Hill was clever but he was not Uncle George. By 1948 he had spent half his life behind bars. He went down for burglary and Jack Spot met him when he came out of Wandsworth a few months before I was born. As always, there are two versions of that. Either Spot wanted Hill as his Number Two because of the man's street cred or Hill wrote to Spot begging him to take him on. I wonder which version John Pedlar believed.

Hill's role was to control Spot's spielers, which meant he was working closely with my granddad. The black market had transformed those places. They were now open 24/7 and the war and post-war years created a 'live for today' mentality that meant that ever more people were out to enjoy themselves. In 1945–6 there were 20,000 deserters somewhere in Britain, 600 of them Yanks who didn't want to go home. Trouble was frequent but few people wanted to tangle with Billy Hill. He stabbed his first man when he was fourteen, with a pair of scissors, and was surprised how easy it was. He always carried a knife and called it his best friend, living by the 'law of the chiv'. When a mate of his, an old-time villain called Dodger Mullins, was being beaten up by two young thugs, Hill gave one tearaway his favourite stroke, a V for Victory sign on his cheek. He cut the other one to ribbons.

By 1951, the opposition had got the message and Hill settled down to relative quiet with Gypsy Riley, a tart with a legendary temper. He took the girl from her pimp, Belgian Johnny, by slashing him in a West End café – they'd never use that restaurant again.

The Sturley boys had met their own girls by this time. George had known little Marjorie Petchy since they were both seventeen. They married and spent their honeymoon in Madeira, the romantic Portuguese island that was still faraway and exotic, not on every other bugger's list on the way to Lanzarote like it is today. It was one of those rare occasions when Uncle George pushed the boat out and spent money from his ill-gotten gains. He and my dad had teamed up for a while, carrying out various frauds and dodges before going their separate ways.

I'd like to tell you that Dad met Ineze Victoria at a dance hall in the Balls Pool Road in Leytonstone and that my dad, 6ft 2ins and immaculately turned out, had swept her off her feet. In fact she was a nurse at a local dentist where he had gone to have all his teeth out (as you did in those days, usually to save money) and he sweet-talked her into nicking some cocaine off the dentist. I was thirty-two before I found out that they had never actually bothered to get married and even with all the other shit I've put up with in my life because of them, this still rocked me. Neither of these women knew what they were taking on by hooking up with the Sturleys. Rita Comer and Gypsy Hill come across as feisty, larger-than-life characters. So, in their way, do Marjorie and Vicky Sturley, but I can vouch for what it does to you, being married (or not!) to a ruthless conman whose only motive is making a buck at the expense of somebody else. And there would be no escape for either of them.

When the bombs started raining down on Plaistow and the East End in general, the Sturleys were evacuated to Shrewsbury. With his one lung and diabetes, there was no way that the dreaded brown envelope was going to land on George's mat. My dad was a different matter, however. He was twenty-five when war broke out and certainly fit enough for active service. All right, he had a young and growing family – my four brothers were all older than me – but that applied to thousands of blokes who got the nod. How he escaped the call-up and got away with his family I don't know.

In the late Thirties Dad had got himself apprenticed to a Savile Row tailor – hence his own flash turnout in good clothes – and he set up business in the border town where the bombs never fell. News travelled fast and his clientele came from Manchester, Wales, Leicester and Yorkshire to be fitted for suits. They were farmers and businessmen, the younger ones already missing the extra wide Oxford Bags that were *verboten* thanks to the new clothing regulations. Now it was all straight legs and no turn-ups (the end of the world, surely?). Dad got the cloth at knockdown prices and only dealt with the wealthiest clients. He always had this skill to fall back on, but with the end of the war, London drew the Sturleys back like a magnet. There were other scams and if you had the knack, the streets were paved with gold. Jack Spot and Billy Hill were running criminal London and were still, at that point, mates. John Pedlar was wheeling and dealing in their spielers. The horizon looked rosy.

And nobody could see that more clearly than my uncle George.

CHAPTER 2

PROMISE LAND AND THE CORNER GAME

I learned a lot from Uncle George and my dad. They were the greatest pair of conmen the East End of London ever produced and the lessons they taught me will stay with me till the day I die.

It's not rocket science. It's plain old common sense and it's carried out every day by politicians, bankers and businessmen all over the world. You know that TV series *Hustle*, the one where a gang of conmen take on a mark every week? All right, it's escapism and some of the plots are a bit over the top, but look at the psychology behind it. What's the common factor in each of the marks that dear old Adrian Lester is out to get, apart from the fact that they're horrible bastards who deserve what comes their way? That's it – greed. My dad told me, and so did Uncle George, you can't con an honest man. If a bloke isn't interested in money and material things, there's no point in trying. This is why so many cons have worked in the stock market. Remember Barlow Clowes? The company was a 'bond-washing' operation that promised a sure-fire return, though in fact most of the money went to funding the director's platinum-edged lifestyle. It was no surprise when it all went pear-shaped. Investors whinged about it, claiming they'd been sold a pup and so on. The plain fact is that business ventures like this are just forms of gambling. There's no such thing as gilt-edged, no absolute guarantee of a profit. But some people are like kids in an amusement arcade, like the ones I grew up with in Southend. They love the flashing lights, the pinball machines, the one-armed bandits. They know the rattle of cash out of the bottom only happens once in a blue moon but by then, you've spent a bloody fortune feeding the thing.

Greed. You got nothing? You want some. You got some? You want more. The love of money of course is the root of all evil. And that's where my dad, Arthur, and his brother George come in. It's important we understand how the Sturley mindset works. Only that way does George Stanley's success become clear. I should explain something else about George that will make more sense later. To make a career in the law, which he did, it wouldn't do to have the Sturley name around his neck. Change two letters and you build yourself a barrier a mile wide.

My dad, however, was a Sturley through and through. And he had the family gift for finding a weak spot and working out how to take advantage of it.

Take an ordinary bloke – let's call him Roy Wiggins. He was medium height, medium build – Joe Public, Everyman, just like you and me. Only Roy was real and he was one of my dad's marks. He had shoulder-length black hair – this was 1957 and he must have looked a right prat when short back and sides were still all that were on the hairdressing menu. He had teeth like dustbins – one in every yard. His nose was pointed and he had absolutely no dress sense. But that didn't matter because he was quite a successful businessman with a bakery and a large property portfolio in the Southchurch area of Southend.

My dad was running a scrap metal business in the same town – Sturley and Sons – and was always on the lookout for a mug ... er ... investor. Such a one was Roy Wiggins and he was introduced to Dad via a mutual acquaintance, a local small-time thief called Bill Collins. A meet was arranged at the old Victoria hotel on the corner of Southend High Street. I can't tell you how important venues like this are. Pubs and bars are where it's at. When I was eleven I met the Kray brothers outside the Grave Maurice in Whitechapel. Bruce Reynolds and several of his team discussed plans, *sotto voce*, over a pint or two in hostelries various. Eastcastle Street, the Great Train Robbery, the Mountnessing bullion robbery, Brinks-Mat, heists and scams great and small owe their origins to quiet chats in pubs. It helps of course if Arthur Sturley or George Stanley are buying the first round; it puts mugs at their ease, gives them confidence. It says, 'This man thinks I'm important. He likes me. I can trust him.' And with Arthur or George, it worked every time.

The Victoria was an upmarket place, gleaming with mahogany and polished glass. Businessmen met there frequently; so did villains. Bill Collins did the introductions, outside on the pavement, after which he was sorry, but he had another engagement. That was because my dad had told him to sling his hook. When Arthur played the corner game, he wanted no distractions. He shook Roy's hand and sussed him in a second. It was almost as instant as that – and both Arthur and George had the knack. They could tell if a man was straight or bent, reliable or a liability.

So what did Roy Wiggins see that morning as Arthur Sturley led him into the snug of the Victoria? A six-foot man in his mid-thirties, with an easy-going patter. But look at his gear. Prince of Wales check suit, silk shirt, immaculate tie, knotted just so, cufflinks (gold but not gaudy), brogues you could see your reflection in. The man oozed money and success; Wiggins could smell it. Yeah, right.

This was the corner game and Arthur and George were the past masters – the place and the appearance were only the start. With Collins gone, Dad could get to work. Bill would have put his foot in it, said the wrong thing, perhaps even put Wiggins on his guard. And men like Bill never learn. As somebody once said, 'You can't polish a turd.'

The drink flowed and Arthur was as plausible as ever. He had dreamed up an investment proposal for a business that did not actually exist and promised Roy 25 per cent on all the money he invested. This was Promise Land, a la-la place where money grows on trees and the fountains piss pennies. If Roy Wiggins was the donkey, braying away happily that morning in the Victoria, my dad had the longest stick in the world and tied to the end of it was the carrot that mugs like Roy just have to get hold of – money. And more money.

The Promise. The Dream. Dad planted the prospect of wealth in Roy Wiggins' head and now he moved into Phase Two of the corner game: playing hard to get. Days went by, weeks. Roy phoned my dad on a regular basis – how was it all going? Fine, said Dad, although of course he was very busy on a scrap-metal contract in Bournemouth (which was actually partially true) so he wouldn't be able to set up another meet till the following week.

So far, Roy had stumped up £10,000 (no mean sum in 1957) and it was now approaching Phase Three: time to up the ante. 'Well, you see, Roy' – I can hear Dad talking on the phone now – 'something's come up. I'm under a lot of pressure my end. I've got other offers. I do my damnedest to be discreet, but you know how it is; word's got around and everybody wants in. I've got two contracts now.' This was true as well, because Felixstowe council had just given Dad another scrap clearance deal. The fact that Dad didn't need any money at all for this was by the by and it was a fact that Roy Wiggins didn't need to know about. 'It'll need to be £20,000 now, Roy,' Dad said apologetically. Wiggins couldn't wait to part with his money.

One of the most bizarre things about Roy Wiggins and his type is that they can't let go even when they realise they've been conned. I'm no psychologist but it's like the Stockholm syndrome, where you form a weird bond with the bloke who's ripping your fingernails out. And Dad had one more pair of pliers to use, metaphorically, on Roy Wiggins. It was time to Work the Jar.

Dad rang Uncle George. Did he know a good jeweller? Of course he did, he knew everybody; he was George Stanley, he had a heart of gold – everybody said so – and he was the favourite lawyer of every villain north (and sometimes south) of the river. George recommended Carlo's in Hatton Garden, a relatively new company with an excellent reputation. So that Dad wasn't directly linked to this purchase, he arranged for a ring to be made and sent to George's law offices in Stratford, already the hub of much of the organised crime in London.

It goes without saying, perhaps, that George was in the process of organising a major armed robbery at that moment, but Dad would have expected little else. When most brothers get together, they talk over family or football or the state of the nation. George and Arthur talked the corner game, Promise Land and van heists.

'Got anything lined up, George?'

'Stand on me, Arthur.' Cue for winks and nose-tapping.

Armed with the ring, Dad set up another meet with Roy Wiggins. By this time (months have gone by), Dad had got most of the money that Roy had made by selling off his portfolio of properties and he remained as upright, immaculate and cool as ever. He told Roy he had just bought the ring (the Jar) for £5,000. However, he had just discovered – and he was deeply worried about it – that it was hooky. It had been stolen, he believed, from a country house and was actually worth £20,000.

An honest man would have recoiled. Hooky gear? Stolen rings? Country house break-ins? He would have run a mile. But Roy Wiggins just sat there, enthralled, exactly as Dad knew he would. Hooky gear? Stolen rings? Country house break-ins? This was the big-time, the Promise Land full of easy-gotten gains. That promise of £20,000 was a life-line to Wiggins, who had already watched a large portion of his wealth disappear down the toilet with nothing to show for it.

Again, Dad broke off the meeting. Again, he made Wiggins wait. The following week he told him he had a prospective buyer who was willing to pay £20,000. Roy offered him £5,000, cash, no questions asked. And it was a pity that he asked no questions because even someone with the most basic grasp of logic would find it odd that Dad was about to accept four times that amount from some other punter, but settled, reluctantly, for Roy's offer. I later found out how much the ring actually cost Dad – just £500. And it was just possible that his brother George had pulled a flanker on him, too. But Dad pulled out this trick time and time again, victim after victim, whenever money was tight and he needed to dip in 'the jar'; it was basically a license to print money!

Roy Wiggins ended up penniless. Did he go to the police and report the scam? No. Why? Because he was not the honest, upright citizen he appeared to be and perhaps too because he couldn't bear the world knowing what a fucking idiot he'd been. 'Arthur,' he said to my dad when it was all over, 'I've been a silly boy, haven't I?' My dad, who never did find out what the word remorse meant, looked the sad bugger straight in the eye and said, 'Yes, you have, my son.'

If my dad had a weakness (one he inherited from *his* dad) it was that if he had it (which he often did) he liked to splash it about – flash clothes, flash cars, the works. Uncle George was altogether more circumspect, which is why, unlike my dad, he never did time.

I still have mixed feelings about George Stanley. In some ways, he was like a father to me, especially when my real father was in Winchester or a similar criminal university at Her Majesty's Pleasure. A diabetic who had had tuberculosis as a kid, he never approved of me smoking, so maybe he did, as all the villains said, have a heart of gold after all. And maybe his motives were of the best when he offered Dad a trifling sum to buy me off him. And I don't know what emotions were going through my head the day I poked a sawn-off up his nostril. 'You fuck everybody over,' I remember screaming. 'Well, you ain't fucking me!'

Ah, happy families.

George worked with Dad carrying out long firm frauds in

Essex and Kent. They would set up a bucket shop, order stock and build up a credit rating with suppliers. Once they'd done this, they'd put in a huge order for goods, take possession of them, then shut up shop and move on. They'd sell the goods, not having paid for them in the first place, and start all over again under a new name. They also ran an estate agency in West Ham, drawing up leases on flats and shops that were actually owned by the local council. Dad did the face-to-face, oozing charm and charisma; George, who had a head for such things, did the paperwork.

And that, essentially, was the key to George's success. He was the boffin, the brains behind, a scrawny little git you wouldn't buy a newspaper from. But behind that slightly seedy exterior, there was a mind like a razor and an organisational ability second to none. He went into the law, a profession he always referred to in the same way – 'Trust me, Lee: the law is robbery without violence.' He became an articled clerk at the law firm of Maurice Lesser, Lesser & Co at 21–23 Broadway, Stratford [not to be confused with the Chingford solicitor's firm of Lesser & Co], a Mock Tudor building that isn't there any more. His meticulous attention to detail meant dozens of successful outcomes for men who, by every law of morality, should have gone down for what they did. Word got around that Lesser & Co were the boys to engage if you were a villain in a spot of bother and very quickly, the Lesser & Co was dropped and baddies asked for George Stanley in person. Let me give you one example. The godfather of London crime today is Freddie Foreman (he even looks like Marlon Brando on the paperback cover of his autobiography) and he says there, on page 182, 'I engaged George Stanley, solicitors from Stratford Broadway' as though that was actually the name of the firm. Villains who found themselves in interview rooms in police stations across the Metropolis wouldn't say, 'Get me a lawyer.' They'd say, 'Get George Stanley.'

So, given the situation, Uncle George was like a fox in the henhouse. He had access to key people and key information and all the time he was hedged round by legal mumbo-jumbo and the law itself as protection. Of course, it wasn't that simple. We'll come across two lawyers – John Wheater and Brian Field – who *should* have been in the same position George was. Both men were involved in George's Great Train Robbery and both got done. Wheater was given three years for conspiracy to obstruct justice. Field got twenty-five years for that and conspiracy to rob. What did George Stanley get for planning the whole caper and pocketing and laundering most of the loot? Fuck all. And a whole lot of money.

I remember as a kid watching the old Perry Mason series on black and white TV – Raymond Burr getting people off every week while an incredibly stupid DA called Hamilton Burger stood there in the courtroom open-mouthed while Perry worked his magic. One thing I found puzzling, as the nephew of George Stanley, was that Perry would only take the case if he believed his client was innocent. If that was so in real life, lawyers would be on benefits. I'm not going to get into a debate on lawyers, how everybody from Shakespeare onwards hates their guts and sees them as the ambulance chasers and shysters that they are. But let's just have a look at what being on the 'right' side of the law gave George access to.

George handled probate business, involving property and antiques. He handled divorce, bitter disputes between aggrieved parties with scores to settle. He worked with businessmen, shady and otherwise. There were contracts involved, import and export, haulage shipments, valuable commodities rattling through the night by train or struggling around the country's pre-motorway roads. He hobnobbed with bank managers at the highest level, finance companies, building society people. He even had a man – Gordon Bray – in the Royal Mint.

The common denominator to all of this was information. That, in any walk of life, is crucial. It is power. It gives you the edge over the other bloke who hasn't got it. When it came to the Great Train Robbery, who knew about the English Electric Class 40 locomotive that left Glasgow Central at 6.50 p.m. on 7 August 1963? My Uncle George. Who knew where the High Value Packages (HVPs) were stashed? Ditto. Who knew a man who could lead a gang, a man who could fix a signal, a man who could destroy all evidence that pointed his way? That would be Uncle George again.

And, of course, legal aid dropped like manna from heaven into George's lap. It was still called Poor Persons Defence in the early days and it was a licence to print money. His success went before him and villains queued up for his services. 'Oh, yeah, I can get you off, son, but it's going to cost' – George might just as well have had this pre-recorded for his clients to save time. Forgers, fraudsters, heavy wheels men, old-fashioned crims – all of them turned up at 21–23 Broadway like it was a bloody job centre. He was getting men off the very crimes he had planned in the first place. Robbery without violence. A lot of criminals will tell you – and Bruce Reynolds, Buster Edwards and Charlie Wilson would be among them – that crime does not pay. I'd have to say that's true, in terms of what it cost me and the rest of my family. But George Stanley? Well, he led a charmed life. If he rolled in shit, he'd come up smelling of roses.

CHAPTER 3

'STURLEY AND OTHERS ...'

When I first came across Sturley and Others v. Powell, I thought it was confirmation of the only time when Uncle George had got into actual trouble with the law and because of that he changed his name from Sturley to Stanley. Having tracked it down, though, it's nothing of the sort. I looked it up in the law books after George died. The clue is in the title – Sturley v. Powell is a civil case, not a criminal one. George changed his name because John Pedlar had already made the name Sturley a dodgy one and the future lawyer in the family wanted to make a new start.

Even so, the Sturley case is so peculiar that it has to be an example of an early scam by George, an example of the corner game that he took to law to sort out.

Picture the scene. It's 1930 and the country is still reeling from the fallout of the Wall Street crash. Leaping forward into the twentieth century, MPs approved a bill abolishing the offences of blasphemy, atheism and heresy – great; that must have been a load off a lot of people's minds. We were scrapping submarines and battleships like there'd never be another war and unemployment topped two million. The British Board of Film Censors turned down 300 films, half of which showed criminals getting away with their crimes. Income tax went up sixpence in the budget and the heatwave in August killed twenty-four people. What has this to do with Uncle George? Probably nothing; but ask yourself this: what has a nineteen-year-old conman from the East End got to do with the fishing business off the coast of Wales? I deal with it here because it shows how deep he was into dodgy dealing. On the face of it, he seems to be the aggrieved party – the plaintiff – but this is my Uncle George; it can't have been that simple.

The account, from the records of Pembrokeshire County Court sitting at Haverfordwest, makes it clear that George and others – and I haven't a clue who they are, but since he is the only named plaintiff, they must in some sense have worked for him – owned a 40-ton steam fishing boat called *Fleck*. This was a drifter, but in legal terms (confusingly) it was called a liner because that was the fishing method it used. George and his mates employed agents J. Hellings & Sons of Milford Haven who in turn had Thomas Powell as the *Fleck*'s chief engineer from May 1924 until November 1927.

The financial arrangements were complicated, if only because so many people had a share in the *Fleck*'s profits. After each voyage, allowing for the expenses of actually running the boat, the net profits (no pun intended, of course – these blokes are lawyers and have no sense of humour) were split into 12½ shares – five for the owners (George et al.) and

7½ for the crew. This last bit was not divided equally; Powell, as chief engineer, got 1⅛ share. In the event of the catch being small, with losses involved, the owners paid a sum of money to each crew member – which legally was a loan – so that whatever happened, each bloke got three quid.

In February 1929, George must have realised that he was being conned by Powell, who had drawn certain sums from the plaintiffs to the tune of £106 10s. 4d., the best part of six grand today. In 1929 that was serious money and it's no wonder that George et al. weren't going to let Powell get away with it. They were prepared to waive the £6 10s. 4d., but they wanted their hundred quid.

Powell's argument was that he didn't owe George anything. He also said that the county court had no right to try such a case. The Merchant Shipping Act of 1894 brought it squarely under the remit of the Board of Trade. The county court judge wasn't having any of that. He pointed out that he had complete jurisdiction, implied that Powell was a conman and ordered him to stump up the hundred quid.

The thing about bent people is that they keep banging on until they get what they want. Today they quote human rights; in 1929 Powell just said the judge was wrong and took his case to appeal. This of course is where it gets heavy. The Court of Appeal was set up in 1907 to give people facing the death penalty a chance to have that overturned. The idea spread to lesser crimes and such cases can drag on for years (although I've got to say that justice was swifter then than today). A KC (King's Counsel) called E. A. Digby with T. Jenkin Jones as his second represented Powell and George got himself a KC, too – T. J. O'Connor with G. Clark Williams in tow. The judge in the Divisional Court was Lord Justice Henry Slesser, a part-time poet who had been Attorney General in Ramsay MacDonald's Labour government, and he had Lord Justice Thomas Scruton with him.

I won't bore you with the legal gobbledegook, the heretofores and the prior precedents, but the bottom line was that the appeal was dismissed and Powell had to fork out, no doubt with costs as well. So there it is; Uncle George's first court appearance and a result, clearly. Twenty years later he might have dealt very differently with Thomas Powell. I have heard him say – to one of his own clients, in fact – 'If there's any fishy business or stroke-pulling, you'll finish up on the deck with a white chalk line around you.' Yes, he smiled as he said it and there would always be a cup of tea or a glass of Scotch on hand at the same time to soften the delivery, but the message was clear.

How come a nineteen-year-old had part shares in a fishing boat at the height of the Slump right on the other side of the country to where he was living? And how come he had the nous to go to law over the con? That much at least I can answer. George was soaking up the law books that had come his way via his dad from Lincoln's Inn and he was already, by that time, getting his knees under the tables of various law firms in and around London. And that was just the start.

CHAPTER 4
OUT OF THE JAWS OF DEATH

Don't ask me what one of my granddad's associates was doing breaking into offices in Lincoln's Inn along Holborn. Maybe he was a cracksman hoping to find a few bundles. In the event he came away with a bundle of law books and no doubt felt a proper loser. The police certainly thought so. It was some half-brained low life trying to get his own back in his own little way by nicking the source of the lawyers' knowledge. What a waste of time.

Actually, of course, it wasn't and that little bit of larceny put George Sturley, as he still was then, on the yellow brick road to a fortune. John Pedlar could see that and advised both his eldest boys to go into the law. My dad didn't want to know; he had his own salvation in mind, the corner game and Promise Land. All he wanted to know about the law was how to break it on the one hand and evade it on the other. George thought differently.

Lincoln's Inn was one of the four Inns of Court that served as a sort of university for London before they invented the real one and just about every government nob from Thomas

Cromwell onwards was educated in one of them. Knowledge is what they sold there – or, in this case, was lifted by a light-fingered burglar at dead of night. John Pedlar would sit night after night looking things up and checking angles. Ordinary libraries didn't have technical stuff like this and there was no such thing as the internet for ease of reference. Somehow George got the bug and immersed himself in the books, too. He would never be an upright citizen. Bent genes were in his blood. But what if he could get himself into a position where he could set up a crime and, if necessary, defend the very foot-soldiers he had sent on the caper in the first place? That would be a corner game and a half.

Before the war, there were two ways to become a lawyer and in those days, the division between solicitor and barrister was clear cut. A solicitor took a case, prepped the client and found a barrister, a brief who would plead in court. The best ones were KCs, who had taken silk. You can still see their QC descendants ambling around the Temple Law Courts carrying their notes and books in little bags – the sort of books that George was reading. Most lawyers, whether solicitors or barristers, read law at university, came out with a law degree and joined a firm or chambers, as they still call it in that old boy network.

Have a look at the four blokes who made up the Prosecution team in the train robbery. Arthur James and Niall McDermott were QCs (Queen's Counsel). They, as well as Howard Sabin and Desmond Fennell, were public school. And there was a scattering of QCs among the Defence team too – Joseph Grieves for Tommy Wisbey, R. Kilmer-Brown for Big Jim Hussey, Sebag Shaw for Gordon Goody. Almost to a man – and of course, they *were* all men in those days – they had public school and 'Oxbridge' backgrounds. They all belonged to the same clubs and hobnobbed in the same bars in the Wig and Pen Club. And for that, you needed money and lots of it. The days of student grants and student loans lay in the future and many was the talented young man who ended up on the scrap heap because such an education was beyond him. Uncle George and my dad both left school at fourteen and I'm not making excuses for them when I say they entered the world of 'work' at a particularly bad time. When he was fifteen, George faced a London crippled by the General Strike with armed pickets and strike breakers facing each other over the barricades. When my dad was fifteen, Wall Street crashed, heralding the biggest depression of the century.

Ironically, of course, with the amount of cash that John Pedlar was earning from Jack Spot and Billy Hill, he *could* have financed a university career for George and *could* have set Dad up in business, but that was not the Sturley way. Where, people would have asked, would a working-class family from Plaistow have found the fees to put one of their seven kids through college? And anyway, university was seen as the privilege of the elite few and not the universal stepping stone of today's generation.

So the only other way for George to enter the law was to

become an articled clerk and to work his way up. Occasionally you see examples today of blokes who have done this and ended up on the Bench as high court judges but this is very rare and the path is long and hard. George Sturley didn't harbour ambitions like that, not because he didn't want to succeed but because he knew the higher you get in the legal profession, the less cash came in. Judges are poorer than briefs. They get their names and pictures in the paper more often, sure – but that was the last thing George Sturley wanted. Starting as a tea-boy was common then though it doesn't happen now and George was a tea-boy with a difference. He was already a petty criminal, on first-name terms with the kings of the underworld, Spot and Hill, whose exact contemporary he was. He tried his hand with various East End law firms before he found Maurice Lesser.

Maurice was a homosexual Jewish solicitor working out of 21–23 Broadway in Stratford and he already had underworld connections of his own when he hired George Stanley. He was an old-fashioned gentleman whose tendencies were not at all obvious. Ever since Henry Labouchere's Criminal Law Amendment Act of 1884, homosexuality had been illegal in Britain and it carried a custodial sentence. This was the 'blackmailer's charter' because it gave observant low life a chance to clean up from men who wanted to keep their hobbies private. Uncle George never actually got money from Maurice but it gave him leverage, as the Americans say today, and he used it mercilessly.

At first, though, it was by the book and money up front. A lot of legit business and careers had to be paid for in a way that would be called corrupt today and the 'entrance fee' to Lesser's was £400; £400 that George did not have. He turned to my dad – 'Arthur, can I borrow some money?' My dad didn't really have it either – £400 in 1939 would be over £22,000 today. Somehow, he and my mum scraped it together on the strict understanding that this was a loan to be repaid. That was how it went with the Sturleys. Blood was thicker than water but watermarks on money were thicker still and a debt was a debt.

So George was in. It seems unlikely today that a mere clerk could call the shots in a law firm, but they were different days. Because of his links via my granddad, George knew half the villains in London and Maurice Lesser knew the other half. The office in Broadway became the go-to place for anyone with the law breathing down their necks. We've seen already what it gave George access to in terms of money-making. He would earn that entrance fee several times over, on top of what Maurice Lesser paid him for introducing clients on a bonus basis.

And Uncle George got his knees under the table when Maurice asked him for a little help, which had nothing to do with the law but everything to do with making money. The venture changed George's life. It was 1940 and all Hell was breaking loose on both sides of the Channel. Maurice and his mate Harry Isaacs – who would prove useful after the Great

Train Robbery – knew a family called Simons who were holed up in Nazi Germany, definitely an unhealthy place if you were Jewish.

The Jews of course had been the scapegoats for everything since the dawn of time. They had killed Christ, some people said. They had caused the First World War, bent as they were on world domination. In the Middle Ages, they ate babies – the nonsense just went on and on. With such a big Jewish population in the East End we didn't think anything of this. You just rubbed along with everybody as best you could. And now, of course, there was a war on.

Since 1933 when Hitler came to power, German Jews like the Simons had had it rough. The Nuremberg Laws, spelt out by Göring and Hess, took away German citizenship from Jews. The chosen people were now chosen for a different future. They were removed from the professions, teaching, medicine and the law. They were banned from marrying Aryans or having sex with anyone outside their race. The Nazis spent a fortune sorting out exactly what a Jew was and defining what rights each gradation had. *Kristallnacht* in November 1938 was a government-backed punch-up in which synagogues and Jewish shops were attacked and the pavements glittered with broken glass.

After that, the deportations started, a systematic removal of Jews from Germany's streets. Banners appeared in country villages – 'Jews not wanted here' – and there was talk about resettlement in the East. The Lublin plan, the Madagascar idea – both areas where Jews were to be herded to work as slave labour for the Master Race – fell apart as being impractical. By the time war broke out in September 1939, concentration camps were being built all over Germany to house the 'undesirables' who, Hitler was saying, had started this war too.

Wherever the invincible Reich marched, bringing the terror of Blitzkrieg – lightning war – in its wake, the anti-Jewish policy followed. It started first in Poland where hit squads called *Einsatzgruppen* routinely machine-gunned men, women and kids just because they were Jewish.

God alone knows how the Simons family coped during those years. There *are* examples known today of Jews who kept their race and faith so secret that they got away with it, but these examples are very few. Something like that must have happened to the Simons, however, because they still had property and antiques – and this was very much the carrot that got Maurice Lesser and Uncle George involved. Neither of them was exactly made of Scarlet Pimpernel material, nipping across the Channel to save the Simons from certain death on a whim or for a noble cause. There had to be a cash incentive.

I heard the following tale as a kid and grew up with it. Only as an adult did I realise how near-impossible it must have been to pull it off and I don't know the exact details to this day. But reflect for a moment. How was Nicholas Winton, the Englishman of Wenceslas Square, able to smuggle out so many Jewish kids on the *kindertransporten* without getting caught? How did Oskar Schindler save the lives of 1,100 Jews right under the Nazis' noses in his metalware factory in Kraków? And what about that French bloke who pole-vaulted out of a prisoner-of-war camp and kept on running until he got to freedom? Bizarre escapes *did* happen, however much they seem to be made up for the *Boys' Own* comic.

Communication must have been hell. All conventional post effectively stopped with the outbreak of war and telegrams and letters used by spies went via circuitous routes involving neutral Spain, Portugal or Switzerland. Just flying over occupied Europe was inviting suicide with the Luftwaffe on nightly patrols. The key to the Simons' escape is that they had somehow got to France and had been able to bring at least some of their worldly goods with them. And in 1940, France was in chaos.

By 4 June, the British Expeditionary Force, with not a single Sturley among them, had been driven off the beaches at Dunkirk. Churchill, the new Prime Minister, was talking big about fighting the Germans on the beaches but the French were on their own. It was still possible on the 11th of the month for Churchill to meet with retreating French generals at Briare, so crossing the Channel even under the risk of being blown out of the water was still doable. Paris fell on the 14th, but evacuations of Canadians, British, Poles, Czechs and Belgians continued from various ports for the rest of the month. By 5 July, most of France was occupied by the Germans. The bit that wasn't – Vichy – was run by Marshal Pétain, a hero of the Great War who, to everyone's disgust, was firmly in bed with the Nazis.

I don't have any dates, but it makes sense that these summer months, before Europe shut down completely, were George's window of opportunity. The military-style expedition he set up was a foretaste of things to come and he should have got a bloody medal for it. He picked a team of villains, hard men from the East End who didn't mind taking the odd risk if the money was right. I don't know who they were but by definition they were lads who didn't want to fight the Germans officially or they would have not dodged the draft and would have got stuck in already. While the rest of the country braced itself for invasion, and Spitfires and Junkers fought it out over the south coast, George's team (minus George, you won't be surprised to hear) took off from the coast under cover of darkness one night. I'd love to think they were on board the *Fleck*, George's Welsh fishing boat, but I really have no proof that they were.

And this is where it all gets a bit hazy. Coastal Command and a million snoopers protecting the beaches might have seen or heard them go. Out at sea, there was always the risk of a U-boat pack or a Luftwaffe patrol, but that was a chance the boys were prepared to take. Switch off all navigation lights and cut the engine noise and trust to luck. These blokes hit cash-vans, post offices, even banks for a living, often in broad daylight. What could be nicer than a little jaunt across the Channel under cover of darkness? How hard could it be?

I doubt any of them could speak French, let alone German. What was an English crew of trawlermen doing approaching the French coast in the middle of a war? It would have been the first question on the lips of any Wehrmacht patrol on the beaches. They came ashore somewhere near Bruges (technically in Belgium, of course). I have no idea how they hid the boat or how they contacted the Simons, but I bet the Maquis did. By this time, there was already an organised Resistance movement in France and Belgium. The groups often squabbled amongst themselves but their common hatred was reserved for the Bosche. It was the Maquis, this band of rural guerrillas, who were hiding the Simons family. You've got to hand it to those blokes (and women). We know from memoirs written after the war by the Resistance themselves and the SOE/SAS agents who dropped behind enemy lines, how cool and organised they were and how often they ran rings around the Nazis. Exactly how contact was made I don't know but once the Maquis had found them, they would ensure that the Simons and their valuables (George was most insistent on that) could be hurried through the French night to the waiting boat. George had provided forged papers for everybody, using the skills of one of his underworld contacts, so that if they were stopped, all would seem to be in order. The Simons, with their native German, might be able to talk their way out of trouble, but for a bunch of villains from London's East End it would not have been so straightforward.

Disaster almost struck at a checkpoint when a suspicious Wehrmacht officer got a bit nosey. Six people travelling together in wartime was unusual, but whoever the firm boss was rightly believed that to split up was even more dangerous, so they kept together. Greed, though, is a wonderful thing, isn't it? The Nazis might have believed that the Aryans were the Master Race and that Adolf Hitler was some kind of god. But that didn't stop the officer taking the fags and Scotch he was offered, not to mention the stonking wad of French cash. His suspicions disappeared immediately.

Then it was back on the high seas and a dash for Hastings as the nearest 'friendly' port. Like every other seaside resort in the country, the holiday season was over – and would be for another five years. The place was all barbed wire and beach obstacles and searchlights but the fishing smack made it and the family – Mr and Mrs Simons and their daughter – were free.

Or were they? Germans, Austrians and Italians, even those who had lived in Britain for years, were interned on the outbreak of war under Regulation 18B on the grounds that they were enemy aliens and probably sending secret messages back home. Three Germans who had just arrived under cover of darkness *had* to attract suspicion. Even ferrying them around the country was risky. Petrol cost money and people were constantly being asked if their journey was really necessary. Travel by train was even dodgier. What if some innocent fellow-traveller asked the Simons the time? One hint of an accent and it would be a prison camp. Besides, there were valuables to be moved as well.

Somehow George's firm got the Simons to a semi he rented in Ilford. This was a safe house he used for business. Jack Spot and Billy Hill had similar hideaways for their most delicate transactions. After all, however accommodating Maurice Lesser was, he couldn't condone George setting up dodgy deals and jobs at 21–23 Broadway and because of the people he was dealing with, George didn't want them at his home either. You couldn't exactly call Ilford safe, of course, not in 1940. When the Blitz started in September, it was right under the Luftwaffe's flight path. But it would do. George let the Simons settle in for a few days, confident, no doubt, that his neighbours weren't going to ask any questions. Then he went to collect.

Edith Simons was one of the most beautiful women George had ever seen and he couldn't take his eyes off her. He had come for his payment, which he got, having passed the relevant rake-offs to the blokes who had actually run all the risks, but he also got much more than that. He got a partner-in-crime who would stay with him to the end. And of course, he had Marjorie already.

When I was old enough to understand these things, Uncle George said to me, 'Lee, when it comes to women, the only way to handle them is to have two on the go at once.' There's that old toast in the Navy, isn't there? 'To our wives and sweethearts; may they never meet.' That was certainly George's philosophy and he kept it up for the next fifty years until Edith's death. Marjorie was suspicious, of course, and probably guessed that George's prolonged absences from home weren't all work-related. Eventually, she twigged what was going on and hated Edith with a passion, but the point was that George genuinely loved Edith, whereas he just tolerated Marjorie. And Edith knew where the bodies were buried. It's the East End way, especially among the criminal fraternity, not to include wives and girlfriends in business. If you've a job to pull, deals to discuss, send the missus out with her girlfriends or go to see her dear old mum. Gangsters' molls are just that, often eye-candy and not much more. That sounds sexist, doesn't it, today, but it was the way of it. Women like Edith – women like my mum – who encouraged their men and worked with them, were not the norm.

I always think that George's little raid into Nazi-occupied France was a sort of blueprint for what was to follow. He had hand-picked a team of footsoldiers, provided the necessary – false papers, cash and other inducements – and had sent them to carry out Mission Impossible. And they'd fucking done it. They'd whisked three of the *Untermenschen*, people the Nazis classed as 'life unworthy of life' out from the jaws of death. George got his handsome bung for doing it, the undying gratitude of Maurice Lesser and a soul-mate for life.

Now it was time to move on to something that would make him some real money.

CHAPTER 5

GEORGE'S DEBUT: THE EASTCASTLE STREET JOB

It might have been Sonny Sullivan or his brother Slip, although Sonny always denied he was ever there. It might have been Tel Hogan, although at twenty he was a bit young for a job like this, one that required nerve. It might have been 'Taters' Chatham himself, although cat burgling was more his thing. On the other hand, it might have been somebody else entirely. Anyway, one of the gang, wearing a GPO uniform and whistling nonchalantly, wandered across the yard of the Post Office Headquarters at St Martin le Grand that spring morning and nodded and waved to the duty man.

Not that he'd seen the man before in his life, but it's amazing what a nod and a cheery grin will do. Especially if the bloke doing the nodding and grinning is wearing the uniform and carrying a mailbag. He must be on the payroll, one of us. He walked up to the van in question, the one with the number plate he'd committed to memory, lifted up the bonnet and pulled free a switch. Then he shut it again and walked back, still whistling, still nodding to the guard. Sweet, we'd say today, as a nut. That was it. His part in the proceedings was over. He would go home now and wait for a call.

It was two o'clock in the morning of Wednesday 21 May 1952 and all around the Post Office Headquarters bustled a world that's all but vanished now. On the world stage, French paratroopers were in battle against rebels called the Viet Minh north-west of Saigon. Allied fighter-bombers were limbering up for an all-out attack as a kind of finale to the Korean War. The Americans blew an atomic crater in the Nevada desert watched on TV by 35 million viewers. At home, the Labour Party took control of twenty-one councils and the Tory government announced an increase in the meat ration to 1/7d. a week. Newcastle United became the first football team since 1891 to win the FA Cup two years running, beating Arsenal 1–0. The Arsenal were robbed, of course. So were the millions still struggling under rationing seven long years after the end of the war.

But on that Wednesday, a robbery of a different kind was about to take place. It was the first of the so-called 'project' crimes, a meticulously planned heist organised like a military operation. Anybody you bumped into at the time, whether it was in Soho or at the race tracks, thought they knew who was behind it. If you asked them who planned the big mail job, they'll all have told you, 'Billy Hill … Only he could have done that.' Not quite. There's a line in that brilliant Ealing comedy *The Ladykillers* in which one of the crooks says of their innocent old landlady, 'If they get us, I'll tell 'em she planned the job. I'll tell 'em she planned the big one, the Eastcastle Street job.' Ancient Mrs Wilberforce, a.k.a. the actress Katie Johnson, is not at all what you'd expect in a criminal mastermind. But then again, you probably wouldn't expect my uncle George either. He was, remember, a nondescript 5ft 8ins or so with diabetes and only one lung. But most deceptively of all, he was a solicitor's clerk and solicitors are supposed to be the good guys, aren't they?

The press, in late May 1952, spoke in awe of the Eastcastle Street robbery – it was carried out 'with Montgomery-like thoroughness ... it went off as smoothly as any of our commando raids during the war'; that was hats off to George as far as the Sturleys and a select band of villains were concerned.

Of course, there was no way that George himself was going to get his hands dirty. What, a diabetic? With only one lung? Get real. No, the general in the field was Billy Hill, careful to give himself an alibi, but the Field Marshal back at HQ was George Stanley. He had all the t's crossed and all the i's dotted. Planning, checking, rehearsing, going through it over and over again at Hill's flat up West. Nothing was left to chance, yet everything could go wrong. And if it did, it wouldn't be George Stanley with a balaclava over his face, wrestling with postmen on the pavement. He'd be miles away with an alibi as unshakeable as the Rock of Gibraltar.

I never knew exactly who made up the six-man team in the Eastcastle Street job because it all happened before my time and I only heard the story in snatches over the years. I was still in nappies when George recruited Billy Hill as the gang leader. In many ways he was the obvious choice. Hill had gone down for two stretches during the war and had even got himself into bother in Johannesburg in 1948. There is no doubt that he was a force to be reckoned with, inspiring loyalty and fear in equal proportions from his own mob on one hand and the Whites, whose crime empire he basically destroyed, on the other. In 1952 he was still on friendly terms with Jack Spot but that was a temporary marriage made in hell. Both men saw themselves as kings of the underworld, so there would be a day of reckoning coming.

Hill's style, in the context of robberies, was smash-and-grab raids, usually of furs or jewels in broad daylight, relying on shock and the speed of the getaway to confuse the hell out of innocent bystanders watching it all unwind. He was on oddly cordial terms with the police, skirting carefully around Ted Greeno and Bob Higgins and remembering to call them 'Mr'. Funnily enough, neither of them mentions Billy in their memoirs, probably because they couldn't catch him. Hill was put up in more identity parades than I've had hot dinners but he was never picked out. He had a tight team of heavies who could be trusted with any hands-on rough stuff and to keep their mouths shut. George knew that. If it went wrong and the boys were caught you could rely on Billy Hill's mob not to grass anybody up. If it went well, he could be relied upon to take the credit for himself. And so it proved.

But Billy Hill was always very coy about his involvement in the Eastcastle job. He wrote that it was the one perfect crime that will always be remembered. He thought Scotland Yard knew who actually carried out that job, but any evidence to prove it had gone.

Of course it had.

Even if Hill hinted that the job was his – and today most books simply state that it was – that was fine by George Stanley. He didn't want kudos; he wanted money. In his own way, George Stanley was the first of a new breed: a careful, quiet manipulator of situations, a mover and shaker. Not for him the ghosted memoirs followed by a lavish gangland funeral with flowers sent by sobbing heavies.

George's plan depended on an insider, someone working in the Post Office who could provide the necessary details. How much was being carried in the High Value Packages, from where to where and when? How many men 'rode shotgun' on the van? What were the security arrangements inside? What was the exact route? I never found out who this insider was. Those who believe Billy Hill orchestrated Eastcastle speculated on a mug who'd got in over his head at one of his spielers and whose debt would be wiped in exchange for certain information. We don't have a name of course and without that the link must be pure speculation. But George was *the* expert at the corner game and Promise Land. If an insider could work for Billy Hill he could also work for George Stanley.

The big money – and nobody could be *quite* sure how much – would come in on the mail train from the north and its terminus would be Paddington. From there, the HVPs were loaded into a van with a driver's door, passenger door and double door at the back. The thing was locked and if the doors were forced an alarm would ring which could only be silenced when it was re-set or the battery ran down; there was no other way to turn it off. No other way, that is, unless early in the morning, a gang member in a GPO uniform sauntered into the marshalling yard where the van was kept and disabled the alarm before it even set off for the station.

George made sure that the heist was rehearsed so that any snags would present themselves beforehand and could be worked out. Two cars were used to act out the van heist in some anonymous streets well away from London. Any nosey neighbours would be told that a film company was shooting a movie. And there was, after all, a precedent. Two years earlier, Jack-the-Lad Dirk Bogarde had shot good old Jack Warner, a.k.a. PC George Dixon, outside a London cinema in *The Blue Lamp*. Only a year after that, Ealing Studios had cinema coppers chasing all over the place in their black Railtons in *The Lavender Hill Mob*. Londoners at least were quite used to celluloid cops and robbers. Nobody would ask too many questions.

On the night of Wednesday 21 May, Billy Hill and his chosen six were cooped up in his flat in west London. They all had their parts to play and now it was all about timing. The 'A' feature was about to start.

Around the corner, in the darkest streets, two cars waited. One was a dark green Vanguard belonging to Eric Hartwell. The other was a 2½-litre Riley, the property of Michael Forte. They had both been stolen the day before from lock-up garages in Bathurst Mews, Paddington and their registration plates had been changed. Like the alarm-disabling postman, the car thief had no connection with what was to follow.

At 3.30 a.m. the phone rang in Hill's flat. The man George had hired to watch at Paddington Station told Hill that the train had arrived and the van was loaded and moving. We have to remember that this kind of robbery – a van hi-jacking – was a new kind of crime on Britain's streets. And nobody, except George Stanley, his inside man and the boys who now dashed to the stolen motors, was expecting it.

But there was a snag. There were roadworks on the van's usual stretch and a detour took it off Oxford Street, along Berners Street and onto Eastcastle. By now it was 4.20 a.m., nearly dawn on that late May morning. Some nifty driving had brought the cars into their relative positions in a mews off Eastcastle and now their occupants pounced. The Vanguard pulled out in front of the mail van and jammed on its anchors. Suspecting trouble, the driver toyed with reversing but the Riley had blocked him from behind. In a blur of movement, boots clattering on pavements, all six men piled out of their respective cars and wrenched open the van's doors. The three occupants, W. C. Johnson, H. A. Symes and F. Rogers, were hauled out and coshed severely, two of them lying unconscious on the ground while the gang helped themselves to the van. All three vehicles snarled away into the early morning.

I have no idea whether this heavy-handed approach was George's idea or Billy Hill's. At the time, of course, George was fast asleep at home in Theydon Bois, Essex, light years away from the scene of the crime, but in any case violence was not his style. The law, as he so often said to me, was robbery without violence. And actual robbery should be without violence, too. Violence was certainly Hill's style, but he is at pains in his autobiography to point out that the coshing of the postmen was not particularly severe. I suppose it depends on which end of the cosh we're talking about.

There are a number of sections to a robbery. First comes the inside information, then the planning, then the carrying out of the event and finally – often most difficult of all – what to do with the loot. I don't think anybody – not George, not Billy Hill, not even the inside man – knew exactly how much the mail van had been carrying that night. It turned out to be anything between £236,000 and £287,000, depending on which version of the events you read. Today that's nearly £6.5 million. It was the biggest cash robbery in British history. And the shock waves reached America where the US press had a field day, smugly pointing a finger at *another* nation whose crime rates were soaring.

The first step in removing the money was to transfer it to a safer place. Seven armed men, some of whom were known to the police, tearing around London in stolen cars and a Post

Office van was a sure way of attracting attention. They might just as well have gone to Bow Street and given themselves up. The van was found abandoned later in Augustus Street, Camden Town, near Regent's Park. The loot itself had been transferred and hidden under fruit on a 'railer', the kind of fruit lorry that delivered early every morning to Covent Garden, then the capital's largest fruit and veg market. *This* is why Hill's boys only took eighteen sacks – the lorry could not carry more. The police and press later speculated that the gang had been interrupted and panicked but this never happened. The sheer size of the haul made the thirteen remaining bags redundant. And the lorry was kosher – it belonged to Jack Gyp, who really was a fruiterer. He'd been recruited by Sonny Sullivan to make his truck available and ask no questions. Only the number plates had been changed to protect the guilty.

Throughout this night, George Stanley had insisted that a fog of confusion descend over the events. Misinformation was the name of the game and he knew that the Flying Squad would be all over Eastcastle Street like a rash. So Hill's boys had dropped 'careless' clues at the scene – a Sheffield-made set of bolt cutters (unnecessary because one of the van's doors was faulty) and, more bizarrely, a belted trench coat with a cleaner's label ZD 662 C19. There were no prints on either object of course and the police spent futile weeks trying to trace their origins. Likewise, the railer's journey was convoluted. It went first to Spitalfields Market, in the heart of the old Ripper territory, then to the Borough where George Chapman had once run a pub and murdered his wives, then back to Covent Garden. But by the time it reached there, the only thing that the lorry contained was fruit. Why? Because another stop on the itinerary was Stratford. Why there? Because that was where Maurice Lesser ran his legal practice and because his chief clerk, George Stanley, was always in first to open up the offices. And he was expecting a delivery. Hill's account has a vague mention of the loot being taken to the country and divided between the fifteen men involved. I don't have to tell you who did the counting out.

The media circus began the next day. Without the saturation coverage of today's television and radio, not to mention social networking sites, the story of Eastcastle Street was told via newspapers, still based exclusively in Fleet Street, and pompous news bulletins from John Snagge on the wireless. In a way, though, George Stanley made history here, too. The job was the first to see robbery as a glamorous enterprise, drawing on the fiction of gentlemen crooks like Raffles and knights of the road like Dick Turpin. It was the start of the popular notion of the common man striking a bit of a blow against the Establishment, a mood change that would become much more marked in the next decade. In the Age of Austerity, with its nasty Utility furniture, coupons and cities still full of bomb craters, seven men moving like commandoes through London's streets and getting away with *so* much money looked like fiction too. It didn't help that the Prime Minister, Winston Churchill, insisted on daily bulletins to be kept abreast of the situation. It gave the average street crook ideas above his station. A van raid almost in broad daylight in the glitzy West End had something of the Mona Lisa heist about it. The System was not working and in the corridors of power there were demands for heads to roll. You can be sure that George Stanley bought a *lot* of newspapers the next day to see what the media were *not* saying about him.

In the real world, spanning that and the newspaper flights of fancy like a colossus, stood Percy Hoskins, crime reporter for the *Daily Express*. He and his oppo Tom Clayton got it right that there had to be an inside man involved in the Eastcastle job. The Flying Squad were sure of it, too. So was the Post Office's Investigation Branch. The Met's Flying Squad, formed in John Pedlar's day soon after the Great War, had been set up to counter armed robbery and was given the fast cars and the streetwise coppers to do it. In the Fifties they were normally called the Heavy Mob by the underworld (and they, in turn, gave the same title to Hill's gang). The man in charge of the Eastcastle case was Superintendent Bob Lee, then second-in-command of the Flying Squad and a no-nonsense copper you crossed at your peril.

As for the Post Office's Investigation Branch, don't think that was just a bureaucratic formality. Set up originally in 1683, they had a reputation for cracking down hard on their own. Tampering with the Royal Mail was a serious offence. On a single day – 20 May 1795 – three of the six men hanged at Newgate were postmen. Another twenty-nine faced the drop before 1837 when the death penalty for postmen guilty of tampering was reduced to seven years' transportation.

Lee, the IB and Percy Hoskins were able to draw up a list of potential Eastcastle Street robbers that was not far from the real thing. Billy Hill was in the hot seat as the organiser. The head of the IB was so convinced that Hill was involved that he tailed him personally for days. The Post Office police became Hill's unofficial minders – it would have been impossible, he wrote later, for him to have been murdered or even attacked because of this protection. The highest profile suspect was George 'Taters' Chatham, who styled himself 'burglar to the gentry'. He used London's notorious pea-soupers to nip up the sides of buildings a spider would think twice about and during the course of a long career nicked a couple of the Duke of Wellington's swords from the Victoria and Albert Museum. Other names on the list were also well known to the law. Billy Benstead had been a burglar all his life. Mike Donovan, Jock Gwilliam, Patsy Murphy, Sonny Sullivan and Joe Price were London thieves typical of the criminal flotsam that Billy Hill could call upon for a job like Eastcastle Street. The man who would most have enjoyed swinging the cosh was Teddy Machin (who later became a neighbour of ours in Inverness Avenue, Southend), although he was more at home with a razor blade. An enforcer for Jack Spot, he had taken an axe to Jimmy Wooder four years earlier. Jimmy ran a protection racket out of Islington and he and Jack had never got on. Just an everyday story of criminal folk.

In that year, Machin and Benstead had been involved in Spot's bungled robbery on a bonded warehouse at the new airport at Heathrow. Somebody grassed and the pair were lucky to get away. Those who didn't got twelve years. I don't doubt for a moment that the gang for Eastcastle was selected by Hill, drawn from men he could trust and who he had worked with before. Uncle George would have been happy to leave the selection to him on condition that one name involved, again not mentioned in the official record, was Charlie Sturley, George's cousin. He was the vital go-between who worked with Billy Hill, so Hill did not need to have direct contact with George. He was the one who brought the mail sacks to George in his Stratford office after the event.

But there was one crucial difference with the Eastcastle job that marks it out as being beyond even Hill's considerable powers. The mock postman who fixed the van's alarm; the bloke who stole the drags (getaway cars); the man with the phone call from Paddington Station; Jack Gyp with his lorry; each of these men carried out a separate, yet vital, part of the operation, unbeknownst to the others. There is nothing in Hill's previous criminal history to match anything as skilful – or as careful – as this. This is pure George Stanley. Keep your foot soldiers apart, keep them guessing. The only team that needs to work together are the blokes with the coshes and the balaclavas – that was where Billy Hill came in.

Another name missing from any list of likely lads was Terence 'Lucky Tel' Hogan, probably because he was the new kid on the block and the Heavy Mob had never heard of him. His dad was a bookie; his mum a milkwoman. Both of them drank heavily and neglected the boy. Like the Sturleys, the Hogans were what today's social workers would call dysfunctional. Billy Hill recruited the lad in 1952, maybe for the Eastcastle job itself. He drove the van away from the scene.

Knowing the likely lads was one thing. Pinning it on them was something else. Apart from the planted clues, there was no forensic to help. The cars were stolen. The lorry, as far as anyone knew, was hijacked. The money – all £287k of it – had vanished. Those were the days of police interrogations, without the benefit of brief or tape-recordings. PACE (Police and Criminal Evidence Act) was still thirty years away. Suspects habitually fell downstairs in police stations. But Billy Hill's men were, with the exception of Hogan, old lags. They'd done their bird and would do more. Hill actually volunteered himself at Scotland Yard once the press hue and cry was on. He was in a nightclub at the time of the heist – thirty witnesses would swear to it. The crime journalist T. A. Sandrock of the *Daily Telegraph* reminded everybody that in those days there was a different kind of villain, accepting his bird, if he got caught, as a hazard of the job. But these men had no intention of getting caught. They all followed the advice given to me by my dad and by my uncle George – 'Give the police nothing, Lee,' they would say, 'and they'll get nothing. You'll walk.' They did.

Superintendent Lee's Flying Squad concentrated on the inside man as the potential weak link. The likelihood was that he was not a hardened criminal but a greedy man with a fatal weakness. That was undoubtedly true, but Uncle George never revealed his name and to this day I have no idea who he was. The staff in the van came under suspicion, especially since the alarm had been de-activated, one door was not secured properly and the driver, Johnson, had left his keys on the seat rather than hand them to the guard, Rogers, contrary to protocol. On the other hand, would anybody *so* involved in setting the job up actually be present on the night? In the event, the law talked to Johnson and let him go. George Stanley knew only too well that sheer numbers were on his side. The number of Post Office operatives who *could* have leaked the information was huge; there were over 3,000 working at the East Central Delivery Offices alone.

There were the usual noises about preventing a repetition of this sort of raid. Guards were to be armed with police-style truncheons from now on but the feasibility of patrol car support was rejected as unworkable because of a lack of manpower. So next time you see a security van with the legend 'Police follow this vehicle', don't you believe it; there aren't enough coppers in the country!

If George was masterly in the organisation of the Eastcastle Street job he was pure genius in the distribution of the loot. If a man lights his fags with stolen fivers; if he buys a fleet of limos; treats all his mates in a West End nightclub, the Heavy Mob are going to come calling (and I don't mean Billy Hill). The only two men ever put on trial over Eastcastle were Robert Kingshott and Edward Noble, both accused of receiving stolen money from the job. Since Noble had previously been fired from the Post Office for petty theft, he appeared to be a strong suspect – an employee with insider information; an employee with a grudge. But both Noble and Kingshott were acquitted of the charges in July 1952 and no more were ever brought.

You couldn't really expect Billy Hill to own up to Eastcastle Street, especially as early as in his autobiography, only three years after the event. In it, he wrote, '[Scotland Yard] suggested that I was the brains behind the robbery. I had to tell them, of course, that I was not.'

George Stanley 1; Rest of the World 0. And the game had only just begun.

CHAPTER 6
A LIFE OF POVERTY

I hated my parents. I hate them to this day. Yes, I know, your mum's your mum and your dad's your dad; they gave me life; blood is thicker than water and all those other clichés that miss the point entirely.

I first saw my mum on 3 October 1950. My dad wasn't there, of course; not because it wasn't the thing then for dads to be present at their kids' births – which it wasn't – but because he was doing a stretch in Winchester gaol at the time.

What else was happening? You've got to see it in context because in some ways, the world I was born into isn't there any more. The Korean War had begun that year on the world stage and in London three generations of the Bowler family attended a celebration marking the centenary of the hat they'd invented. There was a plane crash at Mill Hill with twenty-eight fatalities; and another one in the fog at Heathrow. They still had pea-soupers then – the London smog would become a casualty of the Clean Air Act later but in the meantime played merry hell with Uncle George's one remaining lung. The King officially opened the House of Commons which had taken a direct hit in the Blitz nine years earlier and Princess Elizabeth christened her second child, Anne. A lot of people must have thought the world was coming to an end when teachers got a whacking pay rise up to £630 a year (only £504 for women, of course, as you'd expect back then). And Hugh Gaitskell became the new Chancellor of the Exchequer in Attlee's government.

None of this had anything to do with the Sturleys. Except that it was the Age of Austerity and times, for straight people, were hard. I don't remember our first house in Leytonstone, but I soon got used to the older kids around me – they were my brothers, Arthur, Lennie, John and Vic. They told me all about Dad and I remember, when I was three, meeting him for the first time. I walked with Mum to Chalkwell Station and I was fascinated by the trains. They were big and black, hissed steam and belched smoke. I was hooked. Years later, I would meet the great and the not-so-good on trains like these and would meet some blokes who stole rather a lot of money from them. But the bloke I met that morning was huge. He towered over me and had these enormous hands, one of which he used to shake one of mine. I don't think he kissed me or picked me up. The only time my dad ever made a fuss of me is when there was some ulterior, money-making motive for it. That was just as well at the time because I didn't exactly take to him. This stranger wasn't just somebody we met on the platform; he was living in my house.

There were rows with Mum, rows with my brothers. Dad could sulk for England, but he wasn't always around. I'd ask my brothers where he was and it was always more or less the same answer – 'He'll be in the boozer, Lee, down the Old Vic' or 'Down the dogs' or 'Putting a few on the gee-gees, I shouldn't wonder'. I didn't know what any of this meant; I just went along with it because I didn't know anything else. It would be years before I realised the Sturleys weren't like other people.

Dad had been the breadwinner and for four years he was in gaol. Mum had gone to see my uncle George, with his knees firmly under the table at the solicitors Lesser & Co by this time, and asked him for help; after all, he was Arthur's brother and these were hard times. George was not forthcoming. 'Your husband,' he said to her, careful not to use the 'my brother' phrase, 'has had more money than I will ever see. It's not my fault you've squandered it.' Mum was carrying me at the time and George made an extraordinary suggestion – always helpful, was my uncle George. 'I'll put it to you straight, Vicky,' he said (I found out later). 'Marjorie would love kids but she has a problem; women's trouble, you know. In a nutshell, I'd like to take little Lennie and the kid.' He pointed to the bump that was me. 'They'll be raised as our own. Shall we say five hundred quid?'

Now, in the past, kids were often moved from one branch of a family to another as the need arose, but this was 1950 not the bloody Dark Ages and the fact that cash was involved made it even more sordid and hard-edged. Anyway, Mum was having none of it – 'Over my dead body, George,' she told him. And she never spoke to him again.

If Uncle George wouldn't help, what about Uncle Clement? Attlee's Socialist government had set up the Welfare State so Mum asked for something out of the National Assistance budget. No joy there, either – Arthur Sturley had gone to prison over a £40,000 fraud; did his wife *really* expect the authorities to believe he had made no provision for his family? Clearly the pin-striped arsehole who made that decision had never met my dad.

All I knew about any of this is that I was looked after by a neighbour most days. Mum got a part-time job as a receptionist at a dentist's (which of course is how she'd met Dad in the first place). Within weeks of his release from Winchester – a place he vowed he'd never go back to – Dad was up to his old tricks again. This time it was scrap metal. Because the name Sturley was less than squeaky clean, Dad reinvented himself under Mum's maiden name and called the new enterprise Blamey & Sons; a bit like Uncle George Sturley had become George Stanley. Dad would literally pick up bits of scrap in the streets, because the 1950s saw the end of the tram – the last one ran into the New Cross Depot when I was two – and there were tram lines everywhere, waiting to be ripped up and sold off.

When Mum and Dad had cash, they spent it like water (always against Uncle George's advice) and even with the modest takings from the scrap metal so far, they celebrated the birth of Blamey & Sons by going out (without the kids, of course) to the Grand Hotel on the front, then the swishest place in Southend. My dad was a magician, there was no doubt about that. He'd mesmerise people so that they just threw money at him. He was the sort of bloke who could dominate a room just by walking into it. The first time I saw him in action, I couldn't believe it. He took me along Leigh's high street, the Broadway, and I noticed the shopkeepers calling him 'sir' and treating him with respect. He was a conman with a prison record, but you wouldn't know it to look at him and to hear his patter.

One man who went in awe of him was Toby, who cut people's hair in North Street. I remember Toby plonking me down on a board resting across the arms of his barber's chair because I was too small for the chair itself. Toby wanted to be a wheeler-dealer like Dad and whenever we went there, the conversation followed the same pattern, 'Toby,' Dad would say softly, 'you stick to cutting hair, old son.'

Dad even had a chauffeur who everybody called the Duke and most of Southend and beyond seemed happy to give him credit. He would carry rolled-up fivers (big bits of paper in those days) but only the top was a five; the notes underneath were ones. He bought everything this way, dressed in his smart, re-tailored suit, and he would say 'Keep the change' like he was lord of the manor. Which of course, in a way, he was.

Judas Iscariot had his thirty pieces of silver; Arthur Sturley got his £30 out for every ton of scrap metal he bought. His profits went through the roof. The tram line contract brought Dad into contact with a local Southend councillor,

Monty Schwarz, a dapper little Jew. He wasn't bent in the usual sense of the word, but he did have a weakness – for my mum. I knew nothing about this and didn't understand the looks my brothers sometimes gave each other when his name cropped up. I learned all about it later. Monty would pop around when Dad was out – I was at school by this time and my brothers were too, or at work. Mum played him like a fiddle, laying it on thick about how grim her life was with Dad (not *that* much invention there, then). Monty wasn't very original either, coming out with the age-old cliché of the womaniser, that his wife didn't understand him. He suggested that he and my mum elope together. They talked it out and got down to dates and times. Sure enough, at the appointed hour, Monty arrived looking like a puppy with two tails. Mum had gone to the lengths of packing two suitcases and he carried them down from our upstairs flat.

At the bottom of the stairs was my dad and another man. 'What's going on here?' asked Dad, as if he'd just come down with the last rain shower. Mum blew the gaff, still stringing Monty along, and Dad suggested they all go back to the flat and talk things over. Mum made the inevitable cup of tea but Monty was way beyond all that – 'I could use a large Scotch,' he said. Dad duly obliged; out came the Johnnie Walker. The rivals for my mum's affections sat together on the sofa. 'This doesn't look too good, Monty,' Dad said. 'For you, I mean. By the way, I haven't done the introductions, have I? This is my solicitor.' The other man beamed like he was meeting the vicar. Dad claimed he had hired a private investigator to watch the pair of lovers and he had the photos to prove it. The solicitor nodded gravely. The councillor's mind was racing as he gulped the drink. 'I could lose my job on the council,' he muttered. Dad and the solicitor nodded again like those dogs in the back of cars that were all the rage a few years back, faces straight as pokers, all concern and angst.

'And of course,' my dad didn't really need to add, 'if the papers get hold of it ...'

Monty put his drink down and looked Dad squarely in the face. 'I will do anything if you keep this quiet, Arthur.'

Dad milked the moment for all he was worth, pretending he was weighing up all the outrage of the situation, all the agony of a cheating wife, all the gloom of betrayal. 'All right,' he said at last, like he was taking on the National Debt for the greater good, 'I won't do anything ...' Everyone waited for the other shoe to drop. And it did. ''Course,' Dad went on, 'I expect a few favours in return.'

That went without saying and once Monty had gone, sweating and glad to be out of there, Mum, Dad and the solicitor poured themselves large ones and laughed their heads off. 'Silly bastard. A grown man eloping.'

With Monty Schwarz being very accommodating on the council, the scrap metal business went from strength to strength. Where did it all go, this money? To the dogs, to the gee-gees, to the chauffeur-driven cars and the nights out on the town. And then it all came to bite us in the arse again.

The scrap metal business was in Mum's name so it was Mrs Blamey who ended up in court. Frauds running up to £46,000, bankruptcy, ruin. Dad may have asked Uncle George for help, but he didn't get any. I can just imagine the conversation. 'You've made your bed, Arthur; now you've got to fucking lie in it.' The Sturleys had been here before and would be again. With the Ministry of Defence involved there was no opportunity for Dad to work his magic and in court the Prosecution tore Mum to shreds. Lawyers are clever bastards and of course the law is weighted on the side of the Establishment; there's no wiggle-room. At least one of the barristers had the decency to admit that it should have been Arthur Sturley in the dock and not Mrs Blamey. Even so, she could hardly claim to have been blameless. Ironically, my dad *was* in court that day, skulking up in the gallery. He knew a shot over the bows when he felt the wind of one and went on the run, hiding out in London.

By now it was 1958. There were bubble cars at the Motor Show, race riots with the West Indians in Notting Hill and the hit songs of the year, which I used to listen to on the radio, were very appropriate to the Sturley family – 'Who's Sorry Now?', 'All I Have To Do Is Dream' and 'Magic Moments' (not that we had many of these). With Blamey & Sons a thing of the past, consigned to the scrap-metal heap of history, those sons rallied together against the world and two of them turned to crime in all its varieties.

Although they never communicated directly, Mum took belated advantage of Uncle George's kind offer and Lennie and I went to live with him in the big house at Red Oaks in Theydon Bois. Auntie Marjorie was knee-high to a grasshopper and feisty with it but she could bore for England and Lennie and I realised that this was what normal life was like. There would be no knock at the door at Red Oaks, unless it was the police consulting Uncle George in his official capacity. The place had been a pig farm so it was huge, especially to a kid of eight. There were barns and outbuildings and, after a lifetime in a semi with six other Sturleys, *space*.

How George had ended up in that house in Theydon Bois in the first place is an interesting tale of brotherly love. Uncle George had never repaid the £400 he had cadged from Dad to buy his way into Lessers and soon after the war, Dad was in one of his occasional periods of desperate dire straits. He called at the Broadway to remind his brother that there was still money owing nearly six years on. He had called early in the morning while George was opening up.

'If you want to see me,' George stood on whatever dignity he had, 'you have to make an appointment with my secretary.'

Now, at 6ft 2ins, Dad could have put one on George and that would be that. George had trouble raking a gravel drive, let alone defending himself. But violence was not Dad's way and he resolved to get even rather than get mad. A mate of Dad's worked for Strutt & Parker, the estate agents, and they had a house on the market in Theydon Bois, a pig farm that was an inheritance. The new owners wanted shot of it so the price was a knock-down £1,600. So, for the usual backhander, Dad got George to buy Red Oaks and by a little bit of financial finessing, made that £400 ten times over in the months that followed.

I often wonder what my life would have been like if I'd stayed with George and Marjorie Stanley; having a different name might have helped. Looking back, I'm not sure George actually liked kids. When I was an adult he would glowingly refer to me as the son he never had – 'Oh, Lee; yes, he's good as gold' – but that was much later. He bought Lennie and me because Marjorie wanted us and he wanted to keep Marjorie sweet. It was only in my late teens that George started to open up about his life of crime. I was a man by then, at least in his eyes, and I had won my criminal spurs. The 'big reveal' of George's Criminal Vitae wouldn't happen until later. All I knew was that Uncle George and Auntie Marjorie didn't expect me to go out thieving and passing the proceeds to them, unlike Mum and Dad at home. As it was, my stay with them was short-lived.

About nine months after we'd moved in, Mum turned up in the Duke's black Jag, complete with the Duke at the wheel (this, of course, from a woman who had been declared bankrupt and was lucky not to be doing time). The Duke was a small-time conman who worked with my dad. He had his chauffeur's uniform, with cockaded cap and plastron-fronted tunic, and he looked the bee's knees. His Jag was something else, too, all polished and gleaming. All of it was a front, of course, for when Dad went out on the corner game. George was at work, no doubt fleecing people with the full backing of the law. Mum knew that and she told Marjorie all about the little deal George had struck with Arthur for the grand sum of £500. Marjorie had no idea about this and was horrified. Mum was good at the crocodile tears, claiming that she had been as much in the dark about it as Marjorie was and sobbing that she desperately wanted her boys back. That part was true – Lennie and I were good at making money for her. So back to Victoria Drive we went.

Somewhere in the corridors of power there must have been warrants out for the arrest of Arthur Sturley, but the charge was fraud so I doubt there would have been mugshots all over the place and he didn't exactly fit the image of Public Enemy Number One. As long as he and Mum were careful – and they usually were – he could stay on the run and survive. He got himself a straight job – as far as I know the only one he ever had in his life apart from the brief tailoring business – as a cook in a posh private school in Leatherhead, Surrey.

My own life of crime, which began when I was six, was going well. Drainpipes, soil pipes, window ledges, bring them on. There was a banana warehouse in North Road, Westcliff – don't ask – and my mate Norman and me got £35 from the till. I'd never seen so much money in one place in my life.

What happened to my brother John should have been a warning to me, but I suppose every thief and conman thinks he's better and smarter than all the others and It Will Never Happen to Me. It happened to John, though, and all through that twisted fuck Andy Hempstead. The two of them were burgling a TV and radio shop in London Road, near Westcliff's library, when the alarm went off. The police were called and it turned out that Hempstead was carrying a gun.

Firearms were still pretty rare on the streets in 1960. A lot of blokes came back from the war with guns as souvenirs but there was a huge outcry when I was two and a small-time wannabe crook called Christopher Craig shot and killed a policeman in Croydon. His oppo, Derek Bentley, not armed and actually held by the police when the killing happened, was charged with murder and they hanged him. This was a world away from the sawn-off robberies of the Seventies and Eighties. In fact, in the late Forties, Billy Hill and the White gang had come to an agreement that shooters were not to be used and they actually dumped a small arsenal in the Thames to prove that they meant what they said. As it turned out, of course, no one was hurt in John and Hempstead's raid and they were lucky to get two years in Borstal. 'Our parents are crap, sonny boy,' Lennie said to me. 'Get away from them as soon as you can.'

It was soon after that when I met a couple who were anything but lovely. That summer, Dad got word to me that he wanted me to spend a week with him. Let's draw a veil over the fact that a fraudster on the run wants to have his eleven-year-old son at his elbow and the field day Social Services would have with that today; I knew full well that there was some scam on and I'd have some role to play in whatever scheme my dad had in mind.

Me and Mum met him in the Lyons Tea Rooms at Aldgate tube station on the edge of Spitalfields. They gave each other a hug and a kiss that seemed to go on for ever and all I got was a pat on the head and a 'Hello, Lee'. While Mum went back to Southend via a series of detours in case the Old Bill was about, I was off, with the king of the corner game. 'What we going to do, Dad?'

We were going to Hoxton, a place I didn't know. There used to be a lunatic asylum there in the good old days and the poet and playwright Ben Jonson killed a bloke in a duel there once upon a time, so it seemed the right kind of place for villains like my dad. We were going to meet Red Face, a mate of Arthur Sturley's from way back. His real name was Tommy Godfrey and he lived in a high-rise block of flats. I'll never forget the sight of all London at my feet from his front room window on the eighth floor; I don't suppose I'd recognise half of it now. The docks were still just about going then and there were holes in the ground everywhere where they hadn't patched up the bomb damage from the war.

But that wasn't the only extraordinary view I had that day. Tommy Godfrey had a face the colour of a letter box, glowing with the demon drink. Or, as Bruce Reynolds so colourfully put it later, 'He had a face with the pigmentation of a baboon's bollocks.'

'This is my youngest son, Lee,' my dad said and our host held out his hand.

'Pleased to meet you, Lee,' he said.

'Pleased to meet you, Red Face,' I said and instantly felt my dad's elbow in my ribs. 'Er ... that's Tommy, son,' he said, through clenched teeth. I apologised but Red Face was laughing. 'It's OK, son,' he said.

Then they got down to business. Tommy knew two blokes who were about to open a new nightclub in Bow Road. I knew nothing about London's nightlife then, the wide boys and Jack-the-Lads who hustled for a living, the booze and the call girls. That was going to change. The blokes wanted gear for the club, glitzy lights, upmarket furniture, paint and wallpaper.

'Can you get what they want?'

'Of course I can, Tom,' Dad said, 'but are they all right? Connable?'

'They're a pair of hard cases,' Red Face said, 'but not that clever.'

'OK,' Dad said. 'Set it up. I'll give you a bell tomorrow.'

They talked over old times. How Red Face had been a fixer for Billy Hill in the good old days. He was well impressed that Uncle George had an excellent cover with Lesser & Co, Solicitors and said what a great bloke he was. Dad laughed. 'Maurice Lesser didn't know what hit him when he took George on.'

Tommy agreed, his face getting redder as he laughed. 'Thing about George,' he said, 'he couldn't walk straight if he tried. Be in touch.'

The next day, Dad took me to Bow Road and finally to the Grave Maurice pub in Whitechapel High Street. The place was still Jewish then, as it had been since the days of Jack the Ripper, and it was poor and down at heel. A badly painted bloke in an Elizabethan ruff scowled down at me from the pub sign as I waited outside. This was Grave Maurice himself – actually the Graf or Prince Maurice of Nassau – although I didn't know it at the time. Dad was inside talking to two of the biggest men I'd ever seen in all my eleven years. After a while they all came out and I noticed the plumper of the two looking me up and down very closely. I didn't like him or the other one. There was something about their eyes … They wore sharp, Italian suits with highly polished shoes, trying to look like a couple of ordinary businessmen.

Dad had just struck a deal inside. He would get a monkey (£500) off these two – they paid up there and then – and he would see to it that their new club was furnished tastefully.

'See you soon.' Dad shook their hands. 'I'll ring you.' And he watched them go, striding along the pavement towards Vallance Road. People on the street seemed to part for them like the Red Sea did for Charlton Heston and when they'd gone, Dad whispered, 'They've got no chance.' He beamed at me with what passed for pride. 'You pulled that off, Lee. Here's a pound pocket money,' and he slipped me the note.

'Thanks, Dad,' I said, realising what a rare gift this was, 'but how did I pull it off for you?'

'The fat one's a poof,' Dad said. 'He liked you.'

I don't recall ever having a man-to-man chat with Dad. With big brothers, you don't need to. But at eleven I knew what a poof was and I felt suddenly cold. 'What if it had gone wrong?' I asked him and probably wouldn't have quite understood the answer if he'd told me.

'It didn't,' he grinned. 'So don't worry.'

'Who are they?' I asked. 'They look evil.'

'That's the Kray twins,' Dad said. 'They're a couple of mugs and I've just taken a monkey off them.'

In the years ahead, Uncle George didn't tangle with the Krays. There was the tough, no-nonsense smacking that went hand-in-hand with the gangs. And there were psychopaths. When George Stanley had the opportunity to defend the twins, he passed.

That day, it was back to Aldgate and Lyons Tea Rooms and Mum. Arthur Sturley vanished into the crowds.

But he didn't vanish for long. The police caught him. The upshot of that? Four years in Pentonville. Like all London prisons, Pentonville was old-school, all Victorian brick and high, tiny, barred windows. Before visiting time, Mum and I would stop off at the little café across the road and she'd fold up a pound note in the silver paper from her fag packet and put it in her mouth. We went through gate after gate, through corridors gloomy and cold, into the visiting area. Old lags in prison outfits waited to greet their nearest and dearest and when Mum and Dad kissed, I knew the quid was switched. Dad picked me up and hugged me, as if he did this all the time, and I was told to act normal and not show any surprise. I felt him slide something down the waistband of my trousers. Then we would all sit down and talk family. I noticed Uncle George never featured in the conversation.

Outside again, Mum took a small packet out of her mouth. How she'd been able to talk normally with that in there I have no idea. 'It's platinum,' she told me. 'Your dad's stripping down the phones inside. This bit here's worth £30.' I remembered the paper in my trousers and gave it to Mum. It was Izal toilet paper, shiny and smelling of chemicals. Mum told me that this was the next chapter of Dad's book – the story of his life. For some reason he was going to call it *Hymie*. The family rumour ran that the plotline was pinched later by Sid James's agent. Certainly I remember Dad watching him on telly in the years ahead and whenever Sid came on, he would mutter 'the thieving bastard'. Pots and kettles.

11 June 1964. Lennie had got eighteen months for thieving and he had got out of Brixton earlier in the year. He had a score to settle with Andy Hempstead. I had first come across this shit years earlier watching a Punch and Judy show on Chalkwell beach with Mum and he started throwing pebbles at us. He must have had it in for the Sturleys for reasons

best known to himself. Carrying a gun on a radio shop job had sent John to Borstal and now, with Lennie inside, he really hassled my sister-in-law, Jill. I never knew Lennie to have a temper, but being inside gives you a mean streak, I guess. You don't know what's going on and accurate information is hard to come by. Anyway, Lennie went straight round to Hempstead's house in Beedell Avenue and threw rocks through his window. Days later he found him in a pub and beat the living daylights out of him, almost biting off his nose. Honour satisfied. Or was it?

On the night of 11 June, Len and Jill, together with John, who had been newly released from Borstal, met up with Hempstead and his girlfriend. They were drinking at the Grand Pier pub at the top of Pier Hill. Lennie and Hempstead shook hands warily and made small talk. While Hempstead was sipping halves of cider, my brothers were downing pints of bitter like it was the Prohibition Era in America – Hempstead's treat. At the end of the evening, it was everybody back to Andy's. The girls took one cab; Hempstead and my brothers took another. Lennie was out of it by the time they got to Beedell Avenue and they carried him in and laid him down on the settee. Jill and Hempstead's girlfriend went to the lounge to fix more drinks and when John nipped upstairs to the toilet, Hempstead made his move. He whipped out a coal hammer and smashed it down on Lennie's head four times.

His skull shattered with sickening cracks and blood spurted everywhere. It was all over the settee, the floor, the walls,

Lennie, Hempstead and his hammer. It was also all over the knife that lay on the floor – the knife that Hempstead said Lennie had used to attack him with. The problem with that for me was that, as far as I knew, Lennie never carried a knife.

The first I knew about it was a knock at the door in the wee small hours. It was the police and they had some bad news. The bottom fell out of my life. I was thirteen and a half years old and the person I loved more than everybody else in the world was on the brink of death. They wouldn't let me see him in hospital but the signs were not good. Andy Hempstead was tried for attempted murder but got off on the grounds of self-defence. Back in 1964, nobody tried too hard when it came to defending the Sturleys. As far as the local police were concerned we were a one-family crime wave and the removal of one of us was fair enough. Uncle George had his hands full, as it turns out, defending the blokes who had robbed the Night Mail and laundering the money from it. But I learned later that George and Dad had considered bringing in a hit man. George had his pick of London's underworld, hard men not averse to giving people a smacking for a reasonable outlay. In the end, Hempstead got away with it because George's love of anonymity was more important to him than revenge.

'It's not going to change Lennie, is it?' he said to Dad. And Dad agreed that was true.

Lennie made it. But only just. The severe brain damage he received that night meant that he was physically and mentally destroyed. He came to live with us for a while but nobody could handle it and he was sent to Runwell Hospital in Wickford. The doctor explained it all to Dad when he got out of prison. 'The condition your son is in, Mr Sturley, he must be with his own kind. It's torture for you at home and it's even worse for him because you are all normal. It's a form of jealousy, I suppose. He doesn't need that.'

So, for thirty-four years until his death, I visited my brother in Runwell every week. Every week, my heart was broken all over again. Lennie's friends got together after the Hempstead verdict and left him bleeding in an alleyway, but they didn't kill him and they didn't give him the life sentence he'd given to Lennie.

Part of Leonard Sturley died that night, 11 June 1964. And some part of the rest of us died too. That was the last time I cried. Since then, I became hardened. The police, the Establishment – they were the enemy and nobody gave a toss about my brother.

From that day on I would do all my crying on the inside.

CHAPTER 7

CRIME SCENE: UK

By the middle Fifties, when I was just starting school, London's underworld was squaring itself up for a showdown between Jack Spot and Billy Hill. My dad and Uncle George knew them both well but it's fair to say that they were both savvy enough to realise which way the criminal wind was blowing. Jack Spot was on his way down; Billy Hill on his way up – which is why George had recruited the man for the Eastcastle Street job.

Many years later, Reggie Kray wrote of Billy Hill that he was the ultimate professional criminal. Reggie liked to think that in some ways he came close to emulating him but in other ways Hill stood alone. There would never be another Billy Hill. Probably, deep down, Jack Spot felt the same. 'I made Billy Hill,' he told a reporter in 1965, 'then he got to be top over me. If it wasn't for me he would never had got there. I should've shot Billy Hill. I really should.'

All Hell broke loose on a morning in August 1955, in Frith Street, Soho. The place had a bad reputation then – strip-tease joints, the new Espresso bars and juke-boxes. Perverts in long macs scurried about the streets, dodging street traders and looking at the 'French lessons' postcards pinned to door frames that led up rickety stairs into dingy rooms. Amsterdam's Red Light District it was not. Neither of the men who faced each other that morning had anything to do with the vice trade. Money and power was what motivated them both. One was Jack Spot, the king of the underworld who, for a year or two now, had felt the throne sliding away from under him. The other was Albert Dimes, who had grown up in London's Little Italy and had worked for the Sabinis. Now he was Billy Hill's chief minder and it had reached Spot's ears that Dimes wanted a word with him. That was not how it worked. It was a serious breach of gangland protocol. Dimes was a nobody. *He* should have gone to Spot, not the other way around.

As with most confrontations of this kind, it's difficult to know who struck first. The smart money is that Spot provoked Dimes who pushed him. Spot hit him on the chin with his fist and Italian Albert went down. A couple of not-so-innocent bystanders got involved and tried to pull them apart, but Dimes and Spot were having none of that. Dimes pulled a knife and slashed Spot in the arm before stabbing him in the side. The pair fell, grappling and cursing, into a greengrocer's shop belonging to a Mr Hymes, whose wife, thirteen-stone Sophie, yelled, 'Stop it, you silly boys,' and proceeded to clobber Spot over the head with a pair of cast-iron weighing scales and split his head open.

When both men were bleeding and exhausted (Spot may have grabbed a knife from the greengrocer to defend himself with), Dimes was helped away in a taxi. Spot collapsed into a barber's shop – 'Fix me up,' he gasped to the barber before passing out. His six-guinea shirt, £15 shoes and 100-guinea suit were ruined and saturated with his blood.

Both men had instant amnesia – 'It was a tall man,' mumbled Dimes to the police. 'I don't know his name.' But Spot later decided to get even and the case came to court. He had an apparently impeccable eyewitness to events, an 88-year-old vicar, Basil Andrews, who had seen Dimes start the attack. Spot was found not guilty, but then so was Dimes when it emerged that the reverend, living on £250 a year, had a serious gambling problem and owed money all over the place. The implication was obvious – Spot had passed a bung to the clergyman to buy his testimony. No wonder Andrews had asked that his name not be mentioned in the press – 'I am pretty well known in London and have groups of friends and it is rather a disgraceful affair to be mixed up in.'

That fight in Soho was in many ways the beginning of the end for Spot. The following May a gang led by 'Mad Frankie' Fraser, who had been working the race tracks from the age of eight as a board cleaner, turned up on the doorstep to Spot's mansion in Hyde Park and slashed his face with razors. He needed a transfusion and seventy-eight stitches and carried the scar from his nose to his forehead for the rest of his life.

He had the brass neck later to claim that the surgeons ran out of thread at the hospital, so he put them in touch with his tailor! Billy Hill said, 'I'm the boss of the underworld – Jack Spot was very cut up about it.'

Honest people were getting tired of the publicity given to the Spots and the Hills. Their stories sold papers but there was always an air of disapproval. And this, of course, was where Uncle George came in. While my dad was fleecing Roy Wiggins and various councils over scrap metal deals, George was operating out of 21–23 Broadway and had found a nice little love nest for Edith at 85 Hermitage Court, Snaresbrook. The place is still pretty unchanged today, at least from the outside. In its day, it was an upmarket Art Deco set of apartments, like something off a *Poirot* set, all wrought-iron windows, rounded exterior corners and sharp interior angles. When George was staying there, Edith would drive him to Wanstead tube station every day and see him off to Stratford, just like any loving wife and husband. They were not husband and wife, of course, any more than my mum and dad were, and I'm not sure in the end how much love had to do with it. I know that in later years, George could be abusive to Edith – as he was to Marjorie, once throwing her down the stairs in a fit of the temper that he usually kept tightly concealed. But Edith owed him her life, so what was she supposed to do? George had, at the very least, a whacking share of £287,000 in his back pocket from Eastcastle Street and this was no doubt where the rent for Hermitage Court came from. But it may be he was also getting money another way – and if not actual money, then at least perks.

George showed Hermitage Court to Maurice Lesser, who fell in love with the place. So much so that he rented a flat in the same block where he could spend time with his boyfriends. As I've said, Maurice was always a gentleman, but as I've also said homosexuality was against the law and a solicitor had a lot to lose, even a solicitor whose clients came from the wrong side of the tracks in most people's eyes. I don't know what sort of deal George had struck with Maurice, but you can bet it was to George's financial advantage to carry on turning a blind eye to the comings and goings at Hermitage Court.

I don't want you to think that George Stanley was unique in the annals of crime. He was just better at it than most. In fact all the known dodgy lawyers in this country are simply the ones who were caught. Any book on the subject should leave several pages blank, representing those who weren't. Someone like George needed a foot in both camps. A public-school, Oxbridge type would never gain the trust and respect of an old-school villain. George hailed, like all the Sturleys, from the East End and was brought up to a world of sleight of hand that people like that could never grasp.

One of the first bent lawyers you'll read about in the history books was James Townsend Saward, a barrister who was also a forger of some merit. He was also a putter-up of robberies, like my uncle George, and was the brains behind what is often referred to as the first Great Train Robbery. That's because that was the name chosen (for obvious commercial reasons) for the Sean Connery film. It was actually called the Great Bullion Robbery at the time and took place in 1855 when gold bars being sent to pay our brave lads in the Crimea were hijacked en route by an adventurer called Edward Agar (played in the film by Donald Sutherland). He was a client of Saward. Does Saward get a mention in the film? Of course not. And that's probably how he would have liked it. All the attention was on Agar, as it would be on Billy Hill after Eastcastle Street and Bruce Reynolds after the Great Train Robbery. George wouldn't have it any other way.

Twenty years later, another bent lawyer hit the limelight. A bunch of plain-clothes men from Scotland Yard's Detective Branch were involved in racing scams called the turf wars. It wasn't the first or last time that bent coppers got their fingers burned in the fires of greed and they all did time. So did their brief, Edward Froggatt, who had a law practice in Argyll Street in the West End. He had a sideline as a receiver of forged cheques. The Yard, by the way, was in such a shambles as a result of this that they basically had to start again and a clever dick called Howard Vincent suggested – and ran – the Criminal Investigation Department the following year.

'In our profession,' wrote Arthur Newton (and he could have been speaking on Uncle George's behalf), 'it is so difficult to keep one's hands clean.' He had dozens of pairs of grey doeskin gloves to help him along but they didn't do him much good. He was a solicitor who got caught up in the Cleveland Street homosexual brothel case in 1889 when various members of polite society were caught with their trousers down in the company of errand boys from the General Post Office. He served six weeks in Holloway (then a male prison) for that, but, amazingly, stayed a solicitor. In fact, rather like George, his career went from strength to strength, mostly by defending underworld characters. He got himself caricatured in *Vanity Fair* by Spy, which today is like grinning out of the cover of *Hello!* and being invited onto the *Graham Norton Show*. So much did he think of himself that he offered his services to Dr H. H. Crippen in 1910, just before Uncle George was born. The doctor turned him down – perhaps a wise move, but they hanged him anyway. Newton ended up in Parkhurst prison in the Isle of Wight, as librarian, offering legal advice to the cons.

William Hobbs was, like George Stanley, a managing clerk who ran the practice of Appleton & Co in Portugal Street behind the law courts. He also blackmailed homosexuals. All this is historical stuff, but of course it doesn't end there. George was already working for Maurice Lesser when Rayner Goddard became Lord Chief Justice in January 1946. He was a throwback, fond of sentencing blokes to the lash and insisting that women wore hats in court. He was oddly tolerant of bent lawyers, however, and overturned a case in March 1948 in which the defendant was an MP and a barrister. The grounds for doing this was that the man should have been charged with only one count of conspiracy, not three. He also said he knew the names of a dozen dishonest criminal lawyers in London, but did not name names. Was George Stanley on that list? What do you think? Benny Carter was certainly one; he worked for the Messina brothers, the Maltese quintet who ran an upmarket vice industry in Shepherd Market, Bruton Place and New Bond Street. Their girls had their own maids who rigidly enforced the 'ten-minute' rule, knocking on their doors to remind clients that time was money. Gino Messina's own mistress, Marthe Watts, earned him £150,000 between 1940 and 1955 (including her now infamous record of forty-nine clients on VE night!).

We have met some of the criminals already who became George Stanley's clients in the 1950s and '60s and we'll meet more later. What about the law? I've always had a love/hate relationship with the police, having been told by my dad and uncle that there was a reason for some people calling them bogeys. They were the bogeymen who lived in the darkness under the stairs, the killjoys whose sole purpose in life was to scare the shit out of you and bring it all crashing down around your ears.

There was a half-baked idea soon after the war that developed into the Ghost Squad. Run by DI John 'Charlie Artful' Capstick (and they don't give them names like that any more), the squad's brief was to develop underworld contacts and pass the information on to arresting officers. The problem with this is that the officers (there were only four of them at first) quickly became known to the villains and their days were numbered. The squad was broken up soon after I was born, but I can't claim any credit for that!

Looking back, the time when Uncle George was hiring Billy Hill for the Eastcastle job was like the Wild West. It was a phrase I heard and used more than once when talking with George and my dad. These were the glory days of the Flying Squad, immortalised in the Seventies by John Thaw and Dennis Waterman in *The Sweeney*, roaring around the capital, swearing, drinking, smoking and fighting in a way that made them indistinguishable from the bad guys they were chasing. One old copper I knew gave that show as an example of life imitating art. Before *The Sweeney*, the law used the same ordinary language as everybody else. After it, thanks to the programme's scripts, desk sergeants all over the country could be heard saying, 'Get the DCI on the blower. And get the wheels out. They've got shooters.' The Wild West indeed.

The Squad were led, until I was eight, by Detective Superintendent Reg Spooner who had caught that vicious psychopath Neville Heath for the sex murder of two women in 1946. Spooner would sit in St Stephen's Bar opposite the Houses of Parliament and near Scotland Yard (now a popular tourist venue serving 'authentic' British pub food) and sip a pint while directing his plain-clothes men to all areas of the capital, looking for villains. The Sweeney relied on informants, usually minor underworld characters who kept their ears to the ground. That, of course, was exactly what Uncle George was doing in the same period, except that he was looking at the High Value Packages, train and van times and airport schedules via his own contacts on the inside of various transport industries.

The Met in particular have always had a reputation for dishonesty. It's no coincidence that nearly all of the 3,000 original 'Bobbies' appointed by Home Secretary Peel in 1829 had been dismissed within a year for drunkenness and bribe taking. The bottom line was that the poor bastards weren't paid enough to resist the odd backhander in later years from people like Spot and Billy Hill. But there was almost an old-fashioned natural respect between the law and the lawless in my first decade. Both sides, as we've seen, called each other the Heavy Mob and the Sweeney was certainly a force that got results. In some ways, this love/hate relationship continued until recently. In 1982, Chief Superintendent Peter Croxford retired from the Essex Force. He had arrested my dad way back for fraud and Dad congratulated him on his retirement. Croxford wrote back, 'I think that we have had a good sort of friendship over the years, taking everything into account ... take care, old friend.'

Corner cutting in the name of the law was a dangerous business because it could be – and sometimes was – exposed in the press or the courts. Detective Sergeant Frank Jiggins was dismissed from the Force after admitting that he lied to a magistrate. Detective Sergeant Alec Eist, who made his name as a catcher of lorry thieves, was tried for corruption and conspiracy. He got off but various journalists remained suspicious of him even after that. One man who was *definitely* bent was Detective Sergeant Harold 'Tanky' Challenor, an ex-SAS war hero known as the Scourge of Soho. Two months before the Great Train Robbery, Challenor arrested anti-Fascist demonstrators outside Claridge's Hotel. The kids, not much older than me, were charged with carrying bricks in their pockets to throw at 'Queen Fred', Frederika of Greece, who was staying there. At a subsequent trial, it turned out that Tanky had planted the bricks himself, thereby putting the cause of police officers back a hundred years. The defendants were released and Challenor was put on trial himself. Mysteriously he was found unfit to plead, being as 'mad as a hatter for years' (and that's not my phrase – that's what his psychiatrist said). 'Excessive zeal' was the official phrase, but for all the Met's attempt to portray Challenor as a one-off rotten apple, the corruption-hunting Sir Robert Mark found other examples of blue-coated wrong-doing when he took over as Commissioner in 1972. Eighty officers 'retired'.

Uncle George's style was shadowy. Only two books on the Great Train Robbery mention him at all and whatever he was up to, he was careful to remain well out of the limelight. He didn't have the gift of the gab like my dad and I often wonder whether he watched with a sense of rival satisfaction the collapse of barrister Patrick Aloysius Marrinan, who represented Billy Hill. This was shortly after the cutting up of Jack Spot when Hill's heavies, including Frankie Fraser and 'Wild' Billy Blythe, went down for seven years. Detective Inspector Tommy Butler, of the Flying Squad, who would spectacularly fail to catch Uncle George in the years ahead, denounced Marrinan in court, telling the world that he had an improper relationship with Hill's gang. He had told one of them it was in his best interests to escape.

The upshot was that Marrinan was kicked out of Lincoln's Inn. Unlike many of the men he defended, who shrugged, said it was a fair cop and served their time, the barrister sued Butler and his number two, Peter Vibart (the press at the time called them the 'terrible twins') – and failed badly. All this was no doubt a salutary lesson for Uncle George. Keep your head down and your mouth shut. 'Don't worry about the fucking police, Lee,' he said to me more than once. 'They've got nothing on me.'

And he was nearly right about that.

CHAPTER 8
INFORMATION OF THE HIGH VALUE PACKAGE

When the signals changed at Sears Crossing, I was still a kid. The Great Train Robbery, as it has come to be known, was *Boys' Own* adventure stuff and the size of the pot was out of a fairy tale, Monopoly money. But the job itself was not that much of a surprise. In fact I'd known for nearly two years that something like it was going to be pulled off because Uncle George was a fucking genius and because he'd done this sort of thing before.

'Keep your eyes open, Lee,' he would say when we met from time to time, 'and your mouth shut.' I was already two-thirds of the wise monkeys.

It's already quite hard to picture the scene in 1963. That was the year the BBC let comedians tell jokes about politics, royalty and sex. I know what you're thinking – what the hell did we laugh at before? Harold Wilson – who I'd meet later – took over from Hugh Gaitskell as leader of the Labour Party. Can you imagine a pipe-smoking politician today? Harold Macmillan – 'Supermac' – was at No 10. To me, he looked about a hundred. In March, I drooled, along with every other schoolboy, at the juicy stories involving Christine Keeler and Mandy Rice-Davies. They were mixed up in the sex-and-politics scandal of the Profumo Affair, but the men at the top denied all knowledge of them. Keeler had gone to bed with John Profumo although he said she hadn't. But then, he would, wouldn't he?

The older members of my family talked about the country going to the dogs because Dr Beeching, the Chairman of the British Railways Board, was going to close over 2,000 railway stations. That would mean the loss of 68,000 jobs. No wonder people turned to crime. I saw Peter O'Toole's *Lawrence of Arabia* at the pictures and Sean Connery's *From Russia with Love*. The world came to an end in June when Buckingham Palace admitted that Prince Charles, only two years older than me, had bought a cherry brandy in a hotel bar. That was the month Henry Cooper floored Cassius Clay, the world heavyweight boxing champion – good old 'Enry! A fifty-mile-an-hour speed limit was brought in on the roads, although none of the Sturleys paid any attention to it. I don't remember taking in any news from the world stage. Kennedy was at the White House; Martin Luther King had a dream and there was a new Pope – none of it very likely to upset the equilibrium of life in Southend. We hadn't even heard of the Beatles then and now half of them are dead and the other half are wrinkly old has-beens.

*

'I had a couple of ideas about trains,' Bruce Reynolds wrote in his book *The Autobiography of a Thief*, but if he did, they were ideas sharpened and made real by George Stanley. No doubt the events of 1960 and '61 gave George the impetus he needed because thieves were targeting the London to Brighton line, establishing a precedent. By comparison with the Sears Crossing caper, of course, the results were paltry, but they whetted George's appetite as never before.

In August 1960, nine mailbags containing High Value Packages to the tune of £7,500 (over £150,000 in today's terms) disappeared from the 2.25 p.m. train. Three hooded men tied up the guard and vanished into thin air. In September another train was hit at Patcham Tunnel, Preston Park and £9,000 disappeared. This one, George noticed, was carried out by fixing signals to stop the train. The sort of hold-ups we all watched at the pictures and on telly, where the James and Younger boys and the Daltons put brushwood on the tracks to stop the train in Arizona in the late 1800s and then pointed their guns at the driver, just wouldn't work in twentieth-century Britain.

Despite internal memos whizzing from department to department within the Post Office, memos that talked about the urgent need for upgrading security, bugger all was done and another heist took place in the following April. This time a gang dressed as railwaymen ambled along the platform at Brighton and helped themselves to a bag containing £15,000. It can't have been lost on George that these sums were getting ever larger and although they were back-pocket change compared with the Eastcastle Street job, they had far greater potential. He would have noted two things in particular. How do you stop a train? You fix the signals. How do you lull the locals going about their business? You dress like them by putting blokes in railways slops. But then, he'd already done that with the alarm-removing postman in the Eastcastle job. And he also already knew the vital importance – perhaps the clincher – that you had to have somebody on the inside. He'd had that for Eastcastle and he needed it again. This is where Keith 'Annie' Oakley came in. I met Keith later – in fact he gave me my first job on the railways. He was a dapper, ex-Army Catering Corps bloke and we got on famously. He had blue eyes as cold as ice and always wore a smart blazer and British Rail issue shirt.

I don't believe this man was George's insider for Eastcastle, but he probably met him via that contact. Remember the corner game? And Promise Land? Remember Maurice Lesser and his hobbies? It all came together in the shape of Annie Oakley. He knew that millions of pounds were carried on TPOs (Travelling Post Offices) all over the country. Stationed (no pun intended) in Rugby, he had access to times, schedules, amounts and technical information like signals. Was he a greedy man? You'd have to say, definitely. He didn't have the expertise to rob a train himself, but George Stanley knew blokes who had – they would become the footsoldiers to carry it out. Such blokes had got Edith Simons out of Nazi-occupied France and had got away with the biggest haul in British history in 1952. But there was something else about Annie and you may have guessed it from the nickname. It wasn't just that he had the same surname as 'Little Miss Sureshot', the gun-toting show-woman of Buffalo Bill's Wild West Show. Annie was homosexual. And that, remember, was still against the law. Oakley could lose his job, his social standing, everything. Did Uncle George put the squeeze on him? Do bears shit in the woods?

In January 1962, while a dream of riches beyond avarice was crystallising in George's head, another train was hit, or very nearly. In the early hours of the 26th, a detonator blew up on the line between Colchester and Marks Tey in Essex. The train stopped, but it was the wrong one. There had been a last-minute delay to a goods train and it was that one which had taken the hit. George Drinkell was the signalman in the box at Marks Tey and he got a phone call at 2.30 a.m. to say the goods train had just left Colchester. But it had not reached him. Colchester rang again moments later – the goods train had been stopped by detonators. There were fourteen more such devices on the track and the assumption was made that a gang of robbers would jump on board the mail train, help themselves to the cash and get away by road, probably along the A12, the London–Ipswich Road.

George must have read his *Daily Express* the next day because that was the only daily that carried the story in detail and I can just picture him smiling as he came across the words, 'British Railways Police and Essex detectives met yesterday to discuss the Great Train Robbery that never was.' Well, Uncle George could do something about that. If it was a *real* train robbery the press and the police craved, he would give them one. And the *Express* article gave him other ideas, too. A lonely railway line in the small hours of the morning, alongside a major road that led in two important directions. Had the gang been able to stop the train – and George already knew how to do that – they could have driven north to Colchester and Harwich and then caught a boat to the continent. Or they could have driven south and disappeared into the crime capital of the country or nipped down the Thames to the open sea.

Again, there was a panicked buzz in the Post Office and the IB insisted changes were made to security. Again, bugger all actually happened.

And that was a pity because in August 1962 somebody tried a new tack. George really should have passed a grateful bung to the crime writers of the *Express*, especially their leader Percy Hoskins, because he was virtually giving him – and any other wannabe train robber – a blueprint on how to do it. A fire was started on the relevant train two miles out of Brighton and while the guard dashed to deal with it, the gang pounced. 'Coshing a lone unprotected guard is out,' said the *Express*. That was fine, because violence was not George's style. 'It is old hat to dress up as a railwayman to rob the mails.' Well, George would reserve judgement on that.

'Tampering with the signals to hold up the train – a technique used twice before' is too complicated. He would reserve judgement on that, too.

By the time the blazing train rattled into Preston Park eighteen minutes late, the fire in the empty compartment was too large to contain and the fire brigade was sent for. The fire had almost certainly been started at Haywards Heath and the money was taken during the ten minutes the guard was out of his carriage.

It all got much nastier in February of the following year and good old *Express*; they were there in detail again. The Irish Mail was minding its own business travelling on the Euston to Holyhead run when somebody pulled the communication cord near Boxmoor, Hemel Hempstead. That somebody was one of eight armed men wearing masks who had just coshed the guard, a Mr Owen, and tied him up before helping themselves to the contents of fifty mailbags. The ticket collector was also coshed but he was able to raise the alarm and a couple of dining car attendants came rushing over to find out what was going on. Years later, I could have been one of those dining car attendants, dressed in a crisp bum-freezer waiter's jacket serving the Brown Windsor soup in the days when British Rail was still in existence and still civilised. A running fight broke out in the compartments with plates and tureens going all over the place.

When the train stopped at Boxmoor, people tumbled out of the carriages covered in food and blood. Five of the train crew were wounded but refused to go to hospital. The police were called and local roads sealed off. Nobody was caught.

Enter Bruce Reynolds to show you how *not* to rob a train. As I've said, I got to know Bruce around this time and I liked him. I've also said he wasn't a genius. What he did have was a certain organisational talent and some loyal mates. No doubt he too had read all about the Irish Mail because later that year, he and a few 'chaps' decided to have a go at the same train. He'd just done two and a half years for having a go in a different way against two police officers and he recruited his mates Buster Edwards, Gordon Goody and Bill Jennings, known as Flossy, to help him in his latest escapade. There was, of course, no such person as Flossy Jennings but because the man was also with Bruce on the Great Train Robbery, Reynolds invented this alias for the purposes of his book *Autobiography of a Thief*. As we've seen, Edwards' criminal record was lightweight up to this point – his fourteen days' jug in Brixton for driving while disqualified seems *very* harsh by today's standards. Goody was far more heavyweight; he'd been done last for possessing a firearm by Richmond Magistrates' Court, fifteen months earlier. For that, however, he had only received a fine.

Edwards had got a tip from somewhere that heavy boxes were routinely loaded onto the Irish Mail at Paddington and that these contained wages for workers in Swindon – good, old-fashioned folding stuff. He and Goody did a dummy run, following the cases on and off the train and realising at once that security would be a problem. The solution was to pull the communication cord, grab the boxes' contents and drive off in a waiting car.

Edwards and Jennings were on the train for a second trial run, this time pulling the cord. It worked like a dream and the pair jumped off the stopped train, over a fence and into Gordon Goody's waiting van. Then, the real thing and … oh dear. Four of them were all on the Mail this time, Goody with a crowbar under his coat. The van was driven by a new man, Denis Marlowe, known as Bonko. Jennings hid in the toilet with Edwards outside, as though patiently waiting his turn while Reynolds and Goody smashed the lock on the guard's van and threatened the guard with the crowbar. What nobody expected was that the boxes had more chains on them than Houdini and the bolt-cutters they'd brought weren't doing the business. According to plan, Edwards saw the Hayes signals and banged on the door. Flossy pulled the communication cord and nothing happened. He did it again. Still nothing. Both men dashed for the guard's van to find the others still beavering away at the chains. Edwards grabbed what he hoped was a control wheel and spun it like a lunatic. The train came to a stop a mile away from Bonko and his drag.

'We're fucked,' Goody said. Had a way with words, did Gordon. Everybody leapt off the train, taking as many boxes as they could. The things were lined with lead and everybody but Goody dropped them as they ran through a farmyard watched by an incredulous farmer. 'The train's stopped,' Buster said cheerfully. 'We're going to get help.'

Bruce's gang had got away with one box – £700.

Unbeknown to Uncle George, rumours were spreading in the Post Office's IB and Scotland Yard's Intelligence Branch, then called C11, that a seriously big job was being planned. Reynolds' botched shot on the Irish Mail clearly wasn't it, which meant that the tension continued to build as the year went on. What nobody knew except the IB was the sheer scale of the tempting pot on offer. Between 1962 and 1963 the Travelling Post Office carried more than £4,000 million. If even a small part of that fell into the wrong hands, it would be a national disaster.

Long before the summer, George told me later, he had all his ducks in a row. He would put together a team – the word 'gang' was for kids, according to the Krays – and they would hit the Up Special, which ran from Glasgow to London. There would be sixteen men involved, some to work the train, others to drive the drags. The train would be stopped somewhere in the country and the money transferred to waiting vehicles that would roar off into the night. Signals would be tampered with to stop the train, and the locomotive and HVP coach would have to be uncoupled and moved to minimise the number of Post Office operatives who could stand in their way – Oakley had told George there could be seventy of them. The lads should go mob-handed of course, but there was to be no unnecessary rough stuff.

The telephone wires would have to be cut so that the Up Special would be isolated for long enough for the mailbags to be removed. All this would take planning, specialists and impeccable timing, but George Stanley had been this way before and he knew it could be done.

After the heist ... but let's not run before we can walk. George had it all worked out and if he could have programmed sixteen robots to carry it out, it would have been the perfect crime. As things turned out, some of the wheels came off, but George Stanley...? Remember what I said about shit and roses?

The essential problem in putting a team together is that there is a built-in weakness. If you take a group of unknowns, like Jack Hawkins did in *The League of Gentlemen*, you run the risk that they're too honest to get involved or don't know what the fuck they're doing. If you choose men for their expertise and savvy, chances are they'll be known to the Filth. And that was exactly how it fell out. It was the train robbers' bad luck that the man sent out to catch them was the grey fox, Detective Inspector Tommy Butler, one of the most single-minded policemen in history. He knew most if not all the men who hit the Up Special and it would only be a matter of time before he caught them.

In fact, it was Uncle George's good luck that Tommy Butler was on the case, because he was so focused on tracking the robbers down, he took his eye off the ball in the context of what happened to the loot. In my more wistful moments,

I like to think of the fox and Uncle George trying to outsmart each other. Both men were, in their different ways, geniuses. George with his one lung, his diabetes, his bent law practice and his mistress in Snaresbrook; Butler, the friendless workaholic, living with his dear old mum in Barnes with a girlfriend somewhere on the side. You could admire them both, but you couldn't love either of them.

George's choice as team leader was Bruce Reynolds, the antique dealer. Why, given the fiasco with the Irish Mail you've just read about? Well, three reasons. Things weren't going too well for Reynolds in the spring of 1963 and he owed Uncle George some money; not much, it's true, but enough. Promise Land. Everybody fell for it. And George was good at getting his money's worth. The second reason was Reynolds' personality. He couldn't stand in the same line-up as Billy Hill and he never tried to but in one sense they were two cheeks of the same bum. They were both vain and saw themselves as a cut above. They could both be relied upon to claim the glory if the job went well and to keep schtum if it didn't. Tight-lipped loyalty was their trade mark. So George was on to a winner with Bruce. If the job came off, he'd be swanning around in some exotic part of the world claiming he'd pulled off the crime of the century. If it went pear-shaped and he was rotting somewhere at Her Majesty's Pleasure, he wouldn't blab. Either way, there would be no mention of George Stanley.

And that was doubly odd and leads us to the third reason. George had worked with Reynolds before. On Tuesday 27

November 1962, while James Hanratty was on trial for the A6 murder at Dead Man's Hill, four blokes, complete with bowlers, striped trousers, umbrellas and false moustaches, carried out a daring raid on a strong box containing £62,000 (£1.2 million today). They were hiding in the lift at Comet House at Heathrow, London's newest airport and, knocking security guards left, right and centre, bundled the wages box into a waiting 3.8 Mk II Jaguar. Then they were gone, roaring away along the Great West Road. The whole BOAC raid took three minutes and it was planned and organised by Uncle George, using inside information. He had already selected Reynolds to lead the 'City Gents', as the press called them.

Bruce saw himself as a T. E. Lawrence figure, another train stopper and a maverick genius who could pull off the impossible (in the case of Lawrence he led the desert Arabs to kick seven kinds of shit out of the Turks in Aqaba in 1917). He saw himself as Cary Grant in *To Catch a Thief*, all glamour and suavity. He looks, in most of his photographs, like Michael Caine playing Jack Carter, complete with wavy hair and horn-rimmed glasses. And I'm sorry to bang on about it but he must have seen himself as Jack Hawkins in *The League of Gentlemen*. This underrated little film, black and white and shot on location in London's still bomb-damaged streets, came out three years before the Great Train Robbery. I don't think Uncle George saw it like this, but I bet Reynolds did. Hawkins' team is made up of military misfits, ex-officers with shady secrets from manslaughter to indecent exposure on their consciences. Hawkins knows this and does a number on them. He knows they're down on their luck and they're greedy – just like George knew the same about the train robbers. All right, so the heist in the film is a bank job, not a train job, but the idea must have appealed to Reynolds. Hence the army uniforms, the army vehicles. The details that Bruce came out with in his 1995 autobiography are often unsubstantiated. They are his memories and his take on events. And he was, for at least part of the time, in la-la land.

He wrote in 1995 that he looked exactly like 'the Major' in brown jump boots, olive drabs, a camouflaged Airborne smock, gold-rimmed glasses painted black, a close-cropped military haircut crowned by the sand-coloured beret of the Special Air Service with its dagger badge and motto, 'Who Dares Wins'. It stood for everything he believed in. And remember, this was the bloke who ran away from military service!

If you got Bruce Reynolds, you'd almost certainly get his partners in crime, Buster Edwards and Gordon Goody, both of whom were among the City Gents at Heathrow. Reynolds had met Edwards at the Mary Ann in Peckham, a club owned by Charlie Richardson, one of the family that ran south of the river. Edwards in turn introduced him to Goody, known as Footpad because of his height and street-mugger appearance. Their first meeting had been at the Castle in

Putney where Goody was the 'unofficial guv'nor of the manor' (Bruce's words).

So that was three of the team George had got in his pocket. I must stress that it was only Reynolds who ever met George in the context of planning the robbery. The others never knew who was pulling the strings because Reynolds' conversation, at Buster's flat or wherever they met to finalise the job's details, led them to believe *he* was the brains behind. That puffed him up no end and kept George in the shadows. Result.

The fourth man was Charlie Wilson, who had known Reynolds since they were kids during the war. A heavy who knew everybody in the underworld, he was a natural to team up with Bruce because they'd been smash-and-grab merchants in the Fifties. Uncle George came to like and respect Charlie.

Then there was Roy James, whose fast driving of the Mk II Jag had got the City Gents away from Heathrow in record time. George knew that the drags would be essential. The getaway vehicles, heavy with the stolen loot, would need to be in tip-top condition and at least one of them would have to be driven by an expert. That was where Roy came in. Reynolds waxes lyrical about this genial, cheeky-chappy lad who looks, in his mugshot, like a poor man's Roy Castle, but the facts speak for themselves. When he wasn't nicking stuff (usually car-related), he was driving like a maniac at Aintree and elsewhere. Of twenty races in 1962, Roy won seventeen of them and he only lost the three because of technical problems. He beat the greats like Jack Brabham, Jackie Stewart and Mike Hailwood. Reynolds saw him as one of a new breed – a non-smoking, teetotal fitness freak.

The problem that was uppermost in George's mind was how to stop the train. Edwards had a bloke he thought could do that – Roger Cordrey, who had already pulled six successful train jobs with his South Coast Raiders. He had sunken cheeks and a tight mouth, with a shock of combed-back curly hair, and he came with a mutual friend of his and Buster's, Tommy Wisbey, the brilliant pub singer, bookmaker and gentle giant. This man was gold-plated in terms of street cred. He was the son-in-law of a cousin of Billy Hill's and was brought into the venture as muscle. George was uneasy about approaching a tight, already set-up outfit like the South Coast mob, so just in case he got his own technical expert – Russell-Pavier and Richards' 'Mr Two'. We'll meet him later.

Now they were eight and the ninth was another of Cordrey's outfit, Bob Welch. He only had a couple of previous, but his addiction to gambling meant he was vulnerable, open to all sorts of suggestions for getting money fast.

Who haven't I mentioned? 'Paddy' Daly of course, but the curious thing about him is that he doesn't feature in Reynolds' autobiography at all. It's curious because he was Bruce's brother-in-law and Bruce thought of him as a lucky charm. But in the book he calls him Paddy Ryan because Daly had, bizarrely, been acquitted in the train robbery trial – one of George's more modest victories.

Paddy was one of several big buggers who could intimidate anybody. Jimmy White and Big Jim Hussey weren't there just for the ride either. White, the war veteran, had a reputation for being able to merge with the background (a bit like Uncle George, really). Reynolds says he was the ultimate Mr Nobody. Not quite. He was a first class quartermaster in the complex back-up plan that George had set up and he worked with Roy James on the three vehicles they would use on the Up Special night. Hussey was a mate of Charlie Wilson's from their schooldays, not the brightest apple in the barrel but again, not the sort of bloke you'd want to meet at a deserted railway crossing at dead of night.

Which leaves Ronald Arthur Biggs and his tame engine driver. I can't help thinking that George didn't want Biggs or maybe he didn't fully appreciate what a potential liability he was. I got to know the man personally later, talked to him on the phone and we exchanged letters. Reynolds had met him in Wandsworth prison, which Bruce refers to in his book as the Hate Factory. Biggs had a certain charm about him and a wicked sense of humour. He'd been made a chef during his time in the RAF – 'Not quite the image that I aspired to,' he told Reynolds. 'I'd been looking to be another Douglas Bader, only with legs.' As romantically inclined misfits went, he and Bruce were a marriage made in heaven. And Ronnie owed Bruce five hundred smackers.

The train driver caused problems on the Up Special night and has caused everyone problems ever since, because we don't know who he was. I can't recall George ever using the name, although it's inconceivable that he didn't know it. He'd no more have an unknown on one of his jobs than actually do the job himself, but this was a very technical area of expertise that was difficult to come by in the ordinary way.

'It's the old story, Lee,' George told me later, 'finding a bent bloke with the right cred is tricky. As it turned out, Biggsy's boy was bent enough, but hadn't got the necessary.' Whoever the bloke was, he was greedy and not averse to putting one over on either the GPO or British Rail. Think another celluloid heist movie – the original *Taking of Pelham 123*; Martin Balsam is just such an ex-employee with a grudge, but whereas Balsam delivers the goods in terms of hi-jacking the tube train for the ransom of its passengers, Biggsy's boy froze. We know he was sixty-three and consequently known as 'Pop', or perhaps Peter or maybe Stan – both names are bandied about in various accounts – and the author Piers Paul Read claims that he actually met him when writing his 1978 book on the robbery. With everything that Uncle George told me about this job in the years ahead, he never once mentioned Pop's real name. The closest I got to him was that I did up a property he once lived in in Leytonstone Road, Stratford. Whatever, Pop lost his bottle when it came to it.

And so, to the Night in Question. Train nuts and steam enthusiasts will give you the timetable. The Up Special was a Travelling Post Office of twelve coaches. There were no passengers on board but seventy-seven postmen, all sorting the mail as the train whistled through the night. The engine with five coaches left Glasgow Central at 6.50 p.m. on that warm summer evening. Four more coaches were coupled to it at Carstairs at 7.32. In Carlisle by 8.54, another three coaches were joined on. The train got to Preston at 10.53 for a half-hour stop while the postmen went for a pee and a cuppa. It reached Warrington at 11.36, waited there for seven minutes, then moved on to Crewe. It was at Tamworth by 1.23 a.m. on the 8th and at Rugby by 2.12. This was the last official stop the train was to make before all Hell broke loose.

The seventy-seven blokes who would become the 'victims' of the crime of the century shortly after three o'clock haven't exactly gone down in a blaze of publicity, leaving their mark on history. Some names stand out, however, because they were in the wrong place at the wrong time and because they talked to the police and the press in the days and weeks ahead.

Jack Mills took over the driver's cab in Crewe. David Whitby joined him as his fireman, so these two were in the cab when the lights went out. The train approached Sears Crossing, an ordinary, anonymous place somewhere in Buckinghamshire. The metal sign from the crossing fetched $14,000 at an auction the other day, but back on 8 August 1963, only the locals and a few railway employees had ever heard of it. Mills realised there was a problem. The dwarf signal showed the caution light and beyond it the home signal was red. He slowed the train and stopped, sending Whitby to the nearest telephone box to find out what the trouble was. The trouble was that somebody had cut the telephone wires. It's all different now, of course, with electronics and mobile phones, but at the time that train was stranded with no immediate links to the outside. Whitby had just got back to the train, trying to work out how to contact the Leighton Buzzard signal box, when he saw a bloke lurking between the second and third carriages. He was wearing railway slops, used and well-washed.

'What's up, mate?' Whitby asked.

The man crossed to the down line. 'Come here,' he said. Whitby followed him, expecting to be shown some sort of technical hitch. Instead, he got a push down the steep embankment and rolled into two heavies. A bizarre conversation followed, too peculiar really to be made up. One of the heavies pinned Whitby to the ground, waving a cosh bound with white tape.

'If you shout,' he said, 'I'll kill you.'

Whitby mumbled, 'You're all right, mate. I'm on your side.' That was the side that might let him live. The heavy asked where Whitby was from and promised to send him some money. Then he hauled the fireman upright and pushed him up the steep gradient to the train.

Jack Mills had seen two men to his left and assumed, like Whitby, they were railwaymen. Suddenly, a masked man was in the cab with him, balaclava over his face and wearing a boiler suit. He too had a white-bandaged stick, maybe two feet long. Mills wrestled with him but the intruder was a very big bloke and Mills had difficulty. The next thing he knew he was going down under a barrage of blows from behind, thudding across his head and shoulders. He was on his knees, blood running into his eyes and trickling into his mouth. He was told not to look round and was frogmarched along the passage leading to the boiler room.

By this time, David Whitby had been bundled into the boiler room with a handcuff clicked on his left wrist. He saw Mills with his face a mask of blood. Both men were pushed in and out of the cab. Mills sensed that someone was trying to move the train but it wasn't working.

With Jack Mills out of action with his bleeding head, Pop was shoved literally into the driver's seat to operate the locomotive. It was only 1,100 yards to Bridego Bridge, but if the fucking thing didn't move, it might just as well have been on the far side of the moon. To be fair to Pop, it wasn't really his fault (although as the most technically able bloke there he should have spotted the problem quicker). Roy James and Jimmy White were supposed to seal the brake-connecting pipe when they uncoupled the HVP coach from the other carriages. They hadn't. There again, Pop was a shunter; he had experience of air brakes, but not the vacuum system or the English Electric Class 40 he was expected to drive now.

Pop was surrounded in that cab by pent-up heavies, many of them with a reputation for violence and none of them wanting to get caught, especially by the incompetence of an idiot like him. Where do you lay the blame? Pop the incompetent? Biggsy, whose contact he was? Reynolds for recruiting them? Or Uncle George for letting the wrong one in? Whatever.

'Well, fetch the driver!' somebody shouted and Mills found himself literally back in the driving seat. He was told to drive until told to stop and that was what he did, head down, eyes ahead on his controls but not on the track. The locomotive pulling the first uncoupled coach containing the HVPs and a handful of Post Office workers moved on towards a pre-marked spot near Bridego Bridge, leaving behind the rest of the train carrying the remaining sorters and the ordinary mail at Sears Crossing.

'Stop!'

Mills did. Then he was dragged upright again and bundled backwards to be handcuffed to Whitby. Now they were ordered off the train and down onto the ground, frogmarched between a human chain of 'railwaymen' in balaclavas, throwing heavy mailbags one to the other. At a chosen spot, Mills and Whitby were told to lie face downwards.

The pair now saw everything at an angle, mostly feet. And most of what they heard was cursing, muffled behind the balaclavas. Those mailbags were heavy. Mills could see that the carriages had been uncoupled and only two coaches were still with the engine. The second coach, the one carrying the all-important HVPs, was being systematically emptied of its contents. He counted, despite the pain in his head and the fear that gripped him, fifteen men. He and Whitby were supposed to keep their eyes shut but given the darkness and the fact that the gang were concentrating on the mailbags, that didn't happen.

Another strange piece of dialogue occurred then. One of the gang warned Mills, as they had warned Whitby, 'I'll get your address when this is all over and send you a few quid. Keep your mouth shut. They are right bastards here.'

Whitby had a cigarette and tried to light one for Mills to keep them both calm. One of the gang noticed and said, 'I'll have one if you've got one to spare.' Whitby handed it over. After all, he was parting with 2.6 million quid – a fag wasn't going to hurt. He also passed over his lighter which a gloved hand took and dutifully returned.

Mills estimated it was seven or eight minutes later that he and Whitby were told to get into the back of the almost empty GPO van. The driver couldn't make it because his head was spinning and he felt woozy. He was helped up. Four Post Office workers lay in the corner of the van and Mills was dumped unceremoniously onto a pile of mailbags.

'Stay there for half an hour,' he was told. 'We shall be back.'

The driver heard the kick of a motor-car engine and Whitby briefly caught sight of a lorry with a flat back and a frame for a canvas top. For the record, the three vehicles parked near the bridge were all bought or stolen for the occasion and their plates switched. The light blue Land Rover with the false number BMG 757A was over-painted with khaki. In keeping with Reynolds' imaginary SAS raid, he believed that if anyone asked, the team could claim they were on hush-hush manoeuvres and the public did not have a right to know. A khaki Land Rover made sense in that context. So did the next one – and that *was* ex-War Department. It had been re-sprayed bronze-green and was sold by Cross Country Vehicles to a Mr Bentley who turned out later to be Jimmy White. The Austin Goods Platform Truck (BPA 260) was dark green, blending well into the darkness. Jimmy White had bought this from D. A. Mullard & Co, giving his name as F. Blake. The BPA plates had been stolen from a Ford car in Warner Place, London, E2 between 29 and 30 July.

If you've been the victim of a crime, you'll know how it works. You panic, go into shock. You can't remember little things – the little things that catch criminals. Was his shirt blue or grey? Did he have a moey or stubble? He definitely had a tattoo, but what was the design – and was it on his right or left arm? And don't get me started on colours and makes of vehicles. So each of those seventy-seven blokes on the Up Special at Bridego Bridge or at Sears Crossing, wherever they ended up, had a story to tell. And, you've guessed it, the stories didn't quite tally. Most of them had been left in the other coaches down the track anyway, so they hadn't seen anything. As for those who had, a good Defence brief would drive a coach and horses through their evidence today, but the 1960s were more uptight; the Establishment's doors were more firmly closed. Little anomalies could be overlooked, as long as we all had the general picture.

The bloke David Whitby was trying to contact at Leighton Buzzard when he found the signals faulty at Sears Crossing was Thomas Wyn-De-Bank. The train had passed him, heading south as usual, at 2.58 a.m. Two minutes later the buzzer in his box told him that the Distant Signal lights at Sears were out. He heard nothing of course from Whitby but at 3.10 a.m. Cheddington Signal Box rang him to ask where the train was. Wyn-De-Bank assumed there was a problem either with the track or the locomotive and told his superiors, north and south, that he was going to check via the driver of the next Up train. That was a bloke called Cooper and he found the train by Bridego Bridge. This was the first link with the outside world but men on the stricken train had their own tales to tell.

Assistant Inspector Thomas Kett had been on board the front of the train when it was stopped, in his role of supervising Post Office employees in the second to fourth coaches. He got the time of the train stopping wrong – see what I mean about panic and emotion? – and remembered the hiss of steam as it started again. There was no corridor through the High Value Package coach (the second one in the lineup) so somebody pulled the communication cord and they all started yelling to the driver whose locomotive was moving away from them. Kett realised this was a raid and yelled at his blokes to bolt the doors and pile the mail inside as a barricade against them. Kett's panic may have come into play again because he heard the raiders smash windows and shout, 'They're barricading the doors. Get the guns.' Nobody carried a gun in the Great Train Robbery so either this was what Kett *expected* to hear or it was a nifty piece of psychology on the part of the robbers to put the fear of God into them. Six to eight men broke in and a running battle took place, the blokes with the coshes easily overpowering the unarmed postmen and forcing them to lie down in a corner.

Kett's Number Two in the HVP coach was Frank Dewhurst. He too heard the steam hiss and knew the train had been uncoupled. He too heard 'Get the guns', but his 'Some bastard's putting the bolt on' does not mesh with his boss's memory. Dewhurst went down to what he believed was a blow from an axe shaft and someone drove his boot into the man's ribs before asking him if he was all right.

Thomas Miller was the guard on the train. His position in the last coach meant that he was furthest away from the engine and the HVP coach. When the brakes went on and the train stopped, he took the corridor to the ninth coach and got off, wondering what was going on. He saw nobody, but then he couldn't see the engine or the first two coaches either. He put detonators on the track at various intervals – small devices used to make a loud sound as a warning signal to oncoming train drivers – and walked on towards Cheddington. He found the engine and missing coaches at Bridego Bridge. The HVP door was wide open and Mills and

Whitby were inside, handcuffed together. They told Miller what had happened and he stopped an advancing train and went on to Cheddington to signal for assistance. By now it was 4.15 a.m.

Boiler suits. Railway overalls. Boots. Balaclavas. Whoever these blokes were who had just committed the Crime of the Century in the middle of sleepy Buckinghamshire, they were totally anonymous. Except, of course, they weren't and it's that old maths thing again, isn't it? Bruce Reynolds, Buster Edwards, Gordon Goody, Paddy Daly, Roy James, Jimmy White, Tommy Wisbey, Jimmy Hussey, Charlie Wilson, Roger Cordrey, Bob Welch, Ronnie Biggs and, however reluctantly, 'Pop'. That makes thirteen, but there were sixteen men at that track side in the August of 1963. What about Messrs One, Two and Three? What about the blokes Bruce Reynolds calls Flossy Jennings and Alf Thomas?

Mr Three won't come as a surprise to anybody. His mug-shot stares out from the front cover of Andrew Cook's recent book on the robbery. It was Henry Smith, known as Harry. Eight days after the robbery, his name appeared on two lists as 'likely lads' up to their hocks in the heist. One was compiled by the grey fox, Tommy Butler; the other by his ultimate boss at Scotland Yard, Commander George Hatherill. Neither of those blokes was a fool and if Smith's name was there, there was a good reason for it. Henry Thomas Smith was thirty-three at the time, 6ft 1½ins tall and, in his mugshot at least, looks a mean bastard. He lived at 22 Provost Dwellings,

Provost Street, N1 and had tattoos on his arms – a scroll and the word 'Mother'. According to a statement made by Smith's dad (also Henry) to Detective Sergeant (as he then was) Jack Slipper of the Met, Harry Jnr was the eldest of six sons and he had married Shirley Young in 1950. They had two girls. 'Harry Boy' got into so much trouble with the law that his wife left him, taking the girls with her, and in 1959 Harry moved in with a Margaret Wade who already had two kids of her own. Harry and Margaret had a son, also Harry.

The eldest Henry seemed genuinely disgusted by his son's behaviour. He had gone round to his house on the Sunday before the train robbery to be told that Harry was away 'on a big job that's coming off'. Clearly Margaret Wade was less than discreet in these matters. Instinctively, Harry senior knew what this was all about when he read the headlines days later. Casual chats in pubs in Shoreditch and Hoxton confirmed it. 'What I have said,' the elder Smith told Slipper, 'is perfectly true and although my son is involved I am willing, if need be, to give evidence in court.' Thanks, Dad!

Mr Two is likely to be a new name to many. He was George's choice to work with Cordrey on the signal system and was not one of the South Coast firm. As far as I am aware, he features in none of the books on the Great Train Robbery but the Sturleys all knew him well. He was Leslie Aldridge, known as Electric Les and his nickname says it all. George had known him for years and he could find his way around any alarm system in the world. He was a TV engineer out of

Manor Park and his shop in Hackney was one of the first to rent out slot-machine tellies. On the night, of course, there was some sort of cock-up and either Cordrey or Paddy Daly had screwed up. The idea was to slip a glove over the green lamp signal but somebody unscrewed the bulbs instead. This alerted the railways that there was a problem and Frank Mead of the Signals and Telecommunications Department was sent off at shortly after three in the morning to find out what was going on. I've always assumed that Les was an easy-going sort of bloke who prided himself on his work but was not one to have the gloves on with more senior members of the team like either Cordrey or Daly. He went on to later criminal greatness before moving, undiscovered, to Cyprus for a well-earned retirement.

And so we come to Mr One. And this is where it gets difficult. Mr One has been hovering over this book from start to finish and as far as I know he is one of just three men still standing from that original team of sixteen. He is the Enforcer, the Godfather of Crime, Freddie Foreman. In 1997, Freddie, describing himself as 'Managing Director of British Crime', went into print with *Respect*, ghosted by John Lisners. He paints a picture of a hard early life, not unlike the Sturleys. He was born on 5 March 1932, the youngest of five brothers (I know that feeling!). He was watching street brawls as little more than a toddler and was used to drunkenness and snuff-taking in vast quantities (the 'grass' of that generation). 'Hitting a policeman was acceptable,' he says.

He lived through the violent playground of the war years, with his brothers away in khaki or navy blue, rummaging on bomb sites and punching the kids he played with. He was sitting one day having his tea in the house in Croxteth when a doodlebug hit the railway embankment opposite, blowing the door off its hinges and ripping the lino from the floor. The meal, of rationed bacon and eggs, was thick with soot. But the Foremans had got off lightly; dozens had died on the other side of the embankment.

Freddie lost his virginity to Olive, known as Milky Big Tits, when he was fourteen and he got a job with Southern Railways as a driver's mate when he left school. That was when he first realised how lucrative railways could be. He saw gold bars, neatly packed at King's Cross station and guarded only by him, the driver, two coppers and an official. He cradled the bars lovingly. Boxing his way to a certain notoriety, like the Krays at about the same time, Freddie turned professional in 1954 but by then he had already done time for theft and assault. He worked with the Forty Thieves out of Elephant and Castle for a time at the 'clouting' game (shoplifting for underwear) which was a real eye-opener for him. The Jump-Up followed, pinching goods from reps' cars and in the post-war days of rationing, austerity and the black market, there was good money to be made.

By the early Fifties, Freddie was helping the economy by lifting television sets, washing machines and spin dryers out of electrical shops and into his van. Then he'd sell them cheap to all those desperate housewives out there. 'I'm a saint, ain't I?' he asked his readers in 1996. By the time he and Maureen had their first kid, he'd already met Buster Edwards, who would later become godfather to Freddie's second son, Jamie.

By day he worked in Smithfield, still just a meat market then, but the pay was crap and Freddie set up a little firm on the side with Edwards, Tommy Wisbey and Billy Hart. He confesses in his autobiography that he got Buster into crime, turning the window-cleaner-cum-florist into an old lag, robbing shops all over the capital. In selling the stuff on, Freddie met Charlie Kray, the twins' older brother, and he got in with the Firm as the Krays' outfit called itself (the capital F is important) when it was just starting out.

'Violet Kray was lovely,' Freddie recalled. 'She'd make you cups of tea and sandwiches … she wasn't a bit like they portrayed her in the film with Billie Whitelaw … She was a very gentle woman and of course, she loved the boys to death.'

This was the time when both Jack Spot and Billy Hill were keen to recruit the twins and Freddie did a bit of minding himself for Billy at his spielers. He would have met John Pedlar there and Red-Face Tommy Godfrey, proving what a small family London's underworld were. When a job went wrong in Southampton and Tommy Wisbey was nicked, Freddie holed up in the Krays' flat in Adelina Grove, across the road from the Blind Beggar pub that would become notorious later in criminal history. He was now targeting post offices and banks, looking for wages, payrolls and bullion. His firm had grown to include Micky Regan from Camberwell, Big Tony Sullivan and Alf Gerrard. They specialised in fast getaways, avoiding violence where possible, but these were big men armed with pickaxe handles and they were not going to let themselves get caught by some have-a-go merchant.

There were a number of such firms operating in the late Fifties. Everybody knew everybody else and a specialist from one would occasionally lend his services to another firm for a specific job. By the early Sixties, business was good. The 'pavement artists', as Freddie's firm called themselves, set up clubs up West and betting shops (now they were legal) in Bermondsey, Peckham and Brixton.

Freddie had just pulled off a successful bullion heist from Sharps Pixley & Co in Paul Street near Finsbury Square. It was, said the *Daily Express*, 'the hottest load of loot since Colonel Blood snatched the Crown Jewels'. The gold bullion was buried 'somewhere in England' while Interpol and Customs and Excise were searching every cargo ship from here to next Thursday.

Weeks later, Freddie was having a drink with a couple of mates at the Spanish Patriot, a pub in The Cut, Waterloo, when Buster Edwards, Bruce Reynolds, Gordon Goody and Tommy Wisbey walked in and asked Fred if he was interested in a little job they'd got lined up. This was May 1963 and Freddie needed a rest after the bullion raid, so he turned them down. 'It was none of my business but I wished them luck in their enterprise.'

*

When Freddie collaborated with fellow criminal Tony Lambrianou for their book *Getting It Straight* in 2001, Tony reminded Freddie that there were heavy rumours back in the day that he (Freddie) had been involved in the train job. Freddie explained that that was because of his known associates. After all, he'd grown up with people like Charlie Wilson, Bruce and Buster. Tommy Wisbey had been the best man at his wedding. He'd never heard, he said, of Roger Cordrey, Bill Boal, Jimmy White or Roy James.

Well, that's not how Uncle George described it, Freddie.

CHAPTER 9

GEORGE'S BACK UP: THE FARM AT ROBBERS' ROOST

I f you're planning a heist like the Great Train Robbery –
and remember nobody had ever done that on this scale
before – you've got to cover all your bases and you've got
to cover your tracks. Uncle George did both.

Picture the scene: sixteen villains carrying pick-axe
handles, nearly all of them with previous, roaring around the
Buckinghamshire countryside at four o'clock in the morning
on Thursday 8 August. It'll be light soon and somebody's
going to notice an immobilised set of coaches on the line near
Sears Crossing and a locomotive by Bridego Bridge. Almost
all the robbers were London based or had bolt-holes there so
it made sense to get to the capital quickly. There was no M25
in those days and it would have taken one and a half hours
by road in 1963. Then, the trick was to hide among the nearly
eight million people who lived there.

But think about that. Three army-style vehicles snarling
through the early morning. What if they had been stopped,
not by a road block because they would have been on the

move before the Buckinghamshire constabulary had time to set them up, but just by a routine copper minding somebody else's business? A faulty tail light perhaps or just the natural curiosity of a boy in blue. And inside sat a variety of heavies with balaclavas and the aforesaid pick-axe handles in the vehicles. Oh, and mailbags containing £2.6 million in used notes. It might have worked – in fact, a watered-down version of it did. But George had a back-up plan as he always did and he put it into operation via a man who was very like himself, a George Stanley wannabe called Brian Field.

Bruce Reynolds wrote in his autobiography that the last thing a professional criminal needs is a squeaky-clean solicitor. The best sort of brief, he knew, was one who could dream up good alibis and dispense 'drinks' to whoever required them – usually policemen and witnesses. What is better still, of course, is a brief who can dream up and organise a heist in the first place, because then he has as near to complete control over the event as it is possible to have, bearing in mind the emotionally charged atmosphere of the whole thing and the fact that he himself was miles away.

Brian Field was twenty-eight at the time of the train robbery. A psychologist would have had a field day (no pun intended) with the fact that he was put up for adoption soon after birth in December 1934. He was always a bit too eager to please, maybe because of that. An intelligent kid, he worked as an office boy in a solicitors' firm before National Service kicked in and he became a driver for the Royal Army Service

Corps, ending up in Korea when that Cold War flashpoint got hot. Here he met John Wheater who would eventually, thanks to his own greed and Field's powers of persuasion, become as much a victim of the train robbery as the driver Jack Mills. Wheater had attended Uppingham, the posh public school in the tiny county of Rutland. He was mentioned in despatches serving in Italy in the war and nearly got the Military Cross. After the war, Wheater trained as a solicitor and went back to the army three years later, working for the Army Legal Service – that was when Field met him.

In April 1959, Brian Field became a legal clerk with G. P. Voss & Son of 247 Bethnal Green Road and it's my bet he met George Stanley somewhere around now. George had been with Maurice Lesser for twenty years by this time and Field was no doubt impressed by the man's skill and more-than-modest lifestyle. As always, when the disciples come along, they can't cut it like the master. George always kept his Hermitage Court home carefully hidden from the outside world, whereas Field bought a flash house in Pangbourne in 1961 and drove a brand-new Jag. They never learn!

In May 1960 Field became managing clerk with a firm called James & Mallors, which was taken over the following year by Wheater. Just as Maurice Lesser was a target, with his over-niceness and his irregular, illegal habits, so John Wheater needed help just to stay afloat (while Field was swanning around in his Jag, his boss Wheater was driving a clapped-out old Ford). He was basically crap at his job and freely admitted that himself later. The office was a shambles, with files and paperwork all over the place. Field was vital in keeping all this together. And that gave him an edge.

According to Bruce Reynolds at least, Field was pretty good at what he did. He already knew Buster Edwards and Gordon Goody – I suspect he'd met them while he was still working in Bethnal Green – and he passed on details of his clients' country houses to the two professional thieves always on the lookout for quick money. Field arranged to get bail for Goody for the Heathrow robbery, by passing key people a few bungs. Then he created an alibi by claiming that Gordon was at his shirtmakers' in Jermyn Street at the time of the alleged robbery. He also discredited an eyewitness who had seen Gordon getting out of his Jag in the airport area; what City Gent?

Brucie might have been impressed by this but I bet, if he knew the details, Uncle George wasn't. What is Goody, an alleged hairdresser, who lives in rented property in Putney with his mum, doing driving a Jag and having his shirts made in Jermyn Street? The story Field had created didn't add up. And Goody had previous as long as your arm, with nine brushes with the law against him. Sure enough, it was all going pear-shaped, so Goody nobbled the jury. He picked on one of the hapless twelve good men and true and gave him a lift to court on the day the trial ended. In the event the man had done some bird himself and recognised a 'chap' when he met one. He didn't even take Gordon's offered bung. Goody was acquitted because the jury could not reach a unanimous verdict. Go, as the Americans say today, figure!

Fast forward to May 1963, three months before the robbery. According to Bruce Reynolds, Brian Field got in touch with Goody and Buster Edwards and arranged a meeting with the Ulsterman. This man is so important to this book that I have given him a chapter to himself, but we can skip him for now because Field's particular skills would be used in a slightly different direction.

George needed somewhere for the train robbers to lie low both before and after the robbery. Somewhere nearby within a short, easy driving distance. Somewhere isolated, off the beaten track, where the neighbours, if there were any, wouldn't notice the comings and goings of sixteen villains and their trucks. Put like that, of course, there are few places in the world that would be ideal and, in semi-rural Buckinghamshire, the place would have to be a compromise. He probably over-estimated the speed of the response time by the cozzers once the robbery was over, but that was all part of his careful methodology. George's Plan A was the robbery itself. His Plan B was to buy the farm. But Plan C – to get the bulk of the money away quickly – is one which no previous account of the robbery has ever mentioned. That's because all accounts follow the trial evidence and Bruce Reynolds's later version of events. None of this mentions George Stanley, of course, so it doesn't mention Plan C either. Secret plans stayed secret in his world.

It would have been the easiest thing in the world for George to make enquiries in the area of Sears Crossing, which he had long ago decided should be the scene of the crime, asking if there were any properties available for purchase. But of course that would have put the name George Stanley on the paperwork – something that he never did if he could help it. What he needed was a patsy, somebody as bent as he was but not as bright; somebody with a zest for the good life, who drove a flash car and had an expensive wife and lifestyle. That somebody was Brian Field of John Wheater's firm. He was charming, plausible, looked good in a suit – but it was John Wheater, for some unknown reason, who actually made the phone call on 27 June to the Midland Mart estate agency in Bicester. He had a client at his law firm, James & Wheater, who was interested in vacant properties in the area. Could they help? Yes, they could. How about Leatherslade Farm, near a village called Brill? It belonged to a Bernard Rixon, his wife and his parents. Midland Mart passed on the phone number and Field rang Lily Rixon that same day.

The next day Field turned up with his 'client', Leonard Field (the same name has caused no end of bother but the pair weren't remotely related) who was actually a steward on the P&O line, a company I worked for later. His brother Harry was a bank robber and horse doper which is how he got to know Brian. Leonard would be a useful front man but, with hindsight – and it's easy to be smart after the event, isn't it? – it must have struck the Rixons as a bit odd that two

The early days. From left to right: Dad, Bill Collins, Charlie Dunmore and the Duke, Dad's chauffeur.

A rare family photo. That's me sat in the middle, between Mum and Dad, and my brothers John, Victor and Arthur (with a friend). There's definitely a family resemblance, isn't there?

My brother Lennie, when he was about 14 years old. His life was really tragic and he spent half of it in Runwell Hospital before his death in 1998.

21-23 Broadway, Stratford – the offices of Lesser & Co. which would play a big influence in George's life and my own.

Hermitage Court Wanstead, where George bought his love nest for Edith. It looks much the same today.

The Eagle at Snaresbrook, one of George's haunts and the scene of many a deal. Pubs like this across south London were crucial to the Sturleys, generation after generation.

The overnight Glasgow to London mail train on Bridego Bridge at Ledburn in Buckinghamshire, the scene of the 'Great Train Robbery', on the morning of August 1963.

The inside of the Royal Mail Coach K30204M where 120 mailbags were stolen and offloaded onto army trucks, their contents destined to line the pockets of my Uncle George.

DC Milner and DCI Faber of the Met searching for clues by the signal post – nothing they found would ever lead them back to George.

Commander George Hatherill leads the investigation at Scotland Yard in December 1963. On the right, DI Frank Williams carries two sacks recovered from the robbery – containing over £50,000 (worth £925,000 today) – which were discovered in a London telephone box after an anonymous tip-off. Freddie Foreman recently claimed this was part of a deal he made with DI Williams to buy his co-operation and silence.

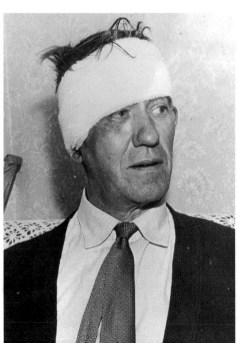

Jack Mills, the injured train driver. Big Jim Hussey apparently admitted on his deathbed that it was he who coshed Mills on the night of the robbery. Jack Mills never drove a train again and he died in 1970.

BUCKINGHAMSHIRE CONSTABULAR

£10,000 REWARD

ROBBERY

About 3 a.m. 8th August, 1963 from the Glasgow–Euston mail train

REGISTERED PACKET

The above reward will be paid by the Postmaster General the first person giving such information as will lead to apprehension and conviction of the persons responsible for the robbery.

Information to be given to the Chief Constable, Buckinghamsh Constabulary, Aylesbury (Tel.: AYLESBURY 5010), or at a Police Station.

The first 'wanted' poster from th immediate aftermath of the robber The police were desperate to catc the robbers – look at that rewar

eatherslade Farm, the robbers' hide-out. Chosen for its isolated location, it was ...ie smoke from the burning chimneys that gave them away.

By the end of August 1963, the owner of the farm was making a killing from opening it up to sightseers – it was half-a-crown for adults and a shilling for children, not quite the stash that the robbers got away with!

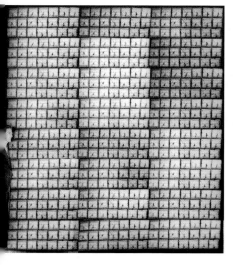

The police mocked this up in 1964 to show just how much money was stolen in the robbery – £2.6 million, worth over £40 million today.

Commander Hatherill created a list of all possible men linked to the robbery and began to arrest them, one by one. This is one of the press shots from August 1963, showing three of the suspects being led out of court.

George wasn't the only solicitor linked to the case – the police quickly discovered Brian Field's involvement in purchasing the farm and arrested him in November 1963. He got 25 years for conspiracy to obstruct justice and rob, and another solicitor, John Wheater, was put in the stir for 3 years. And what did George get? Nothing.

Ronnie Biggs' police record sheet. Biggs is probably the most famous of the robbers and has gained notoriety as the possible mastermind behind the whole thing – you couldn't be more wrong…

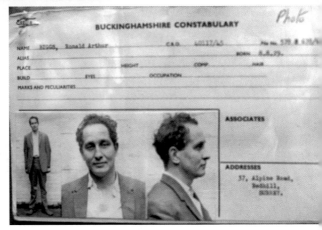

There is such public interest in the Great Train Robbery, anything connected to the case has become hot property. On 5 February 1969, the police held an auction of all the gangs' gear and personal effects that were found in Leatherslade Farm, making thousands. Worthless at the time, the metal sign from Sears Crossing recently sold for $14,000.

Between 1963 and 1968, 29 people were charged with crimes relating to the Great Train Robbery, with sentences totalling 337 years and 9 months. Bruce Reynolds, Buster Edwards and Jimmy White evaded capture for years before finally being arrested – Bruce Reynolds was caught in 1967, Buster gave himself up later that summer and Jimmy White was eventually caught after his caravan was found with £30,440 (worth £568,000 today) stashed behind panelling.

Police cars escorting a group of the convicted robbers disembarking at Yarmouth in February 1966 on their way to Parkhurst Prison, Isle of Wight, to serve out their sentences. Biggs was sentenced to 30 years but escaped after only 15 months.

One of the last photos of the Great Train Robbers, taken in 1979. From left to right: Buster Edwards, Tom Wisbey, Jimmy White, Bruce Reynolds, Roger Cordrey, Charlie Wilson and Jimmy Hussey. George would have been knocking 70 when this picture was taken and his name has still never been connected with the case. There are no surviving photos of him either, which only adds to the mystery. Just as the police said, 'the actual part he was called upon to play is not known'...until now.

London wide boys would be interested in a slightly rundown farm in the middle of nowhere. The place was available for sale and the asking price was £5,500.

Leatherslade Farm was actually an estate agents' nightmare, not a working farm at all and covered with weeds and peeling stucco, but the relative seclusion and outbuildings made it near-perfect for Field's purposes and he felt sure George would approve. Most importantly, it had a 360-degree visibility – Joe Law roaring up the surrounding lanes with sirens blaring would be seen and heard miles away. It was an hour's drive along twisting country lanes to Bridego Bridge. Leonard proved to be even smoother than Brian, linking arms with Mrs Rixon and asking her to imagine a swimming pool on the spot where they stood. Because there was someone else interested, the Fields put in a bigger offer of £5,750 and for a £555 deposit could move in at once to start on 'redecoration'.

The Rixons moved out on 29 July and the key was left with a Mrs Lilian Brooks who lived nearby. All the gang except Gordon Goody, who was late, had got to the farm by 6 August, the Tuesday before the robbery.

Whatever else you could call him, Uncle George was not a country boy, neither were Brian or Leonard Field, nor any of the men who would actually rob the train. They didn't know that a Mr Wyatt would call on 6 August to ask if he could still rent a field from the Rixons. He noticed a lorry parked near one of the outbuildings and the gang knew he had seen it. A public bridleway ran right past these sheds and any number of horsey people could have trotted past at an inopportune moment.

Both Fields would be remembered. Their names – and that of John Wheater – were on the paperwork purchasing the farm. George Stanley? Who's he?

Fast forward to the night in question: 8 August 1963. The crime of the century has just been pulled off and the gang have made for Leatherslade, to be dubbed the Robbers' Roost by the press in the days ahead. Incidentally, some enterprising journalist nicked that from Butch Cassidy's Hole-in-the-Wall gang of train robbers and outlaws in the American West seventy years earlier.

Every account of the Great Train Robbery tells the same story because it was essentially the one that came out at the trial later. They divvied up the poppy (underworld slang for cash), no doubt congratulating themselves on a job well done, then settled down to eating their way through the mountains of tinned food they'd stockpiled and, in the case of a couple of them at least, playing Monopoly. No doubt, there were all sorts of jokes about buying property in Mayfair and getting out of jail free. The assumption was then that each of them buggered off to their homes, safe houses or parts unknown, with suitcases full of loot, to fly to the sun with their financial futures assured. There was only one man who did that and he wasn't at the farm at all; neither was he going to draw attention to himself by flying to the sun. I don't know how Bruce Reynolds explained it to the others, but each man kept only a couple of thousand quid for himself, enough folding to make a quick getaway when the time was right. The bulk of the stolen money was taken straight to London, to a safe house (actually, a safe set of garages) at Hermitage Court, Snaresbrook. This is what I'm calling George's Plan C and when he told all this to me, he was typically cagey about *exactly* where the money went.

Peta Fordham got it nearly right in her 1965 book *The Robbers' Tale*. She wrote that the lorry was to have taken the cash away at once, using roads to the north and east, outside any police cordon that might be set up to wherever Reynolds, Goody and Wilson had decided it should go. Everybody was to make their own plans for getting their share away. But it wasn't Reynolds, Goody and Wilson who had a destination in mind, at least, not in the short term; it was George Stanley. You've got to bless Peta Fordham. She was the wife of Wilfred Fordham who helped defend Gordon Goody and it seems she was really taken by the big Irishman at the time. She was also utterly taken in by Uncle George. In her preface she wrote a big thank you to the solicitors and barristers who helped with the book and above all, to Mr George Stanley, of Messrs Lesser. She points out with wide-eyed respect that George represented five of the accused and held the record of the only two complete acquittals in the case – oh, and one reduction of sentence on appeal. Way to go, Uncle George!

So the lorry *did* get away from Leatherslade before the police cordon was set up on the understanding that at some point, when the furore had died down, there would be a meeting of minds and the splits would take place. George knew full well that of Bruce's team the only one with experience of handling large sums of money was Charlie Wilson. He had been a prime mover in the BOAC Airport robbery the previous year and, almost alone of the robbers, could be trusted not to light his fags with fivers.

Even so, something must have buggered up George's Plan C and I'm prepared to bet it was greed. The nucleus of the robbers – Goody, Edwards, Daly and James – knew Reynolds and trusted him. He may or may not have told them who was going to hold the readies for them against the day. But the others – Cordrey, Welch and Co. – were the second team, as they are often called in train robbery folklore, and they weren't happy. They insisted on keeping their share – which explains the large amounts found on some of them later.

Reynolds' problem now was to hold the team together so that sixteen known criminals weren't all heading out at the same time from a ramshackle farmhouse they had no legitimate business being anywhere near. Peta Fordham has the robbers solemnly handing over a fiver from the share of the take they kept back and giving it to Ronnie Biggs because it was his birthday. They all tried to sleep but Jimmy White was nervous. He had been on the run for four years, according to Fordham, and his paratrooper training made him warier than most. He was also, at forty-three, the oldest member of the team and had tried perhaps harder than most of them to go straight from time to time.

Roy James couldn't sleep either. He fed the three farm-yard cats on a Pyrex plate and left his dabs on it, despite Reynolds' constant reminders that they all wear gloves at all times. Nice that, wasn't it? Reynolds left first and the others followed later by various means, although Peta Fordham contends that there were complications in the evacuation and that the 'chiefs' went back to help their 'labourers' out.

The wheels of the law began to crank into motion early on the morning of 8 August, some two hours after the train was hit. I'm not going through all the ins and outs of these operations, which had nothing to do with George Stanley (yet) and you can read about them in a dozen books on the train robbery. Inspector J. Mellors of the Buckinghamshire police was first on the scene and radioed his HQ at Aylesbury to 'turn the lot out'. He needed cars, road blocks and tracker dogs. Now. He also, with what can only be called a nose for these things – and a lucky one at that – asked for local premises to be searched in case the robbers were holed up somewhere. That of course didn't happen, not at first, and was one of the strokes of luck that villains often have in the carrying out of a job. The dwarf signal that Electric Les, Paddy Daly and Roger Cordrey had tampered with was found and the driver and his number two, Mills and Whitby, still handcuffed together, were taken to Casualty in the Royal Buckinghamshire Hospital. Police photographers and fingerprint experts swarmed all over the locomotive and the HVP coach, now parked at Cheddington, and a GPO engineer found the cut telephone wires that had also knocked out phone communication for four homes in the area.

DC Keith Milner had the job of Exhibits Officer, collecting all the bits and pieces from the train, Sears Crossing and Bridego Bridge. Some of this had been left by the team – string, white tape to mark the train's stopping point and so on. The rest – a broken piece of coupling – belonged to the train itself. The law took 315 photos of the scenes of crime, some of which were used at the later trial, but most of which have never seen the light of day. There were the usual cock-ups by the investigators, if only because so many authorities were falling over themselves to solve the crime of the century. Only now was it dawning exactly how much cash had gone and secretly, the Buckinghamshire police, the Met and the Post Office law enforcement, all wanted to be the ones to bring the culprits in, hopefully still gleefully clutching their bags of folding.

Some of this operation was being picked up by Bruce and Co. at Leatherslade, as they could tune in to the police frequency on portable VHF radios. An incident room was set up at Aylesbury but with only two telephone lines, you've got to ask how hard the Bucks fuzz were really trying.

There was a high-level conference that afternoon at the GPO HQ in Newgate Street in the City. The chain of command of the thirty blokes in the room began with George Hatherhill, Commander from the Met, ironically known as 'Uncle George' at the Yard. The popular old bugger spoke eight languages and had seventeen high-profile murder collars to his credit, including John Christie, the necrophiliac strangler of Rillington Place and the Acid Bath murderer, John Haigh. John Creasey's series of novels revolving around Gideon of the Yard were said to be based on him. Softly spoken and cigar-smoking, his reputation was second to none. However, the train had been hit at a bad time for the Yard, with senior police officers on secondment or ill, and they were short-staffed. Hand on heart, I can't claim that *my* Uncle George knew that.

From day one, Hatherhill had no doubt that the team involved were London men – 'where the cream of the criminal profession live', as he put it in his 1971 autobiography. He also believed the villains would still be hiding out somewhere within thirty to forty-five minutes' drive away. A few names were put forward and a week later the Commander produced a list which is unbelievable in its accuracy. Of fourteen named individuals, only one – Danny Pembroke – had nothing to do with the robbery. The other thirteen were up to their hocks in it.

Financial details were now coming to light and of course the media went into a feeding frenzy. Television and radio coverage in 1963 was nothing like it is today where such a crime (if it could be carried out at all technically) would be covered 24/7 with everybody from Paxo to Clarkson getting in on the act. One hundred and twenty mailbags had been stolen with 636 packets of notes from eight different banks, one of which, belonging to the Midland (today's HSBC), was not even insured.

At Leatherslade, the team heard the midday news. The police knew that an army vehicle had been involved. Whitby, the driver's mate, had seen it and the information was logged at 6.16 at the coppers' HQ at Aylesbury, 8 August. The gang could not be sure who had seen it or where and they panicked. Jimmy White found some yellow paint in an outhouse and started slapping it on over the dark green. It looked crap – the sort of badly-done DIY colour that everybody would notice. Clearly, they couldn't all get away in this without drawing attention to themselves. Roger Cordrey had a bike with him and he pedalled to Oxford, an hour away, to ring Brian Field and a friend of Reynolds', Mary Manson, from Wimbledon, to come and collect them. What had begun so slickly was starting to fall apart.

Reynolds coordinated the destruction of the evidence at Leatherslade, but something went wrong here, too. Burning everything would send up clouds of black smoke – as it was, smoke from the farm's chimneys was observed by many locals – so they hit upon digging a pit behind the outbuildings. Some things, like the three 'drags' involved, were too big to hide, so they had to stay behind, the Land Rovers locked in garages nobody ever found the keys to. Whoever had driven the big truck to George's – and it must have been Bruce Reynolds because, alone of the robbers, it was only Bruce who knew of George's involvement in the first place – had of course brought it back, which explains Peta Fordham's nonsense about the leaders not deserting their men but returning to the farm to help the others get away. Why did Bruce come back with the truck, when that was clearly increasing his risk of getting caught? Because if he hadn't, a lot of blokes at Leatherslade would have feared he'd done a runner with their loot. I reckon that Brucie was back at the farm by the middle of Friday morning, *before* news of the involvement of the army truck reached the team and the airwaves.

Exactly how the robbers left Leatherslade is open to inter-pretation. George Stanley wasn't there so it was something he never talked about. According to one version, Brian Field and his wife Karin turned up and whisked Roy James back to London to organise less conspicuous transport than the army vehicles. Another version has Cordrey and White buying a car – a grey Rover – for £360. White doubled back to pick up another robber, name unspecified, and buggered off to London. Bruce Reynolds' version is that he walked to Thame on the Friday morning (9 August) where he was picked up by Mary Manson and her friend Rene. While the women were on their toes with Bruce's modest cut of the robbery proceeds, Brucie and Daly caught a Green Line bus to Victoria coach station and then on to Mary's house in Wimbledon.

When the police found Leatherslade on 13 August, DC Milner had a field day. There were army uniforms, black hoods with eyeholes, sleeping bags, mattresses, cooking utensils and even instructions for use of the state-of-the-art American handcuffs used to click Mills and Whitby together. In the cellar were thirty-five mailbags with money wrappers and £627 10s. in Scottish banknotes. That was legal tender (and still is) all over the UK but a lot of shops wouldn't take it and the team no doubt considered it was safer to leave such a pathetic sum behind than have questions asked at counters.

Then we come to the bit about the burning of Leatherslade Farm. The original plan was for someone to come and torch the place after the robbers had flown the nest, so all the evidence was destroyed before the law found it. I was nearly the kid with the matches. Peta Fordham's version is that the bloke detailed to do the job had a run-in with the police days earlier and knew he was being tailed, so he couldn't show at the farm. Thirteen years later, some of the robbers told the author Piers Paul Read that Brian Field was supposed to do the job using a friend of his called Mark. After all, he'd been involved in acquiring the farm in the first place and he had no previous. A smooth talker like him could, perhaps, have concocted an excuse if he'd been seen on the premises. The fact was that no one fully trusted Brian Field. He was not one of the team in the accepted sense, but a 'little conspirator' as Peta Fordham calls him. He smiled too much, she said, for most people's tastes and had a curious 'hand-washing' gesture. Don't get me started on the psychology behind this body language. Charlie Wilson in particular sensed that Field was not going to get the job done. So Wilson, Reynolds, Daly, James and Buster Edwards geared themselves up to go back to the farm and burn it down. By now, it was Tuesday 13 August and the police had found the farm with most of its incriminating evidence scattered around; so the plan, redundant, was abandoned. 'We're nicked,' said Roy James, whose dabs were all over the kitties' Pyrex plates.

Many commentators today believe the man earmarked to burn the farm and its contents was a myth concocted by the robbers later in a vain attempt to salvage their reputations. All the evidence is that they intended to stay much longer at Leatherslade – and I believe that was Uncle George's intention – but police broadcasts and the increasing media hype about the robbery put the frighteners on the 'builders and decorators' hiding out at the farm. The list compiled by DC Milner reads like something out of the siege of Ladysmith. Apart from robbery accessories, there were: 9 pipkins of beer (that's 63 pints), 15 sets of cutlery, 15 mugs, 16 plates, 40 candles, 18 lbs of butter, a catering tin of coffee (Maxwell House – no rubbish), 16 packs of sugar, 18 tins of pork luncheon meat, 38 tins of Campbell's soup, tins of peaches, 40 tins of baked beans, 20 tins of peas, a sack of potatoes, 200 eggs and 34 toilet rolls. I could go on … Somebody had over-catered. Why? Because they were supposed to stay longer until things had calmed down.

In the real world of Southend, the Sturley family caught the news wherever we could. Media wasn't saturation in those days with 'Breaking News' every second and endless speculation when there isn't any. There were only two TV channels and the BBC dominated the airwaves. A BBC reporter called Reg Abbis stood under Bridego Bridge talking to camera about events that would become the 'Crime of the Century'. We got hold of the *Daily Mirror* and laughed like drains at Uncle George's success.

Mum got a message from Uncle George. There *was* a bloke tooled up to burn the farm; all part of Plan B. But suddenly he wasn't available. Mum didn't like George, as you know, but there was money involved here for two of her boys and my brother Lennie was briefed (this was before he had been attacked by Hempstead). I was away at the time but due back that day and Mum realised that having me tagging along would arouse less suspicion than a young bloke on his own.

'Drive out to the countryside,' she said to Lennie, who was never afraid to get his hands dirty. 'It'll just be a bloke and his kid brother out for a ride in the school holidays. Take plenty of paraffin and lots of matches. Make sure there's nothing left.' It might seem odd that Mum was so happy to go along with Uncle George's request but she always had pound signs in her eyes and could see that the job had to be done for the greater good – or was it bad? Can you imagine any mother today sending her thirteen-year-old on a mission like this? Come to think of it, can you imagine any normal mother doing it in 1963?

But the law got there first and we didn't have to go. Six days after the robbery, the police found Leatherslade Farm and the BBC News showed uniformed coppers wandering the site and keeping nosey locals away. This discovery was probably just as well; if they hadn't found it and we'd gone ahead, I would have become that much-loved character in Uncle George's legal jargon, 'an accessory after the fact'.

Then, everybody held their breath.

CHAPTER 10
THE ULSTERMAN

Freeze frame. It's 14 August 1963. Uncle George is holding the folding, to the tune of the best part of £2.3 million after the robbers had taken their cuts. Bruce Reynolds' team are holding their breath because the law have found Leatherslade Farm and an awful lot of incriminating evidence.

I'd gone that year on a school holiday, between the job itself and the finding of the farm, to the Lake District. I'd paid for it myself from the hooky gear I'd flogged at school – pens, pencils, bikes and air guns – and I'd run up the princely sum of £7 10s. I loved it. There was always plenty of fresh air in Southend, but you couldn't compare it with Helvellyn. It was actually snowing as we trudged along Striding Edge with our backpacks, but it had stopped by the time we reached the top and the views were breathtaking. We'd started off camping in our tents but a deer had eaten most of our grub during the night and the weather drove us indoors to stay at the YMCA in Keswick. The next morning the town was buzzing with news of the train robbery – they'd found Leatherslade.

The talk up there was the same as at home a couple of days later – the robbers were heroes, not villains and I felt really proud. It was still speculation as to who was involved, although of course I knew Uncle George had planned the whole thing because Dad had confirmed it on 9 August and that a 'big one' was being planned was common knowledge to all the Sturleys. But I never told anyone, not once; not my mates or my teachers or anybody. It was the Sturley way – 'Give 'em zilch and they've got zilch' as we'd say today.

But I've frozen the frame and stopped the film here because we haven't talked about the Ulsterman and it's time we did. He doesn't appear at all in the earliest books about the case. *The Great Train Robbery* by Gosling and Craig was published in 1964 just after the trial and paints a vivid picture of just how much in the dark everybody was back then. John Gosling was the recently retired Detective Superintendent from the short-lived Ghost Squad at the Yard and he wrote, 'The two mighty mysteries of the Great Train Robbery – who planned it and where the main booty is – remain unsolved.' That was fifty years ago, and until this book the authorities have been no further forward.

Gosling and Craig spend sixty pages speculating and include as a possibility an Irishman 'believed to have led three big bank raids in Dublin'. Wrong bloke.

Peta Fordham doesn't mention the Ulsterman either. She speculates furiously on who 'The Mind' might have been who planned the whole operation and the identity of the 'second mystery man' who organised the disappearance of the loot – not dreaming, of course, that this was one and the same person, a one-lunged diabetic you'd walk past without a second glance and somebody she'd already profusely thanked for his help in her preface.

By the time we come to Piers Paul Read's *The Train Robbers* in 1978, the world had turned. That was the year that Bruce Reynolds was released, along with Charlie Wilson, and they were the last of the team to smell the fresh air. As we'll see, that was because Brucie had stayed on the run for five years before his eventual capture and Charlie had done a runner from prison in 1964. The exception as always is Ronnie Biggs, a more famous fugitive than Dr Richard Kimble – the hero of the long-running TV series of the Seventies. The dozy bastard became a folk hero even among people who weren't born in 1963. His official release date was 2009!

Read talked to several of the train robbers when writing his book and everybody agrees today that they strung him along with lurid tales of a Nazi connection and international espionage. Read wrote that there was a Mr Big behind the crime who financed it and got in exchange a million quid. He was Otto Skorzeny – an officer in the Waffen-SS who had led the German commandoes during the war. One of his blokes had been at Leatherslade Farm, Read believed, and more of them had sprung Charlie Wilson from Winson Green later. Read admits he was sceptical and realised that it was not impossible – given the facilities of prison libraries and the time spent alone in a cell – for the train robbers to have invented the whole story. But he goes along with it anyway, at least in part.

He also talks about the Ulsterman. And he tells it like this. According to Read, Brian Field rang Gordon Goody in January 1963 and met him at the Old Bailey the next day. Field knew someone who knew where to find very large sums of money that were there for the taking by anyone with the right organisational credentials. Was Goody interested? He was. He phoned Buster Edwards and the pair went to Field's offices at Wheater & Co in New Quebec Street near Marble Arch. With Field was a fifty-something bloke called Mark, a businessman, the boys reckoned. The money was several million and it was on a train. So far, so vague. Mark, Edwards and Goody drove to Finsbury Park and strolled in the shrubbery. There, sitting on a park bench like something out of a John Le Carré novel, was a middle-aged bloke, ordinary and slightly balding. Everybody shook hands but no names were used by anybody. As they walked together, the balding man told the others what he knew. Money came regularly into London on the night train from Glasgow. It was carried in the HVP coach which was always number two behind the locomotive. He estimated there could be seventy postmen on the train, but none in the HVP coach and the cash could be as much as £5 million.

Goody and Edwards needed time to think about this juicy offer and agreed to meet the man in a week's time.

Mark dropped them back at Waterloo and they set up a meet with Bruce Reynolds and Charlie Wilson later that day. Brucie claimed he didn't believe a word of it so that evening they went to Euston and watched, apparently astonished, as the mountains of mailbags were offloaded onto the station platform.

They talked it over at Reynolds' flat in Putney and agreed it was too big a job for the four of them. Hence Buster approaching Tommy Wisbey, Bob Welch and Roger Cordrey of the South Coast mob at the New Crown in the Elephant – the team Piers Paul Read calls the second firm. The others were drawn in under Bruce's vague coordinating as you've read already and on 31 July, a week before the robbery, they met the little man from Finsbury Park for the second and last time.

The meet took place in Hyde Park this time and again it was Goody and Edwards who went. Both men knew a Belfast accent when they heard one – Goody was an Irishman himself – and the pair were intrigued as to his identity. It was a swelteringly hot day in an otherwise dull and chilly summer and the three stopped at a café by the Serpentine for a drink. The anonymous man took off his jacket and hung it on a chair. While he popped to the loo, Goody ransacked the jacket pockets. Nothing. He checked the lining. Nothing there either. But he did notice a tailor's label and below it the customer's name and address – the Ulsterman. Goody memorised the name and came to the instant conclusion that the man was both a Protestant and a farmer (is this bloke Sherlock Holmes or what?).

The Ulsterman came back; they finished their drinks and shook hands when they parted. 'By the way,' the Ulsterman said, 'if you do well on this one, I've got an even bigger job for you afterwards.'

What does Bruce Reynolds say about all this? According to him, the original meeting via Brian Field took place in May, not January, which sounds a little late for detailed information gathering. They all agreed, the 'chiefs' who met to discuss the proposal, that the Ulsterman's information sounded kosher and Bruce pointed out that Brian Field wouldn't risk his career on a chancer. When Roy James and Jimmy White reconnoitred the arrival of a Night Mail in Euston station a couple of weeks later, they were horrified to note that a different, state-of-the-art HVP coach was in use. But the Ulsterman assured them that, come the night in question, the older type, that he had already described to Goody and Edwards, would be used. Reynolds smelled a rat. Was the Ulsterman an undercover cop, some rogue descendant of Scotland Yard's Ghost Squad?

Reynolds had a tense conversation on the night in question as he checked one last time with his 'chaps' at Sears Crossing. Somebody asked him if the train was always on time. Roger Cordrey knew the score. 'Never more than five minutes late, never more than a minute early.'

'Let's hope it stays that way.'

'Yeah, we don't want any delays tonight.'

'Or strikes.'

'No worries about strikes,' [Reynolds] said, 'our man [the Ulsterman] has guaranteed that.'

'Who the fuck is he, Doctor Beeching [Chairman of the British Railways Board]?'

'Could be. Could be anyone. Who the fuck knows? Who the fuck cares?'

Well, rather a lot of people, as it turns out.

What did authors Russell-Pavier and Richards make of the Ulsterman in their 2012 book? Suspiciously, the details of that first meet differ. The Ulsterman told Goody and Edwards in Finsbury Park that he'd got his information from his brother-in-law (or it could have been brother or step-brother) who worked on the railways. This confusion is important because the authorities could only trace possible Irishmen insiders with brothers. Brothers-in-law would have been research too far. The authors believe, rightly, that the Ulsterman didn't spill all the beans of his vital inside knowledge to two strangers at that first meet. The 31 July meet now takes place in Kensington Gardens and the Ulsterman left the table, not to go to the loo, but to buy a cup of tea. The label was not sewn into the lining but was in a spectacle case sticking out of the jacket pocket, which, according to Goody talking to Piers Paul Read, was empty.

It was the Ulsterman who rang Goody at Brian Field's

house in Pangbourne on Tuesday 6 August to tell him of a last-minute change of plan. The serious money was not going to be loaded until the following night and all the team could do was grin and bear it at Leatherslade.

Russell-Pavier and Richards then get into the speculation game. George Hatherhill's information in August 1963 was that the insider, who gave the team their knowledge, was an Irishman. The Post Office Investigation Branch was specifically working on this angle and identified sixteen operatives who could be called Irish, either by surname, accent or known background. Ten of them had one or more brothers and three of those actually on the train that was robbed had criminal records. Who could you trust in those days, eh? The likeliest of these lads was James O'Reilly and he lived alone at 87 Napier Road, Tottenham. His girlfriend worked in Lloyds Bank. He was watched by members of the Flying Squad and enquiries were made about him in his native Ireland. Nothing. Except that O'Reilly and his brother tried to buy a big Victorian house in Edmonton soon after the robbery. This may, of course, be a coincidence. O'Reilly's file in the Postal Archive stays shut until 2030. Will it bring any surprises? I doubt it.

Bizarrely, Andrew Cook's *The Great Train Robbery* (2013) doesn't mention the Ulsterman at all, although he does discuss Hatherhill's work with Chief Superintendent Ernie Millen, trying to discover the insider working for the Post Office and/or British Rail. The police seem to have overlooked the Ulsterman entirely as a go-between and were much more interested in the man who gave him the information – the true insider. In pinning down this individual, Deputy Controller R. Yates of the Post Office's IB drew up a list of thirty-five blokes, any one of whom could be our boy. This is where James O'Reilly's name came from, although it is listed 'Reilly' in Yates' paperwork. Two other possibilities were Michael Lyttle and Thomas McCarthy on the grounds that they were both Irish and had brothers. Both were investigated and watched. The upshot? Bugger all. And of course, there was no mention of Annie Oakley at all, the operative who was *really* supplying the information.

As I was putting this book to bed, Gordon Goody, now a frail old geezer of eighty-five living in Spain, dropped a bombshell. He took part in a documentary called *A Tale of Two Thieves* and gave the Ulsterman's name as Patrick McKenna. He was indeed a Post Office worker and in a photo from the time looks rather dodgy, complete with combed-back thin hair, shades and a pinstriped double-breasted suit. Gordon's assessment of McKenna was a little wide of the mark. He was not an Irish farmer, but a Post Office operative living in Islington. And as for being a Protestant, McKenna's family believe he gave his ill-gotten gains (his share of the loot) to the Catholic church!

This is the true origin of the mysterious go-between who had such accurate information about the Up Special on 7–8 August 1963. Patrick McKenna worked for Uncle George. It was a clever ploy, really. George had already got Bruce

Reynolds interested because Bruce owed George large, but he had nothing on the others so he needed to lure them a different way. Note that it was only Edwards, Goody and the mysterious Mark who ever met the Ulsterman. Even though they may well have spoken on the phone, there is no evidence that Brian Field ever met him. Bruce Reynolds certainly didn't. All McKenna was doing was relaying the information George had got from Annie Oakley, the *real* insider the Post Office Investigation Branch were looking for. McKenna was just another red herring that George threw into the net to create as much distance as possible between him and the law.

'He's too clever by half,' I remember Mum saying to Dad as the organisation of the train robbery came to light. 'George is going to pick the wrong bloke one day.'

McKenna, who died years ago, was poor all his life. There is a theory that his share of the folding was stolen; his widow and kids think he got an attack of the guilts and gave it all away to the church. Allow me to set the record straight. Patrick McKenna was another in the long list of victims of George Stanley. His money wasn't stolen and he didn't give it away; Uncle George never paid him in the first place. And, in the scheme of things, there was bugger all that Patrick McKenna could do about that.

Back in August 1963 the authorities had some train robbers to catch. In terms of catching Mr Big, they should have paid attention to the *Daily Express* leader on the 9th – 'It is almost certain that one man plotted the raid ... First he gets a tip-off about a train ... Then a small team of "officers" are told to hand-pick the raiders. They are given an assurance ... that if they are caught their wives and families will be looked after ... Afterwards, raiders go their own ways, knowing the haul will not be touched and distributed for several weeks.' This was spot on and makes nonsense of various stories that all the loot was divvied up at Leatherslade.

You have to remember that this was the crime of the century. Never before had such a huge amount of cash been lifted at one time and speculation was rife. Somebody thought Eastcastle Street (right) and mentioned Billy Hill (wrong). In fact, from his yacht in Cannes, the now-retired Hill emphatically denied his involvement and threatened various papers with legal action. It was Uncle George who had advised Hill to quit the rackets while he was ahead. 'Time to give it up, Billy,' he had said, 'you don't need the grief.' And Billy certainly wasn't going to go down for something he hadn't done. His name disappeared overnight. The Irish menace reared itself again – three of the gang were Irishmen wanted in Eire for bank jobs, it was speculated. Perhaps it was the IRA – they were always up to no good. Since the British are obsessed with gentlemen crooks ever since Raffles, the Flying Squad were shadowing a baronet, identity never revealed. The *Sunday Telegraph* had the goods on a miser living alone in Brighton in one room. He had had no convictions for twenty years and when he had concocted a plan, he took it to a master criminal in the Harrow Road who then carried it out. No doubt if the train robbery had happened ten years later, it would have been the work of little green men or greys who had travelled millions of light years just to rob the Up Special.

Commander Hatherhill's list – and there were longer ones, drawn up by, among others, the grey fox, Tommy Butler at the Yard – was now acted upon. Bob Welch's home in Benyon Road was turned over on Wednesday 14 August but he was not at home. Nothing was found. Welch was actually represented at his trial by Lincoln & Lincoln, but the word got around the gang indirectly from George. His client advice rule book could be written on the back of an envelope: don't get caught with cash; have a watertight alibi; say nothing without the presence of your solicitor; remember, coppers aren't stupid, but they are fishing. And you're not biting. Not today.

Roger Cordrey needed somewhere to stash the cash he had hung onto despite Reynolds's advice and found a handy lock-up for rent in his home town of Bournemouth. He paid £7 10s. for three months from a fat wad in his pocket. It was his bad luck that the Mrs Clarke he was hiring from was a copper's widow and she got suspicious, ringing the local nick the same day. He was arrested, along with the unluckiest man in this whole story, William Boal. It didn't help that Boal lost it when Sergeant Stan Davies of Bournemouth CID said he wanted to search him and had to be restrained. Since

Davies was an ex-prop forward, that was the wrong thing for Boal to do. He also denied knowing Cordrey at all and said he lived in the area, whereas his home address was Fulham.

Boal was a Geordie whose family had moved to London when he was fourteen. Short-sighted after an industrial accident and quick-tempered, he had met Cordrey soon after the war in Kingston and they played snooker together. Undoubtedly the fall guy of the train robbery, his only 'crime' was knowing Cordrey, yet he served fourteen years and died in prison. Since the robbery had taken place in Buckinghamshire, anybody arrested for the job was whisked off to Aylesbury nick. Two down (one, to be accurate) and Christ knew how many more to go.

Enter the fox. And with Tommy Butler, a formidable team of Flying Squad blokes led by Ernie Millen, Hatherhill's right-hand man. Millen was the 'overlord', to use his own phrase, on the case but ended up looking a complete pillock when he refused to believe there was a mastermind behind the robbery or that four of the robbers – Aldridge, Smith, Foreman and 'Pop' the driver – were still at large years later. We've already talked about Butler; he was a driven man who would spend years of his life and go all over the world in pursuit of the robbers. He even combed the beaches of Kent and dear old Southend on his holidays looking for unfriendly faces. His 'terrible twin', the bald, bespectacled Peter Vibart, was at his side most of the time. The polite books say that Frank Williams' methods were 'unorthodox'. He was old school, with a wide selection of grasses and snouts who fed him information, some of it bloody useful. Rumours of bribe taking and blind-eye turning came to bite him in the arse eventually and it was said that because of this he was passed over for promotion when Tommy Butler finally retired. These senior men and pretty well all the junior ones below them shared the grey fox's determination to 'get the bastards'.

On the 15th, long before most of the 'labourers' had had their collars felt, the Fraud Squad (the Met's C6 Department) were having a close look at the signatures on the Leatherslade purchase paperwork. There was a Brian Field, a Leonard Field and a John Wheater and two of them were legal men. Oh dear!

The fingerprint evidence at Leatherslade was beginning to tell its own story. Nothing was computerised in 1963 and the workload of counting loops and whorls was enormous. One copper reputedly had a nervous breakdown over it. Some 750,000 print comparisons were made and 243 photographs of 311 finger and 56 palm prints. In the end, nine of the team would be picked up by this kind of evidence. Ironically, one of them was Bruce Reynolds, who had insisted everybody wore gloves. This of course makes it pretty obvious that there *was* a plan to torch the farm.

Some of the robbers jumped before they were pushed, believing this would be taken by the police as evidence of innocence. Billy Hill had often used the same technique. Accordingly, Bob Welch turned up at Scotland Yard to be interviewed by the Flying Squad who were, inevitably, looking for him (his dabs were found at Leatherslade). No, he didn't know Buckinghamshire and was at home with Mrs Welch on the night in question. With their usual cat-and-mouse technique, the Heavy Mob let him go.

On 20 August, Tommy Wisbey went to Scotland Yard and made a statement. He had been at a pub on the night in question – the landlord would corroborate that.

Jimmy White had gone walkabout, but £30,440 in fivers had been found behind a wall partition in his caravan at the Clovelly caravan site near Dorking. A man resembling White in the company of a woman, a baby and a white poodle called Gigi had been seen in the caravan recently. All leave for the Flying Squad was cancelled and dozens of poodle owners were stopped and questioned – who says our police aren't wonderful?

The Flying Squad also turned over Gordon Goody's mum's place in Putney. He wasn't there and it turned out they had no warrant, so it was lose-lose for them, really.

John Wheater realised the game was up because the TV and radio news was full of it. Clearly nothing this exciting had happened in Buckinghamshire for years. The previous owner of Leatherslade, Bernard Rixon, had plans to charge five bob (half a crown for the kids) for tourists to gawp at their leisure. Wheater contacted the fuzz and told them all about his client Leonard Field, about whom he actually knew very little.

There was now a difference of opinion, apparently, among the senior officers on the case. Tommy Butler, secretive, obsessive and determined, wanted a media blanket so the robbers still at large (all of them except Cordrey) wouldn't be spooked. Hatherhill and Millen disagreed. Afraid the team would be on their toes to sunnier climes with large amounts of folding, they wanted names named and photos posted. And they got their way. On Thursday 22 August, the *Evening Standard*, read by felons everywhere, carried the banner headline '3 Men the Yard Want to See' and there were the names Reynolds, Wilson and White, together with mugshots taken at previous social gatherings with arresting officers. It paid off. When they arrested Charlie Wilson on 23 August – Detective Sergeants Dilley and Reid got him at his house in Crescent Lane, Clapham – Wilson said to them, 'I do not see how you can make it stick without the poppy [money] and you won't find that.' From the mouths of babes! No cash was found on Wilson, but since his dabs were everywhere at the farm, that hardly mattered.

Now, I know what you're thinking. We haven't heard from Uncle George for quite a few pages now. I'd like to tell you that he was already in the Bahamas, safe from extradition and richer than God, but it didn't work that way. Nor was it supposed to. He was at Maurice Lesser's office every day, doling out (expensive) advice to villains high and low, having a quiet lunchtime drink at the Two Puddings next door, keeping out of the limelight. But at midday on Wednesday 21 August,

George Stanley went to Scotland Yard in the company of Mary Manson. She was a 42-year-old housewife, vaguely involved in the antiques trade, and she lived in Wimbledon. She was a friend of Bruce Reynolds, some accounts say girlfriend, and the pair had bought an Austin Healey from the Chequered Flag Sports Car company in Chiswick on 9 August. It was an example of Brucie getting carried away with his success, not being able to resist flashing the cash so soon after the robbery. In the event it was Mary Manson who paid – £835 in fivers tied up with elastic bands. The dealer, Dennis St John, had got suspicious as the robbery story broke in the media and called the police. News of the car purchase broke on 19 August and Mary must have called George for help. The statement she handed in to the Yard was undoubtedly written by him and designed to get her off the hook.

Unfortunately, one of the coppers questioning Mary that morning was DI Frank Williams, whose soft Welsh lilt only just disguised the fact that this man was hard as nails and nobody's fool. It didn't help that Williams knew Mary by the name of McDonald, a part owner of Mac's Antiques in the Portobello Road and an a.k.a. immediately set alarm bells ringing. She signed a statement in George's presence but it was obvious that Williams wasn't buying it. He asked her to go back to her flat in Wimbledon and she agreed. 'The solicitor then left,' Williams' report says but you can bet George was worried. And rightly so, too, because although they found nothing at Mary's flat she got a bit blabby in the car.

'I'm scared stiff about this,' she told the DI. 'I saw my solicitor [George] on Monday first thing and he kept me there [21–23 Broadway] all day and then he advised me to hide until he'd sorted it all out.'

'What exactly do you mean by that remark?' Williams asked her.

'Just what I've said,' Mary told him. 'Now what is going to happen to me?'

What was going to happen to her was that she was kept at the Yard overnight while her other premises were searched and the next day she would be taken to Aylesbury police station to be charged with receiving £835 she knew to be stolen. George went with her, no doubt pumping her when he could about exactly what she had said to the police. What she had said, that he had advised her to run, had got the barrister Patrick Marrinan disbarred seven years earlier. Bruce Reynolds' version of events is that, having bought the car, Mary Manson was involved in taking him home from Leatherslade in an antiques van, complete, presumably, with the loot. But we know most of that had already gone to George. Whatever her involvement or not in the getaway process, the last thing George could afford was a loose-lipped woman being less than discreet with the police.

By the time she appeared at Linslade Magistrates' Court, George had got a brief for her – Wilfred Fordham, whose wife Peta would go on to write one of the first books on the robbery. 'This is not a woman on the run,' he told the magistrates. 'This woman went to Scotland Yard to face allegations made against her.' It didn't work; Mary was remanded for two days and sent to Holloway to await trial. The *Daily Mirror* of Friday 23 August had a front page photo of Mary under a blanket like the one which would cover all the robbers' heads in the days and weeks ahead.

'She stood with her hands in her pockets,' the *Mirror* reported. 'She glanced across the courtroom and smiled at a red-haired woman [almost certainly her friend Rene]. Another glance at the red-head. This time a wink too.'

George was sitting there, no doubt glaring daggers at Walter Leach the farmer-magistrate, but the evils didn't do the job this time.

The day Mary's photo appeared, the word went out in connection with getaway driver Roy James. The Weasel – a nickname that actually belonged to somebody else – couldn't have been higher profile at that moment. He had won the circuit at Cadwell Park on the 18th and was up for the race at Goodwood on the 24th in his 1098cc Brabham-Ford. His lap time on the 22nd had been 95.57 mph. Plain-clothes men went to the track, but James didn't show.

They tracked down Gordon Goody at a hotel in Leicester, knocking him up at two in the morning. Butler and Vibart had a go at him but Gordon was a seasoned criminal and, alone of the robbers, had set up a partial alibi for himself. He had been 'over the water in the Green Isle' doing a bit of shooting and fishing. Tommy Butler told him he knew that

Goody's mum and a friend called Knowles, who had gone with them, had got back to England on 7 August. He believed Goody had come back a day earlier. Goody now kept schtum until he had a chance to see his solicitor. Who was that? Oh, George Stanley of Lesser & Co. So they had to let Gordon go.

Goody complained to the press about police harassment, especially on behalf of his poor old mum. 'When I go out it's a certainty that [a detective] is following me. Anyone would think that I was one of the train robbers.' He cited his 'wrongful' accusation over the BOAC robbery the previous year and talked about being set up. 'Either they charge me today or they get off my back.'

They charged him. But not until 3 October at Putney nick and it's interesting that it was not Uncle George who held the Irishman's hand on this occasion but one of his colleagues at Lesser's, a straight bloke called Ray Brown, who handled a lot of George's smaller cases. Perhaps George thought it best to keep a lower profile. After all, he'd chanced his arm with Mary Manson and DI Williams. It wouldn't do to have too much of the spotlight. Goody asked to speak to Brown alone, but Tommy Butler wasn't having any of that. A pair of shoes belonging to Goody had turned up and they had potential links with Leatherslade Farm. He was sent to Aylesbury and charged with the train robbery.

Long before this, other gang members were constantly on the move. Bruce Reynolds moved from Wimbledon to Clapham with his wife Franny. Paddy Daly and his wife,

Barbara (there is a famous photo of the four of them that is reproduced in most books on the robbery), were in a hotel in Margate. Bob Welch was skulking with some mates in a farmhouse near Bideford. There were rewards out for these men and any information on the case, in some instances as much as £240,000. Silence comes at a price and because Uncle George still had most of the assets, serious money was not available to any of those still on the run. This is why, despite Daly or Edwards or both making enquiries in various shipyards in Cowes in the Isle of Wight, nobody could actually get out of the country. The airports and docks were being watched and a more private departure would have cost a packet.

Then Biggsy put both his feet in it again. On Wednesday 4 September, Frank Williams and his boys turned up at Ronnie's home in Redhill. They found nothing but took Ronnie in for questioning. 'That don't sound too good,' Biggs said. 'What are my chances of creeping out of this?' His solicitor, by the way, was George Stanley of Lesser & Co. That didn't even slow Williams down of course and it may be that Uncle George sent Brown along again or perhaps his other dogsbody, Frank Campion, otherwise he'd have been talking to Williams again in defence of a third alleged robber and that was a bit too centre stage for George Stanley. Biggs was charged with the robbery at Linslade on 5 September. 'It's all lies,' Biggs shouted in court. He kept that up for most of the rest of his life.

Two days later, Big Jim Hussey was rounded up at Dog Kennel Hill by DS Jack Slipper, a shifty bastard who looked like a spiv and went on to write his own version of events as Slipper of the Yard. Butler grilled Hussey and told him his dabs were all over Leatherslade. 'In that case,' said Jim, 'it looks as though it's on me. I want my solicitor here.' This was Lincoln Ellis, the *other* famous bent lawyer outfit in London.

Leonard Field was stopped at traffic lights in Haringey on Monday 9 September and taken in for questioning over the purchase of Leatherslade Farm. 'Never in your life,' he told Butler and demanded to see John Wheater, his solicitor. Field was out of his depth. He had not been charged or even cautioned and could have left at any time. When Wheater turned up, Butler saw him first. This was brilliant – two birds with one stone – and they were the weak links, too. Hard nuts like Goody, Reynolds, Daly and Edwards could fence all day with the cozzers, but here were two basically straight blokes who had got in over their heads.

Wheater tried to bluff his way out but against a man like Tommy Butler that was a waste of time. He couldn't remember whether Field was his client or not – 'I'm confused. I'm confused.' He must have been shitting himself, because his legal career was over. But Butler let both men go.

Tommy Wisbey rang the Yard again on Wednesday 11 September and DI Frank Williams went to see him at his betting shop in Red Cross Way, SE1. Taken back to the Yard and grilled by Butler, Tommy made two statements. Then he was off to Linslade Magistrates' Court with the usual blanket over his head to be charged and remanded in custody.

Buster Edwards, his wife June and little girl, Nicolette, were jumping at shadows as the police search intensified and the media made sure that their faces were well known. They moved sharpish from Shepperton to Wraysbury and Edwards rang John Wheater for advice; frankly, for all the good that would do he may as well have asked the cat. On the 14th, the law again picked up Lennie Field who was about to start a tour of duty on board P&O's *Canberra* out of Southampton.

Brian Field was next. A large amount of money (as we shall see in the next chapter) had been found in woods near Dorking and it was definitely part of the train robbery haul. A hotel receipt inside one of the bags linked this with Field and his German wife, Karin. Butler went in person that Sunday to 'Kabri', the Field home in Pangbourne. Field came the 'I'm-a-lawyer' line, maintaining that the purchase of the farm did not constitute the train robbery. Butler wasn't listening and the lawyer got very gabby in the car ride back to the Yard – a sure sign of nerves and guilt. When Butler brought Leonard Field into the interview room, Brian denied knowing him – 'It is decidedly like him, but this is not the man.' Butler had heard it all before. 'Who, me, guv? I wasn't there. I don't know nothing about it. I'm being stitched up. You planted that.' It went on and on and it was just so much hot air.

On 26 September the committal proceedings were held in Aylesbury Road District Council Chamber where a specially set-up courtroom had had to be built to accommodate everybody. Altogether, over time, twenty-nine people would appear in the dock over the Great Train Robbery. At this stage, there were only thirteen and of those, only six were actually robbers. Others were charged with receiving or conspiracy to rob.

At that time, Bruce Reynolds, Paddy Daly, Buster Edwards, Roy James, Bob Welch, Jimmy White, Les Aldridge, Freddie Foreman, Harry Smith and Pop the train driver were still free.

Oh, and George Stanley. Mr Big.

CHAPTER 11
GEORGE'S BEAUTIFUL LAUNDERETTE

You're sitting on £2 million, give or take. What do you do? Deposit it safely in a high street bank? Give it to charity? Buy yourself something nice? Or wipe your arse with it, like John Pedlar after a hard day at the spielers? If the answer is: none of the above, you're very wise and you might even be George Stanley.

The *Daily Express* was helpful again. Just as they'd given George a sort of blueprint for how to rob a train, now they told him how to spend the money. To be fair they were talking not about the total, which they reasonably assumed would be divided at least sixteen ways, but about the £260,000 reward on offer, which they called 'Squealer's Bait'. In 1963, this kind of money could have bought a yacht, a Rolls-Royce, a country house, a world cruise, 2,000 bottles of champagne and a private plane. Oh, and there'd be £171,000 left over, which, sensibly invested, would produce £10,000 a year for life.

The fact that no one did squeal or claim this reward is down to three factors. One, none of the robbers except Reynolds knew who was holding the money for them and even when they found out, they were prepared to wait for their return. Two, George was being minded at the time – and for years afterwards – by Freddie Foreman and there weren't many who would go up against Foreman in his heyday. And three, George could make money disappear like David Nixon, Copperfield or Blaine, whichever generation of magicians you've grown up with.

In 1978, Piers Paul Read had a brave stab at guessing where the money had gone. He got it right when he said that in several cases, the train robbers themselves didn't know what happened to their money while they were in prison but they found none when they got out. He gets the total haul wrong, in fact, and breaks down various sums villain by villain, 'chap' by 'chap'. He assumes that each of seventeen men got their individual whack of £150k. Only the recent release of official papers under the Freedom of Information Act has provided the *actual* sum stolen. Read had no access to this.

Piers Paul Read speculates that in addition to the main gang members' individual portions, other individuals also got one-off payments for their part in the robbery. The substitute train driver (who Read calls Stan Agate) got £20k. Lennie Field, the purchaser of Leatherslade, got £12,500. Brian Field's mate Mark got £28,500, although Christ knows why, because all he actually did was to introduce Goody and Edwards to the Ulsterman. Roy James got £2,000 expenses to buy the drags. An anonymous friend of Charlie Wilson's got £8k – again, why and who the hell was he? And £627 10s. was left at the farm in Scottish banknotes.

I won't bore you with each man's breakdown because the premise is basically false. According to Read, the bulk of the money can be accounted for, so in what sense is £2.3 million still officially missing? His figures are based on chats to the robbers who I don't believe would have said a word about what *really* happened to the money (even though by 1978 we can assume that most of them knew). On his own admission, Read didn't talk to Brian Field, Bruce Reynolds, Charlie Wilson or Ronnie Biggs about the loot. But he does handily point the finger at Brian Field for dumping some cash in Dorking Woods and at Alf Thomas (a pseudonym) for doing the same in a telephone box in Camberwell. Incidentally, if we assume that the team were accurate in what they told Read they paid in legal fees, the total amount comes to £181,100, a reasonable chunk of this going to Messrs Lesser & Co and Uncle George. Taking all the cases together, including later appeals, George earned a legitimate £250,000 for the firm from the Great Train Robbery.

So putting aside various cartloads of bullshit fed to Read by the robbers, what do we *know* happened to the money? The information from Annie Oakley, duly passed to George Stanley, the Ulsterman and the team, was that all the money on the train was in used, untraceable notes. On the day the Filth found Leatherslade, the *Daily Mirror* carried a banner headline 'Big Shock for Rail Gang'. Over half the haul, the paper claimed, was in new, unissued notes with recorded serial numbers. In reality, only 1,400 notes were recorded, so the bulk of the cash was, indeed, untraceable. How could the gang, Russell-Pavier and Richards asked in 2012, know which they were? Easy – they were the new ones, unfolded and crisp. It's not rocket science. And you can bet that George and his fellow-launderers knew which was which.

The problem was that each gang member had insisted on keeping 'spending' money for themselves. That made sense and was understandable, but remember old gypsy George's warning – don't flash the cash; don't spend, spend, spend. And what does Brucie Reynolds do, the very day after the robbery? He buys himself a spanking new sports car (via Mary Manson) with stolen notes. Nice one, Bruce! Cordrey's mate William Boal was picked up on 14 August, the police having been tipped off by the ever-observant Mrs Clarke in Bournemouth. He had £118 10s. ½d. on him (£2,200 today); Roger Cordrey had even more – £159 3s. 3d. (just shy of £3k today). When the law searched the van the pair had garaged with Mrs Clarke, they found £56,047 in a canvas bag inside a suitcase. That would be just over £1,042,000 today, hardly mere spending money. Perhaps I should put a note in here for anyone reading this who doesn't remember money pre the mid-Eighties when the pound coin replaced the pound note for good and all – it was possible in 1963 to have not just odd pounds as notes, but 10s. (50p) as well! So we're not talking bags of change when we give figures ending in odd amounts.

Cordrey, of course, was just looking after this cash for a mate he had bumped into at Brighton Races, the implication being that this was winnings money. The police found a further £78,982 (£1.47 million) in used notes contained in six cases in another car and another lock-up used by the pair. The total haul was £135,306 13s. 3½d., which of course comes suspiciously near to Piers Read's £150k whack for each man.

Two days after the finds, John Ahern and a colleague, Nina Hargreaves, stopped on their way to work in Dorking. His motorbike was overheating and the engine needed to cool down, so the pair wandered in the woods along Coldharbour Lane on Leith Hill. Here they saw three bags wrapped in polythene and opened one. It contained banknotes. Today of course Ahern would have been on his mobile, straight through to 999, but in 1963 he had to flag down a passing motorist who drove to the nearest house and made a phone call. The police and their dogs found a fourth bag near the first three and it was clear they hadn't been there for long. The ground was wet and they were dry. The four bags contained £100,900 (£1.88 million) in notes, thirteen useful fingerprints and some German money and a receipt from a hotel in Hindelang that would tie Brian Field and his German wife Karin to this money in the weeks ahead. At the later trial, Field told the court that although the bags were his, they had gone walkabout a couple of weeks before the robbery, no doubt in the light fingers of the criminal element that tramped through his offices at Wheater & Co on a regular basis. Interestingly, the judge, in his summing-up, said he couldn't decide on this issue and seemed prepared to give Field the benefit of the doubt. He'd already got the bloke bang to rights over the purchase of Leatherslade Farm.

Two days after the Dorking find, police tore apart Jimmy White's caravan at the Clovelly caravan site and found £30,440 (£568k) stashed behind the vehicle's interior panelling. The finds were rising, but it wasn't over yet. Five weeks later, a routine side enquiry by the Flying Squad uncovered £518 (£9,660) from the robbery stashed in an envelope in a house belonging to Martin Harvey in Bower Drive, Dulwich. He was arrested, freely admitting the money was from the train robbery and he was holding it for someone (identity not given).

The search for the missing poppy would have made an excellent Ealing comedy all by itself. 'There is booty to be found in all sorts of odd places,' Superintendent Malcolm Fewtrell of the Buckinghamshire CID told the press and that was enough for enthusiasts all over the country to start ferreting everywhere. The Aylesbury nick switchboard was jammed with calls, up to ten a minute, of people reporting new holes and signs of digging on their property. Quarries and gravel pits were searched, sand-dunes by the seaside. Courting couples were surprised in their cars in the middle of a bit of nooky. Shopkeepers watched carefully how people paid for their purchases or held banknotes up to the light in case the watermark read 'Nicked From the Up Special on 8 August'.

While the preliminary enquiry was going on against the arrested villains, John 'Paddy' Daly was still at large. That all changed on Tuesday 3 December when six black squad cars squealed to a halt around 65a Eaton Square. This was in the heart of Belgravia – Lord Lucan would bash his kids' nanny over the head in his house just around the corner eleven years later – a pretty flash address for an 'antique dealer' with a prison record and eight counts against him in various courts. Nevertheless the tip-off that reached the Yard was that this was home to Paddy Daly and they pounced.

DI Frank Williams couldn't believe it. The plump, clean-shaven Daly had lost the best part of three stone, had a beard and called himself Grant. That subterfuge didn't last long and he said, 'Hello, Mr Williams. Yes, you've got me.'

How did the law get on to Daly? One theory is that he was shopped by Godfrey Green, who was supposed to be minding him. Green, according to Piers Paul Read, seems to have been a piece of work. He was supposed to invest Daly's share of the loot. Instead, he moved to Brighton, changed his name to Hugget and, conveniently or inconveniently, died. Another version says that Daly breezed off to Boscastle, a little village in Cornwall, and buried the loot in the garden of a Bill Goodwin. He took a bloke called Michael Black with him and after Daly was arrested, Black went back, dug the money up again and split it with Goodwin. He then buggered off to Spain, where … guess what? He died. Goodwin stashed his share in the kitchen wall and … you won't believe this … died.

When he was acquitted (see next chapter), Paddy Daly went back to Boscastle with Billy Still, who for a while was in the frame as the bloke tasked with burning down Leatherslade Farm. And this is where the story takes a bit of a twist. Still was a partner with James McDonald in Mac's Antiques of Portobello where, you'll remember, I first met Bruce Reynolds. Still had been arrested in Euston Square on 25 July 1963, a fortnight before the robbery, along with three blokes tooled up for something or other – explosives, a jemmy and nylon stockings (for the face, naturally). This played into the hands of Scotland Yard whose C11 branch later received a tip-off about Still's connection to the farm and it came as quite a blow to Uncle George because he had recruited Still to torch the place. The job then passed to Brian Field's friend Mark who bottled at the last minute and that in turn led to George contacting Mum to get Lennie and me on the road before the law found the place.

George battled long and hard to get Billy Still bail on the going tooled up charge, but it didn't work. With the clear line between Still, Daly and Reynolds, it's not too surprising that it should be Still who went to Boscastle with Paddy looking for his cut. It wasn't there, but Daly bought the story from Kathleen Sleep, Bill Goodwin's niece, that Black had half-inched the lot.

In September 1965, when most of the furore had died down, Tommy Butler went to Boscastle and talked to Miss Sleep. Her story now was that she had burned most of the cash walled up by her Uncle Bill. She did have £9,349 (£165,000 today) in one pound notes, however, that had been in a biscuit tin in the garden, which had been dug up by her dog. Bizarrely, Tommy Butler brought no charges against Kathleen Sleep, nor against Paddy Daly who could have been charged with receiving. Curiouser and curiouser.

Tommy Butler himself rang Mary Manson, whose friend Daly's wife Barbara was, to come and look after Barbara who was heavily pregnant. This doesn't sound at all likely from a man dedicated to tracking down the robbers whatever the cost, but there is another factor. Mary Manson had been released the day before and what she and Paddy Daly had in common was that their solicitor was one George Stanley of Messrs Lesser. There is nothing in the official reports about George going to the Yard or Aylesbury to hold Daly's hand, but, as with Mary, I can't believe he wasn't there, advising, smiling, being nice, looking after his own interests. What I wouldn't give to have seen Tommy Butler, the grey fox and Uncle George in the same room, circling each other like a snake and a fucking mongoose!

Eight days later, the law cornered Roy James. An anonymous tip-off said he was at 14 Ryder's Terrace in St John's Wood, around the corner from the Abbey Road studios where the Beatles were belting out *Please Please Me*. This time, the raid was nearly rumbled. As officers moved in back and front of the house, a figure leapt out of a skylight and ran across the rooftops, his boots clattering and slipping on the tiles.

Police torches flashed in all directions and there were shouts and the sound of running feet. The figure threw a holdall to the ground and jumped down to follow it, almost landing in the arms of DS John Matthews. It was the Weasel himself who had been in the house for four months. He denied having anything to do with the £12,000 (£224,000) in his holdall and of course, there was no law against growing a beard as he had done. All the best train robbers (see Daly) were doing it these days.

That was a day for breakthroughs. While Butler and Williams were psyched up to arrest Roy James, DCI Sid Bradbury of the Flying Squad got a call. A voice told him that £50,000 (£932k) of the robbery money was going to be left in a telephone kiosk at the corner of Black Horse Court and Great Dover Street, Camberwell. Butler and Williams, pretty sure the whole thing was a hoax, went to have a look, just in case.

Remember those old red telephone boxes? They still had Buttons A and B to press in those days and smelt of widdle. But inside this one were two sacks tied with string. The Yard men took these back to HQ and counted out £47,245.

So who dumped this money and why? The who was Freddie Foreman, as he admitted on Channel 4 in 1999. The why is altogether more fascinating. Freddie said he rang the police on behalf of one of the three unnamed blokes who carried out the robbery. He cut a deal with DI Frank Williams that, for a £10,000 'drink' and the return of two sacks of loot, that unnamed member would be left alone.

Williams was a tough, no-nonsense copper, well known in the criminal haunts of south London. That he had dodgy friends and didn't always play by the rules is more or less accepted today. A precedent had already been set: Buster Edwards is believed to have made enquiries of the police (he was of course still on the run at this stage) and a deal was discussed along the lines of his returning £50,000 and he would get a lesser sentence. So Freddie's claim doesn't surprise me. But who was Freddie acting as intermediary for? Harry Smith, slippery as an eel, who didn't really need help? Electric Les Aldridge, *so* anonymous the police seem never to have considered him as a possible train robber? Or Freddie Foreman himself, although he was sure he'd covered his tracks and was never, as far as I know, interviewed by police in the context of the train robbery? Freddie of course was minding Uncle George during this period and in my kinder moments, I wonder if Freddie's altruism didn't kick in here. George Stanley, as we'll see, was starting to blip on the authorities' radar. Was it possible that Foreman put up the money to direct attention away from Uncle George?

Uncle George put his head over the parapet again on Wednesday 11 December when *The Times* ran a story about Mary Manson and a statement from Lesser & Co (George). Back on 4 October, Mary Kazih Manson, aged forty-two, of Wimbledon Close, The Downs, Wimbledon SW19 had been formally accused in court of receiving '£835 in money, the property of the Postmaster General, knowing the same to be stolen'. Laying aside the fairly dodgy assertion that the stolen cash belonged to the Postmaster General, there was not a lot of evidence against her. By the time of the committal proceedings' last day on 2 December, her brief, Howard Sabin, asked the magistrate not to put Mary on trial. It was unfair, he said, to link her with Bruce Reynolds who had yet to be found and arrested and there was no evidence that the cash she had bought the sports car with was *actually* from the train. So Mary walked – a clear result for George who had been arguing along those lines all along.

With her in the clear, he chanced his arm by speaking in public again, telling *The Times* that Bruce's child was being looked after by Mary voluntarily (i.e. without payment from the train robbery) because Bruce's dear old mum was too ill to do it herself. In her book *The Robber's Tale*, Peta Fordham explains that little Nicky Reynolds would have gone into care if Mary had not been available and she also throws an interesting spotlight onto George. He was the sort of person, she said, to whom no unfortunate ever appealed in vain. (Yeah, right.) His home at Red Oaks was one where stray cats rubbed shoulders with an old one-eyed goose and rescued animals of every type wandered in and out of the house. His wife [Auntie Marjorie] was even more determined in her attempts to right the wrongs of any of nature's hard-luck cases. Peta Fordham would not have been surprised to find Nicky kipping down with the goose if Mary had not taken him in.

Mary Manson had also gone to support Barbara Daly, who

was 'ill following the shock of her husband's arrest'. George was quick to paint a picture of happy (innocent) families – 'There is no mystery about this association. John Daly used to work for Mrs Manson's husband [James McDonald] and Mrs Daly and Mrs Reynolds are sisters.' 'It is hoped,' said George, 'that the publication of the facts will prevent further intrusion.' (Doesn't he sound posh when he's got his legal voice on?)

Judging by the photographs of Mary trying to reach her own front door, hidden under a blanket and jostled by a crowd, I don't know how successful George was on that one.

Taking all the finds together, by December 1963, the police had recovered about £300,000 of the missing £2.3 million – that's just under 12 per cent of the grand total. So, what happened to the rest? If you buy Piers Paul Read's theories, it went on incidental expenses, to lawyers, relatives, minders, landlords and other hangers-on who systematically robbed the robbers over the years. Some of that certainly happened, but it's time I introduced you to George's little helpers. To call them the B Team is a bit unkind. All right, they didn't rob a train but they did stash and help launder a great deal of cash, so they were vitally important to operations and, unlike the actual robbers, they got away with it.

Behind the investigations carried out by Scotland Yard, the Flying Squad and Buckinghamshire CID, another, alto-gether more furtive one was going on. This was the work of the Post Office's Investigation Branch (IB) under its controller Clifford Osmond who had been involved in this sort of work for thirty years. According to files released in 2011 (and some are closed until 2017), the IB was poking its nose into Bruce Reynolds' business and three addresses had come to light as being occupied by people who might be helping to keep him under the police radar. The memo, dated 27 August, three weeks after the robbery, gives the name and address of Edith M. Simons, Uncle George's bit on the side, living at 85 Hermitage Court, Woodford Rd, Wanstead, telephone WANstead 5078. The second was Mrs Doris May Golding of 42 Winchester Road, Fulham, telephone RENown 3592 and the third was Mr L. Heller of 69 Belsize Park Gardens, Hampstead, telephone PRImrose 2183 [both innocent of any involvement of course]. On a nostalgic note, don't those exchanges sound romantic? A bit like the Yard's famous Whitehall 1212.

I mention the phone numbers in particular because it's possible all three were already being tapped by the authorities. The laws on this were pretty vague at the time and nobody asked too many questions. Tommy Butler was happy for three IB blokes – Balm, Hood and Grey (spooks or what?) to watch the addresses concerned.

Grey reported that a man resembling an Albert Millbank left the Heller house with a blonde carrying a poodle. He was driving his mum's car, which of course could be traced via its licence plate. The Sturleys had known the Millbank brothers, Albert and George, for years. When I met Albert in his flat in Tilbury ten years later, I couldn't believe it. When he was in funds my dad looked the business. George lived in a big house that was the envy of his neighbours. But Albert Millbank looked like a tramp – 'Come in, boy, I've been expecting you.' He was fat with a receding hairline and he wiped his dripping nose on his sleeve.

'So you're George's nephew,' he said. 'He thinks the world of you, son.'

'I do my best for him,' I said. There was a pile of cash on the table.

'That's for George's clients,' he explained. 'He sends blokes over all the time with hooky gear and George and I split it down the middle, after exes, of course.'

Of course.

What the Sturleys didn't know back in 1963 was that a grass had already pointed the finger at Albert for another job entirely. Bernard Makowski was a Pole who had got to Britain during the war and went straight into the black market business. He had previous as long as your arm but that didn't stop the law from taking his blabbing seriously. Describing himself as an antique dealer – now, there's a rarity – he talked to the IB on Saturday 10 August. 'He often talks in riddles,' Osmond reported. 'He leaves much unsaid and he either forgets or does not know the full names of the persons he mentions.' Why this bloke was given house room by the authorities I can't imagine. His information about his alleged involvement in a hit on a Scotland–King's Cross train was so garbled it made no fucking sense at all. Albert Millbank, Makowski said, was 'an important man behind the scenes' in this planned robbery and that what happened at Bridego Bridge was the actual carrying out of the job with another team.

Albert was not, of course, squeaky clean. He had previous since 1939 and was on the Irish Garda's lists too. He had been arrested in Dublin in September 1955 along with Charles McGuinness who was wanted over a train heist in Glasgow in July of that year. In the end, all the law could charge Albert with was 'loitering at Kingsbridge Station between 7 p.m. and 8 p.m. for the purpose of committing a felony'. God help you if you were a little boy collecting train numbers!

All this was pretty circumstantial stuff, but you have to see the train robbery in context to realise what it meant at the time. There had never been a hit anything like as big as this in British criminal history and it made the Establishment look weak. It came on top of a host of other events that made it look as though the world was coming to an end. In March, John Profumo, the War Minister, lied to the House of Commons about his relationship with the call girl Christine Keeler and that came to bite him – and Harold Macmillan's government – in the arse. There were spies all over the place, like weevils in biscuits, burrowing their slimy way into British security. Burgess, Maclean, Kim Philby, Gordon Lonsdale, John Vassall – they were all at it, defecting to the Soviet Union or passing secrets to them. The success of the train robbery was the last straw for various blokes in the corridors of power and the word went out clearly – 'get the bastards' (Tommy Butler) by almost any means (e.g. phone tapping) and when you do, throw away the key.

George Stanley was in the enviable position to bestride the worlds of the Establishment and Crime like a colossus. He was always John Pedlar's son and raising two fingers at the fat cats who filled the corridors of power pleased him no end. And the fat cats at the Home Office gave their permission to tap Edith Simons' phone. It was 22 August and although I don't know who the 'male voice' was who was doing some of the talking, I'd be prepared to guess it was a one-lunged diabetic uncle not a million miles removed from the current writer – 'Things are a bit fresh. Would you take it over the road and put it in the fridge in case it goes off?' Fifty minutes later, a man called and said, 'Thanks for getting the message through, will try and get another message later.' 'Thanks,' said a female voice who had to be Edith. 'It's a pleasure' and 'Get clothes ready will arrive in the morning.' Edith then rang her friend Doris Golding on REN 3592 and talked to a Mr Brand – 'Coat will be ready today, make arrangements to pick it up tomorrow' and there was talk of Mr Heller in Hampstead.

The telephone engineers weren't quick enough to trace these calls (the technology was slow and clumsy in 1963) but these messages were clearly codes. And they referred to moving money from A to B because the law were getting nosey. Incidentally, I hope George's instruction to Edith to move the money 'over the road' wasn't meant literally. That could mean Maurice Lesser's flat at Number 17 and that would land the old lawyer in it up to his neck. It was now getting a little hot for George Stanley. It didn't take the law long to put the Sturleys in the frame. George might be a solicitors' clerk (not, as we've seen, that that made much difference when you're looking for villains) but he was the brother of Arthur Sturley, a well-known fraudster with a record and the cousin of Charles Sturley, who, it was whispered, had been on the Eastcastle Street job.

It's just as well George didn't see the files from Scotland Yard's Intelligence Branch. They were written by Deputy Controller R. F. Yates and are worth quoting in full and mention another character from George's past – Maurice Lesser's old mate Harry Isaacs.

'This group of suspects [the Millbanks, Heller, Simons and Harry Isaacs] have been kept under observation from time to time by IB officers and this has produced proof of association. Police believe that stolen money is being held or controlled by this group of suspects.'

Association, of course, is a bugger. It led to William Boal dying in prison in 1970 just because he knew Roger Cordrey. Harry Isaacs and his wife Joanna had arranged a safe house for Jimmy and Sharee White – and of course Gigi the poodle that was fast becoming a fucking liability

– in Nursery Lane, Whitstable. The coded messages over the phone mean that George Stanley was aware that there were ears on the line – he already knew from his Post Office insider that this was likely to happen. However, it's doubtful whether everybody in his tight circle realised they were actually being followed.

Yates' report goes on:

'Mr George Stanley is the Managing Clerk for Messrs Lesser & Co, Solicitors, London E15 and came to notice very early in the enquiries.'

I would love to know how this happened, with all the careful plans Uncle George had laid to cover his tracks. Yates' report was compiled in late August so was it merely his work on behalf of Mary Manson that drew somebody's attention to him? And was that somebody DI Frank Williams?

'Stanley is a shrewd man,' Yates' report continued, 'and the Police know him as an able advocate for the criminal classes. The actual part he was called upon to play is not known, but there is reason to think he may be controlling some part, at least, of the stolen monies. Observations on Stanley by Assistants of this Branch [the IB spooks] established that he made regular visits to 85 Hermitage Court, Wanstead, a flat owned by Miss Edith Simons in a luxury block.'

OK, so they'd found George's love nest. There is no hint that Edith was his mistress in the report but that was hardly the point. If they suspected George of handling the train loot, some or all of it might be at number 85.

'Other persons who have also visited the flat (sometimes when Stanley was present) were Harry Isaacs and Albert Millbank. Isaacs was traced by the IB to 10 Saddleton Road, Whitstable, Kent. Millbank was traced to 69 Belsize Park Gardens, NW3, also occupied by a German, Mrs Heller, who is believed to be in touch with Reynolds.'

If she was, Bruce doesn't mention her in his *Autobiography of a Thief*, but then, he doesn't mention Paddy Daly or George Stanley either, so we can't read too much into that. It's too much of a coincidence that Edith and Mrs Heller were both German; they must have become friends because of that at some time in the past.

'Both Isaacs and Millbank are known receivers, or minders, of stolen property and both are associates of James Edward White who is wanted for questioning. Isaacs is somewhat of a mystery man. For some considerable time Albert Millbank has been suspected ... of receiving property stolen as a result of Post Office break-ins. His brother George Millbank has in fact been convicted for Post Office break-ins. Another relative is Amy Millbank who has been seen in White's café at 36, Aldersgate Street, London, EC1. Further enquiries need to be made about this group of suspects.'

Indeed they did, but it was almost as though Commander Yates forgot the bit he'd written about Uncle George. No doubt it was easier to focus on known criminals rather than an adept, organised and streetwise lawyer against whom (unless and until the cash was found) there was no evidence at all. Or am I right about Freddie Foreman's involvement, that DI Frank Williams steered everybody away from George Stanley?

The IB tails concentrated on Millbank and they spent weeks following him around London and down to Sussex and finally chasing their own tails. I assume that the Isaacs, the Millbanks and Mrs Heller got their cut for holding or moving the loot around on George's behalf, although you can't guarantee that (see Patrick McKenna, the Ulsterman). I remember the first time I met Bruce Reynolds in Mac's Antiques in Portobello. 'Always remember this, son,' Dad said to me after we'd left. 'Anyone that does business with George always ends up one way – and that's skint.'

I must have been feeling particularly cheeky that day because I said, 'He's the spitting image of you, Dad.' He stopped in his tracks, right there on the pavement. His huge right hand snaked out and I thought I was going to get slapped around the head. Instead, he shook my hand, winked and laughed. 'No flies on you, Lee,' he said.

Let me show you around Pedlar's Folly. Named after my granddad, it was the only real piece of luxury George allowed himself. His day job – which of course included defending four people charged in connection with the train robbery – would appear to cover the costs of this if anyone asked, but it was certainly built with train robbery money, every brick of it. The new house in Theydon Bois was of Dutch design and all the materials were handmade. In case the law got nosey, George had two building plots at Red Oaks up for sale and got the building firm of John and Gordon Bray to erect a high fence around his own plot while Pedlars went up. If anybody asked, the money had come from the sale of the two plots – dirty money was going in and clean money was coming out, just like a cash launderette. Gordon Bray, needless to say, was in Promise Land to George to the tune of an unspecified amount. The Folly, with its herringbone-patterned porchway and huge entrance porch, cost £6,000 which is £112,000 in money today but of course housing has galloped ahead of inflation for years, so that isn't really a helpful comparison. The average house in 1963 cost around £3k but Pedlar's Folly was by no means an average house! So comparing it to an average house price now of knocking on for £200k doesn't even come close. Remember as well that George was already running the Red Oaks house and Edith's place at Hermitage Court. It was comfortable without being ostentatious, brave but not brash. And there was a cosy little potting shed around the back, next to George's vines. It was completely cut off from the outside and many's the dodgy deal that was struck there.

'If you seek his monument, look around you,' they said about Christopher Wren who redesigned half of London after the Great Fire of 1666. Well, next time you're in Southend, Hastings, Lydd, Theydon Bois or the East End, do the same. But we're not talking Christopher Wren; we're talking George

Stanley. G. A. Stanley Properties was the official moniker of the laundry business. The two building plots in Red Oaks were prime development sites. So was the East End. The bits of it that had survived the Blitz were still standing in the Sixties, rows of clapped-out old terraces that hadn't changed since the days of Jack the Ripper. George got in on the ground floor of the slum clearance that took off in the middle of that decade, with new high-rises replacing the old hovels. Flats were the sought-after properties of the Sixties and that imported French word that covered a multitude of cramped abodes – maisonettes.

Other builders and property developers had to borrow from the banks. George Stanley didn't. The Hellers, Edith, the Millbanks and the Isaacs held the money, passed it around, carried out deals on George's behalf. Tight profit margins? Do what? Villains always needed houses – think Freddie Foreman hiding out in the Krays' spare pad in Adelina Grove or any of the places the train robbers moved in and out of when on the run. Much of the business was by word of mouth. George drew up mortgages and deals, careful that his name was not on any of the paperwork.

So, we're not talking about anonymous Swiss bank accounts or some offshore institution. And we're not talking about burying loot in the back garden either (like Paddy Daly). It suited the authorities to believe that the missing £2.3 million had been spirited abroad because extradition treaties and old-fashioned bloody-mindedness between the world's police forces meant that tracing it was beyond their reach; the problem was out of their hands. How sick would they have been to know that it was still in the good old UK all along? And Uncle George was laughing all the way to the bank (which he never needed to visit).

I left school in the summer of '64. Some bloke called Nelson Mandela was sentenced to life for treason in South Africa. They let Christine Keeler out at the same time but her glory days were over. I listened every night to Radio Caroline, the pirate station that played stuff us kids wanted to hear rather than Johnny Ray and Max Bloody Bygraves. It was nearly a year since the train robbery and the trials were over (see next chapter). I was working full time for Uncle George – tidying up the gardens at Red Oaks during the week and at weekends doing a bit of filing at 21–23 Broadway, Stratford. Lawyers didn't do weekends and anyway, Maurice Lesser being Jewish, you'd never see him in the offices on a Saturday. George was happy to let Marjorie decide on the flower pots and the hedge trimming. Office filing was more closely vetted. Some of it of course was the humdrum legal business of any law firm. Some of it was dynamite and I wish I had it to hand today.

I'd often be sent next door to the Two Puddings pub to get a couple of bottles of Scotch on account. The landlord knew Uncle George was good for it. What he didn't know – at least the fine tuning – was that George repaid the bottles with hauls from lorry hijacks, the details of which he'd got from a haulage contractor client. My God, how the money rolls in! One Saturday morning at nine o'clock, George's reception room was full of fashionably dressed women, with high heels and beehive hairdos. On this particular occasion (it was 30 July 1966), I was painting the outer office, preparing the windows.

'Come in, Mrs Reynolds.' Uncle George was on gushing form. That name, of course, rang immediate bells. I'd met Bruce personally and his name had been splashed all over the headlines, intermittently, for three years. One by one the women went into George's inner sanctum and by 12.30, he'd interviewed them all.

'I'm off, then, Lee,' he said. 'Are you staying on?'

'Yeah,' I told him. 'I want to finish the reception room. It's awkward when you've got clients in.'

'That's what I like to see,' he said, 'hard work. I'll look after you for doing this.' And off he went for lunch with Edith at the Eagle in Snaresbrook. I felt a bit of a shit to be honest, but I wasn't shafting George. I was just curious. I waited about half an hour and then nipped into the inner office and peeked in his desk drawer. There lay a large red accounts book and in it: 'Mrs Reynolds, £25 per week; Mrs Goody, £25 per week; Mrs Wilson, £25 per week' and so on. Their old men might be on the run or serving thirty years in jug, but these women were only the wives of the damned. And so who knows, perhaps George Stanley did have a heart of gold after all.

If I'd had one of those little spy cameras like James Bond carried, I could have photographed those pages, with the usual suspects' names and the weekly pay-offs. If I'd been the blackmailing sort, I could have dangled the photos over George's head and made a killing. But I was fifteen and it didn't dawn on me that the law would give their eye teeth to see that accounts book. Just think of it as the crown jewels King John lost in the Wash way back – a fortune that passed through his hands briefly and was gone. George's accounts book was a bit like that.

CHAPTER 12
TRIALS AND TRIBULATIONS

It depends which set of statistics you want to use in connection with the trial of the train robbers. Biggsy's version is that the thing lasted for ten weeks with fifty-one days in court. There were 264 witnesses (not all called) and 2.5 million words were spoken, which is about a quid a word in the light of the money taken in the first place. There were 613 exhibits shown in court and the transcript ran to 30,000 pages of foolscap (that's longer than the A4 stuff we use today). The twelve good men and true who made up the jury (one of whom was called Mr Greedy, by the way) were paid £2 10s. a day, not a bad screw for sitting there, but of course that paled into insignificance against what the twenty-one barristers got.

Peta Fordham was there and described what she saw. Gordon Goody was 'tall, blond, obviously a "person"' [whatever that meant] and about to marry a pretty little red-head, Patricia Cooper. Charlie Wilson had a 'sudden attractive smile', and one of his daughters had a hole in the heart. These were the chiefs. Jimmy White, 'much nicer looking than the police photographs', was the first of the labourers. He had a great sense of humour and a baby boy. Roy James was very attractive to women, 'very small, something of the expression of a sad little monkey'. Jimmy Hussey's stupidity in court was said to mask his nervousness. He was tough in public but a considerate son at home. Roger Cordrey was married with four boys aged from six to twenty-one. He was a heavy gambler with a 'very protuberant forehead'. Tommy Wisbey looked as if he was a 'jolly fellow; you would like to buy drinks from him or get him to do work in your house' – only, presumably, if you nailed stuff down first. Bob Welch was 'pale, tense and strained-looking. Looks more like a research student than a criminal.' Welch had been watched closely at his farm hideout in Beaford, Devon, and when he went back to London, DI Frank Williams and DS Van Dyck pounced. 'Do you mean the train job?' Welch had said, all wide-eyed. 'I don't know anything about that.' Ronnie Biggs, said Peta Fordham, was 'very tall, dark and mild-mannered' and 'not very bright'. She got that right.

I'm just going to look at the trial from the point of view of the villains defended by George Stanley, that was four out of the thirteen for the original trial – Biggs, Daly, Goody and Leonard Field – the most defended by any one firm. There was some argy-bargy at first about where the trial ought to be held. After all, a high-profile case like this should surely be heard at the highest profile of courts, the Old Bailey. That's not how the law works, though; the crime had been

committed in Buckinghamshire, so Aylesbury had the jurisdiction.

It was pissing down on Monday 20 January 1964 when
the convoy of baddies turned up, all darkened windows
and flashing lights. Among the crowd of interested parties,
snoopers and limelight-seekers was Mary Manson, already
free thanks to Uncle George and the brief. But if the Filth
were hoping that Bruce Reynolds or Buster Edwards were
going to turn up incognito they were going to be disappointed.

George Stanley sat with the other barristers and solicitors
at a long row of desks in the centre of the modified courtroom
in the Rural District Council Chamber in Walton Street.
Everybody was coughing and sniffing with seasonal colds
and there was such a rush for peppermints that the local
shops ran out. Altogether twenty men and women stood in
the dock, which the press likened to Nuremberg because of
its size and the numbers involved. All that was missing were
the white helmets of the Snowdrops, the US military police.
The judge was Edmund Davies, not the usual public school
ponce who sat on the Bench in those days but a bloke from
the Welsh mining valleys. As things turned out, however, he
had as much empathy with the robbers as he would have had
with a Martian.

Those charged with receiving money from the robbery
were suspended until later and they left the dock. So did
Roger Cordrey, who had copped a guilty plea. After the usual
warnings to the jury to keep their mouths shut and report

any attempts to nobble them, Arthur Jones QC opened the case for the Crown – 'There was a train, the Up Postal train ...' It sounded like something out of *Jackanory* and it went on for ten hours. Give that man a carrot.

'Do not think I am suggesting,' he said, 'that there is some mastermind sitting somewhere who worked it all out and placed his men to do this and that.' What a line, with that self-same mastermind sitting not twenty feet away from him, his face like a slab of granite. Off the hook, or what?

On Day Three, Lewis Hawser QC had a go at Lilian Rixon, wife of the owner of Leatherslade Farm. Although he was defending Brian Field, this inevitably focused on Leonard Field too since both men were alleged to have gone to the farm together. And Lennie Field was one of George's. Mrs Rixon became so confused that she identified Jim Hussey as the man she saw, then said she wasn't sure and withdrew it.

On Day Seven, Sebag Shaw QC for Gordon Goody went for DS John Simon of the Yard big time. He had lied to Goody's mum when he turned over the Goody house in Putney by saying he had a search warrant whereas in fact he hadn't. The judge was far from amused. But Sebag Shaw had bigger police fish to fry than Simon. He savaged DCI Peter Vibart, Butler's 'terrible twin', later that day over the questioning of Goody at Leicester. He had not been cautioned as the rules demanded so anything Goody said was inadmissible. Simon and Vibart both had their knuckles rapped publicly – God knows what happened to them at the Yard behind closed doors – and this was a body blow to the Prosecution.

On 31 January, Michael Argyle QC defending Lennie Field used the same tack: Field had been questioned by Tommy Butler without a caution. So both the terrible twins had got their fingers burnt in their eagerness to get results. The judge's decision this time involved a bit of hair-splitting. Verbal evidence given by Field was to be allowed – his written statement was not. If there's a sure way to confuse the simple souls who make up a jury, it's this kind of legal mumbo-jumbo. Malcolm Fewtrell of the Buckinghamshire CID overheard two jury members as they left court one day – 'I can't make head nor tail of it.'

Ronnie Biggs had been due to be defended by a pro bono lawyer as the Americans call them, in that he couldn't afford a brief of his own (laying aside the potential £150k from the train robbery, of course) but Gordon Goody had got a message to him in Bedford nick where he was on remand before the trial to hire George Stanley. That instruction had come via Goody from Bruce Reynolds, still, of course, on the run. George told Biggsy and Paddy Daly, who he also represented, that the most serious evidence against them were the fingerprints at Leatherslade. He suggested that Biggsy tell the police/court that he had been to the farm as a jobbing carpenter doing the place up for new owners, specifically that he was putting up a whipping post to cater for kinky parties to be held there. If this was George's idea, it was a new facet to this complicated man I'd never seen before and I'm not sure, as a fourteen-year-old, I'd have fully appreciated its significance. As for Daly, there was no defence and he should cop a plea. That was a piece of advice from Uncle George that Paddy just couldn't take.

As the trial went on, Biggs became increasingly concerned about Wilfred Fordham, his brief. He describes him in *Odd Man Out* as a 'kindly old gentleman' who nodded off in court during the afternoon's proceedings. In desperation, Biggs went to George and begged for a new brief. This must have been difficult but Uncle George swung it. Fordham became Number Two in Biggs' Defence team under the young and highly capable Michael Argyle QC, Recorder for Leicester.

You know the old joke about coppers and their size twelves? Well, DI Basil Morris of the Surrey police put his firmly in it on Thursday 6 February. He had interviewed Biggsy on 24 August at his home in Redhill and recalled in court that when he (Morris) asked Ronnie if he knew any of the alleged train robbers, he said he had met Bruce Reynolds some time ago when they did time together. You could have heard the bombshell at Bridego Bridge and all points east. Fordham may have been old and doddery but he didn't miss this. He talked in private with the judge and then declared Morris's words 'grossly improper'. It was – and is – a basic maxim of British law that previous is never made known to the jury until after the accused has been found guilty and it then may play a part in sentencing.

The judge adjourned for ten minutes while Fordham, Biggsy and Uncle George went into a huddle to decide what to do. This kind of gaffe – and especially from an experienced policeman – was music to their ears. The upshot was that Fordham asked for a retrial for Biggs with a different jury which of course would cost, but the judge agreed there was no alternative. No doubt George regarded this as a partial victory although the case against Biggs was fairly strong. Now they would have to do it all over again.

Gordon Goody was a different matter. The Prosecution claimed that a pair of suede shoes belonging to Goody had been found at the Windmill pub in Blackfriars where the Irishman had been staying. They were spattered with yellow paint of the same type found in a tin at Leatherslade that had been used to disguise the army truck used in the robbery. Remember Gordon's tactics over the London Airport Robbery, egged on by Brian Field? He had nobbled a juryman and Field had rubbished a witness. Could something similar happen here? Hardly, but the Defence argument, as put forward by George & Co, was that anybody could have put the paint on the shoes after both were in the tender care of the police. The judge wasn't having any of that, but Sebag Shaw was careful not to go too far – 'My Lord, I am not desirous of making any suggestions. I was exploring the situation as far as one could.' They had found no money on Goody and there was no fingerprint evidence against him. How handy that yellow paint was! Even now, living in Spain at the age of eighty-five,

Gordon Goody continues to maintain that he was stitched up by a police force desperate to get him, not just for the train robbery but the airport job too.

But for the Defence team of George Stanley, W. A. Raeburn, Wilfred Fordham and J. N. Speed, the best was yet to come. The fingerprint evidence, as presented by Superintendent Maurice Ray of the Met, seemed open and shut. Biggsy's dabs were all over a plate, a Monopoly box and a bottle of tomato ketchup – and it was that that would get him at his later trial. In the case of Paddy Daly, they were on a Monopoly card. Raeburn challenged this, on the purely legal grounds that it was not possible to say *when* the prints were left on the card. In other words, Daly could have played with that particular Monopoly set *before* somebody else took it to Leatherslade to while away the hours before and after the robbery.

The same could have applied to them all of, course, but the judge allowed this challenge in Daly's case alone. Nobody was more nonplussed than Uncle George, who, after all, had advised the man to plead guilty only weeks before. The jury were ordered to acquit Daly and they did. Walter Raeburn QC's argument was that Daly's only 'crime' was doing a runner. This was silly of him but it was not evidence of conspiracy to rob or of robbery itself. The judge agreed and acquitted him on legal grounds, making nonsense of the whole thing. In theory, on this basis, everybody else who had left prints at Leatherslade should have walked too. Is the law an ass, or what? A press photo later that day showed a clearly delighted Paddy leaving Aylesbury nick with his meagre possessions in his arms. Most accounts today describe his sudden acquittal as a minor miracle. The judge was clearly unhappy about it and nothing could show more clearly what an ass the law was – and is. Mary Manson threw a party for Daly, and the law – watching him as they were – noted that 'criminal associates of both Daly and Manson were present'. No doubt that included Uncle George. So far, he (although he could hardly claim the credit for it in Daly's case) had got acquittals for two of the accused in the robbery he himself had set up. No wonder they invited him to the party!

On 21 February, Gordon Goody appeared in his own defence in the witness box. He wore a Royal Artillery tie, stuck to his 'I was in Ireland at the time' story and was genuinely impressive. A week later, it was Lennie Field's turn. He claimed he had been involved in buying Leatherslade, for which Brian Field said he would get a large wad of folding. He didn't know until 9 August that the place had been used as a 'robbers' roost' and John Wheater told him he would sort it all out. Field was not, of course, a hardened criminal and had seemed as nearly out of his depth in court as Wheater did, scowling at everybody like a schoolboy caught with his hand in the cookie jar.

On Friday 6 March, Sebag Shaw launched his paint defence of Goody by bringing in his own expert witnesses. Criminal cases often end up like this. Apart from the he said/she said evidence of eye-witnesses, there is the he said/

she said testimony of experts. In the days of capital punishment (and of course, for murder, these still *were* the days of capital punishment), that could mean the drop for some poor bastard. This tit-for-tat went on for four days and Sebag Shaw scored a minor victory when he got Dr Ian Holden of the Met's Forensic Science lab to admit that the infamous yellow paint on Goody's shoes *could* be, but was not definitely, the same as that found at the farm.

The Defence summed up on Tuesday 10 March. There was an attempt at jury nobbling when Terrance Addy of Chalfont St Giles received a letter telling him to sway his fellow jurymen. Needless to say the letter was anonymous and nobody ever found out who sent it. The judge ploughed on regardless, his summing-up lasting for six days and running to 4,815 pages. Everybody today says the judge was fair throughout the trial and perhaps he was – Daly would hardly have gone free otherwise – but phrases like 'diabolical crime' stuck in the minds of the jury and nobody seemed to notice when he called Leatherslade Farm the scene of the crime. Then he sent the jury out – 'If you are smokers, bring your smokes; if you are sweet eaters, bring your sweets.' There was to be no telly, no newspapers and no contact with the outside world.

After sixty-five hours of debate, the twelve were back in court on Wednesday 25 March. It had been the longest deliberation in legal history, if only because the verdicts had to be unanimous. The judge later officially exempted them from future jury service for life because this case had been so long and arduous. The seven men charged with the actual robbery – Goody, James, Welch, Hussey, Wilson, Wisbey and Boal – were all found guilty (and conspiracy to rob – Uncle George's crime – was thrown in as well). Brian Field and Leonard Field were found guilty of conspiracy to obstruct the course of justice as was John Wheater.

Bruce Reynolds in the Gloucester Road, Jimmy White on the Derbyshire Moors and Buster Edwards in Wraysbury sat tight and watched the media for news of sentencing. At the time and since, the world, criminal and straight, reeled when the tariffs were handed down. Legal precedent and common sense (and, trust me, the two don't always go together) said that fourteen years would be the norm, with the usual time off for good behaviour. With any luck, the train robbers would be out in ten. But that doesn't take into account the vengeful mood of the Establishment in 1964. These men had cocked a snook at society. They'd said, in effect, we don't give a flying fuck about morality. And as for somebody else's money, we'll take what we want from where we want when we want. What are you going to do about it?

What Mr Justice Edmund Davies did was this (again, we're just looking at George Stanley's clients). The guilty were brought up from their cells one by one. When it came to Ronald Arthur Biggs (who had by this time been found guilty in a separate trial) the judge said, '... you are a specious and facile liar and you have this week, in this court, perjured yourself time and again, but I will not add a day to your sentence for that.' He gave him thirty years.

Davies sounded almost apologetic when it came to Douglas Gordon Goody. 'You have manifest gifts of personality and intelligence which could have carried you far had they been directed honestly.' But he also believed Goody to be 'a dangerous menace to society'. Thirty years.

Lennie Field got a similar tongue-lashing. 'You are a dangerous man,' the judge said, at which point a woman from the public gallery screamed 'No!' He was up to his neck in the conspiracy to rob and got twenty-five years. 'I'm seventy-three,' his old mum shrieked in court. 'Justice is not right.' Lennie Field collapsed after leaving the dock and was rushed to hospital.

'Justice is not right' – you can say that again. All in all, between 1963 and 1968, twenty-nine people were charged with crimes relating to the train robbery, either conspiracy to rob, receiving, harbouring wanted fugitives or conspiring to obstruct justice. Between them, their total tariffs added up to 377 years and nine months. We must move on in a different direction, but let's just pause to look at those done for receiving, one of several crimes George Stanley should have been charged with. I'm not counting Boal and Goody here because their big sentences were handed down for conspiracy to rob (Boal of course being 100 per cent innocent of that). Renee Boal was acquitted on the instructions of the judge. As Boal's wife, she had been charged with receiving £325 from the robbery (which she had, in all innocence, handed over voluntarily to the police). She pleaded not guilty and the prosecuting counsel, Arthur James QC, offered no evidence. That meant Renee walked. So did husband and wife Alfred and Florence May Pilgrim. May was Cordrey's sister and she and Alfred had been charged with receiving £860 of the Postmaster General's loot. So relieved was Alfred at the dropping of charges that he promptly dropped to the pavement outside the court and had to be rushed to Aylesbury hospital. He made a full recovery.

As we've seen, the case against Mary Manson was dismissed through lack of evidence. Robert Pelham was twenty-six and Roy James' mechanic. £545 was found at his home in Notting Hill. At his arraignment he denied all knowledge but had changed his tune by January 1964 and copped to receiving. The judge decided that 'no public good will be served by sending you ... to prison'. Pelham walked.

Martin Harvey was the brother of Ronald, once on the Yard's list as a possible train robber (he wasn't there). Martin was 28 and £518 in used notes had been found in his Dulwich flat. When confronted he told Tommy Butler's men, 'You are dead right. It is from the job but I was not in it and that's gospel.' He claimed he had been paid £200 to mind the £518! He went down for twelve months.

Walter Smith was a Shoreditch bookie who was visited after a tip-off by DS Slipper of the Met. Sizeable amounts of train robbery loot were found on the premises, including £645 stuffed down the front of his wife Patricia's skirt! The total ran to nearly two grand. 'A man,' Smith told the police, had wanted him to change the cash for postal orders. As money-laundering went, the Smiths weren't exactly top-drawer. He got three years.

All in all, a mixed bag, but it shows how difficult the authorities found it to pin laundering on anybody, let alone a crafty solicitor's clerk who knew – and abused – all the angles. One thing you will not have failed to notice in the last few names; George Stanley is not linked to any of them.

From George's point of view, the success in court had been considerable. The firm had defended five clients in all and two of them (Manson and Daly) had got off Scot free – not a bad average in a high profile case like this. The Daly acquittal in particular was unexpected – George had after all recommended he put his hands up for it! And of course G. A. Stanley & Co went on to make several killings, in the rather less harmful sense of the word. There were appeals, which is routine for just about every case under the sun. They ran from 6–20 July 1964. Whatever he thought about Wilfred Fordham, the old boy was still there in the case of Ronnie Biggs and the appeal failed. Fordham was Number Two for Sebag Shaw in the case of Goody and that too was turned down. Lennie Field's appeal, against the charge of conspiracy to rob under the able challenge of Michael Argyle, worked and his sentence was hacked.

For the record, William Boal died in prison of a brain tumour on 26 June 1970. None of the train robbers except for Cordrey knew him and he had nothing to do with the robbery. Cordrey himself, partly because he pleaded guilty, was freed in 1971. Jim Hussey was released in 1975 but his criminal ways never left him and he went down for cocaine smuggling in 1989. Tommy Wisbey got out in '76 and contributed years later to various television documentaries on the train robbery. Lennie Field, 'still young' as he shouted to his dear old mum as he left court, was released in 1967, in time to see Stanley Baker's film *Robbery*, loosely based on the events that Field had been involved with. Brian Field got out that year too and changed his name and bought a sports car. Gordon Goody was released in 1975 and went eventually to Australia before moving to Spain, where he still lives today. John Wheater served all of his three years, disappearing from the limelight in 1966. Roy James got out in 1975 but he was too old and infamous now to return seriously to the racing circuit. That was also the year that Jimmy White got out; so did Buster Edwards; and Bruce Reynolds was finally a free man in 1975 too. These last three stayed on the run for longer than the others and you'll never guess who defended them all. That's right; George Stanley.

They busted Charlie Wilson out of Winson Green on 12 August 1964 just as the nobs were getting ready to blast defenceless grouse out of the sky on the moors. It was an SAS-type operation with blokes in balaclavas abseiling on ropes and climbing over walls. Wilson allegedly knew nothing about the plan and had to be forced to escape at gunpoint. Do what? The jury's still out on all this. Either Wilson organised the escape himself (alone of the robbers, he did not attend his appeal hearing in London) or he was kidnapped. If it was a kidnap, you can bet it wasn't because good old Charlie deserved a break, prison or otherwise. It was because the boys in balaclavas believed he was sitting on £150,000 from the train robbery; which he soon would be, because alone of the robbers except Foreman, George had taken pity on Wilson and given him his entire cut. You'd think there were easier ways to make a living, but since the Winson Green job (pause to listen to the *Great Escape* movie score) resulted in only one coshed screw and took three minutes, there's not much that's easier, is there? Charlie Wilson buggered off, by whatever means and considerably richer, to Canada.

Which brings us to Biggsy. If you believe his account, for example in *Odd Man Out*, he was itching to escape from every prison they sent him to, even when on remand. But to do that, he needed help from outside. Wandsworth Prison is the 'hate factory' as Reynolds called it. Ronnie Biggs refers to it as 'Britain's answer to Alcatraz', the prison on the rock the Americans had closed two years earlier. His version is that he could handle anything the system threw at him, but in Wandsworth he was removed from his old train robbery associates and he was looking at thirty years with fuck all in his pocket. He got word to George Stanley and this means that by now, Biggsy at least had a shrewd idea (or knew for a fact) that George was holding the folding. Ronnie Biggs wanted out.

George told me years later that he called an emergency meeting at Edith's with Harry Isaacs, the Millbanks, the Hellers and Harry Smith, the robber who got away. Smith's name of course had been on both Hatherhill's and Butler's lists of likely lads, but there was no evidence against him. It's rather ironic that not only was he untouchable for the robbery itself, but he got away with the laundry business too. Talk about a man for all seasons.

Tommy Butler and Frank Williams had finally caught up with Harry Smith on 5 May 1964 at an address in Camberwell. As far as the law knew, Harry had lived at Fieldgate Mansions (Jack Spot's old haunt) until 14 August 1963 and had then disappeared. He followed Uncle George's advice and told the officers nothing. He agreed to have his fingerprints taken and there was no match from Leatherslade Farm. Ten people from the area who might have seen him there looked him up and down in an ID parade and failed to pick him out.

Stymied, the Yard sent DS Slipper and DS Shuter to Gosport in Hampshire to check on properties recently bought by Danny Regan, a mate of Harry's who ran a string of betting shops in London. He had recently bought thirty-two houses, a drinking club and a hotel in Portsmouth. He'd also done up his place in Barking Road, Plaistow. Butler wrote to Hatherhill. 'It can ... be said with virtual certainty that the cash expended on all the property is the proceeds of Smith's share of the proceeds of the train robbery.'

He got that right. Just as well no one was looking too closely at the properties George Stanley was buying up.

The team could not risk Biggsy shooting his mouth off in prison. Whether George knew it or not, the police were still interested in the Isaacs for harbouring Jimmy White – they would be arrested in September 1965 – and there was no need to give Tommy Butler any more ammunition. So Biggsy had to be sprung to shut the loose-lipped bastard up.

The man George chose for the job was Ron Leslie, a Geordie who believed, like everybody else, that George Stanley had a heart of gold. He happened to owe George quite a bit of money. While Biggs sorted out the getaway from the inside, using other cons to occupy the screws with rugger tackles, he would nip over the wall into Ron Leslie's welcoming arms – or rather, truck. Incidentally, there were Sturley contacts on the inside, too, via a bent screw my dad got to know well at Winchester and who was now at Wandsworth. The plan could only work in fine weather because the cons would not be in the exercise yard if it was pissing down – and it was on 7 July. So the whole thing was postponed until the next day. Biggs' version places great stress on the role played by Paul Seabourne, an ex-con who had recently been released. He disconnected all the telephones in the kiosks around the nick which would give the team a few precious minutes to disappear into London's jungle. Charmian, Biggs' wife, took the kids to Whipsnade Zoo for the day so that she had an alibi.

Ron Leslie was a motor mechanic and he'd converted the truck he'd bought with George's money (actually Biggs's or maybe the Postmaster General's) so that it had a hinged platform that could be raised above roof level so that the jump from the top of Wandsworth's wall was not fatal. Paul Seabourne got in the same way and threw rope ladders over the top. On the day in question, Ron Leslie drove a Mini (again, courtesy of the same money source) which had been hidden inside the removals lorry and was reversed off via a ramp. The third member of the escape team was Ronnie Black, so there would in later years be all sorts of jokes about the three Ronnies. The only hitch was that two other cons, seeing Paul's dangling ladders, took the spur-of-the-moment chance and legged it as well. They were Patrick Doyle and Robert Anderson.

Ron Leslie put his foot to the floor without attracting too much attention ... and promptly had to grind to a halt when he met up with a prison work party complete with dustcart. The screw with them, not wishing to obstruct Joe Public going about his daily business, waved them through. But George's after-sales service didn't end there. He arranged for Freddie Foreman and another villain, Alf Gerrard, to look after Biggsy. In *Odd Man Out* Biggs claims never to have met Freddie before, but as we know, that can't be right. He was shunted from safe house to safe house, but Paul

Seabourne and Ron Leslie were tracked down and both did time for springing Biggs – in Ron's case, three years. He had, of course, been given a large drink of £2,000 by Uncle George (again from Biggs's share of the loot) and, in common with virtually all of the Sixties underworld, kept schtum about who had hired him.

In October, it was finally safe to get Biggs out of the country (and he wouldn't be back until 2001). Freddie Foreman took him to the docks, dropping him off near London Bridge. Then Biggs was on a cargo boat with a substantial wad of his own cash in his pocket, with dreams of plastic surgery and a new life.

Many years later, Ronnie Leslie turned up in Barbados where Biggs found himself in court facing extradition issues. He had been sent over, according to Biggs, by the *News of the World* to get an exclusive from Ronnie B, but the interview was not to be. The local paper headlines screamed 'What is Ronald Leslie doing in Barbados?' What indeed?

To answer that, we have to look at what happened in March 1981. That was when John Miller, an ex-Scots Guardsman, and a handful of mercenaries grabbed Biggsy from Roda Viva, a barbecue restaurant halfway up Sugar Loaf Mountain in Rio de Janeiro. The plan was to hold Biggs to ransom and start a bidding war with the news-papers. It all went tits up though and the train robber who had become the greatest celebrity of them all ended up in Barbados.

I heard about the kidnap on the radio and rang Uncle George straight away. 'Uh-oh,' he said. 'I've got trouble if they bring Biggs back. Meet me at Edith's in the morning.'

I did. I was thirty-one by this time, fully aware of George's cons, scams and double-dealings. I knew how his mind worked, what he could pull off and what he couldn't. I knew all about the train robbery and a lot more. And, alone of my brothers, I was the one with a good head on my shoulders. I could be trusted. Edith was in full hostess mode, but I could tell she was worried. Out came the Scotch and the fags. She told me that George had rung his usual suspects team – one of the Millbanks, Heller and Harry Isaacs. Electric Les Aldridge was at Hermitage Court that morning and he looked none too pleased either. We all knew that Scotland Yard had tried earlier to get Biggs home by, shall we say, unconventional means – and that hadn't done Jack Slipper's career much good at the time.

I rarely saw George flustered, but he was that morning and I made the mistake of asking him what was wrong.

'What's wrong?' he blurted out. 'I'll tell you what's wrong. If Ronnie gets back to England and blabs to the Old Bill, we're all fucked.'

The problem was that everybody saw Biggs as a cash cow, but all of us in that lounge that morning knew the only money he had was what George had trickled to him from his share of the train robbery loot, mostly via his wife. Biggs had nearly fucked up the robbery itself with his useless train driver; now he was a bitter man who was owed rather a lot of money.

I suppose it was my idea to use Ron Leslie. 'You got him to help spring Biggsy in the first place,' I said. 'Why not send him out to Barbados and give the bastard an ultimatum?'

'Ultimatum?'

'If he spills the beans about the train robbery, he's dead, whether he's in prison or not.' It was always possible to arrange these things on the inside; lifers don't have much to lose. None of us had any intention of actually carrying out the threat, but Biggs didn't know that.

A convoy of cars left Edith's that night for the East End. George liked the idea and there were people to see. The next thing I knew about it was watching the news on TV and there was Ron Leslie walking into the Barbados nick to talk to Biggs. So of course, there was no interview with the *News of the World* – that was just Biggsy's cover story for the benefit of the public. It was the best five grand Ron Leslie ever earned (Biggsy was paying!) and George calmed down again.

If, like most of us, you got heartily sick of the media frenzy surrounding Ronald Arthur Biggs later in life, I'm afraid you have to thank George Stanley for that. Without his money, his initiative and Ron Leslie, the legend of Ronnie Biggs would never have been born.

Many years later, I rang Ronnie Biggs. He was a celebrity by now of course and a lot of water had flowed under the bridge.

It was November 1996 and Ronnie was in Rio. I remember the conversation like it was yesterday.

'Hello. Is that Ronnie Biggs? How are you, Ronnie?'

There was a pause. 'Who wants to know?'

'My name is Lee Sturley. I believe you know my Uncle George.'

'George?'

'You might have known him as George Stanley.'

Another pause.

'Yeah, I know George Stanley. Where's my fucking money?'

I had a similar conversation with the man by letter years later still, a letter I still have. By this time he had come back to face the music and was doing his long-overdue bird at Belmarsh. He had had three strokes by this time and the letter was written by a fellow con:

'Is George dead? What did he die of? Did he remember me in his will? I find it hard to believe he did ...'

You got that right, Ronnie.

CHAPTER 13
RAILWAYMEN

Thirteen months after the Great Train Robbery, my mate Ricky and I cycled over to Theydon Bois to see Uncle George. It took us hours and we had to negotiate a long gravel drive at the end of it – quite a novelty when you live in a house with three feet of garden around it.

'Your uncle's rich, isn't he?' Ricky asked, 'to have a house like this.' (I'm glad he wasn't on the Flying Squad's payroll.) 'Why isn't your dad rich too?'

'Because he's a fucking gambler,' I told him, all my pent-up hatred of the man suddenly coming out. It had only been three months since Andy Hempstead had nearly bashed my brother Lennie's brains out and I hated the world at that moment. 'He's blown it on fucking horses and dogs; he's just a fucking mug punter.' George's place was magic – huge oak trees and immaculate lawns under a cloudless sky. We were invited in for sandwiches, scones and endless cups of tea while stroking the cats and keeping away from the one-eyed goose.

Uncle George took me aside. He didn't know Ricky and what he had to say was personal. He asked how we were all coping with what had happened to Lennie. 'I did have a word with your dad,' he said, 'on the phone … I was going to have that bastard [Hempstead] shot but with all that's been happening lately we agreed not to do anything at the moment; it will attract too much attention.' We didn't use the term 'low profile' then, but that's what it amounted to. Most of the train robbers were doing thirty years, but Jimmy White, Buster Edwards and Bruce Reynolds were still on the run, not to mention the elusive Messrs One, Two and Three. And Uncle George was up to his elbows in the suds of the laundry business.

I told him I understood. 'You've got a good head on your shoulders, Lee,' he smiled. 'I am developing property here and at Hastings at the moment. Come and work for me soon.'

'I look forward to it,' I said.

'None of your father's tricks,' he winked.

'Wouldn't dream of it, George.' And I didn't. I had too much respect for the man for that.

'I haven't developed a poisoned palate for drinking police or prison tea. Make sure you do the same. Don't forget what I said.'

I never forgot *anything* that Uncle George said and decided to get out of the thieving business. I would become, like George Stanley, a criminal consultant, without the law bit. I shall never forget my swansong, though. A mate and I (no names, no interrogation under caution) did over the house of a police chief inspector in Thorpe Bay, just along the coast from home. I still had it in for the world. The police had done fuck all to bring justice for my brother, so it was, in my own little way, payback time. We helped ourselves to cash and jewellery from the bedroom wardrobe and I saw a police helmet.

'Hang on,' I said, knowing we had to be on our toes and I shat in the helmet before quickly (and carefully) replacing it.

'You are a piss-taking bastard!' my mate laughed. And, do you know, that little part of the robbery never appeared in the local paper at all!

Throughout 1965 and 1966 the law were asking questions, if only because Tommy Butler had put off his retirement until he'd brought Reynolds to justice and collared the endless escapee, Ronnie Biggs. The Flying Squad had spread their net wide, interviewing people who were on the very edge of their radar. One of these was Arthur Sturley, my dad. He looked suitably blank, of course, when spoken to, following the old Sturley line – 'Give 'em zilch and they've got zilch.'

Even so, it occurred to Uncle George that it might be better if I was out of the way. I had been working for him since I left school, both at Pedlar's Folly and Lesser's, and one Saturday after he'd fed the 5,000, i.e. the train robbers' wives who had got their weekly housekeeping money, he took me aside. He'd heard from an inspector at Euston that there was a job going on British Rail, in the dining cars. It was only three days a week, which was good because I could carry on working for him for the rest of the time.

'Look here,' he said. 'If all my clients had a legitimate source of income, they wouldn't keep getting nicked, would they?'

'Great, George,' I said. 'Get me that interview.'

It turned out the interview was just a formality because George had swung the job for me anyway. I started on 1 January 1966 on the nine o'clock to Manchester Piccadilly. For the first time in my life, I had money and could afford handmade suits and my first car. The black Barathea four-piece cost me £300 (four-piece because there was an extra pair of trousers). I got £4 10s. a week plus £2–3 a day in tips. I went back to visit Mum and Dad occasionally – 'Come back, son,' they'd say. 'We miss you.' What they missed was the folding I was bringing in. I asked Mum to bank my wages because I was saving for my first car. It's a big step in a bloke's life – more so in the Sixties than now. I picked out the one I wanted from a dealer in Romford and arranged to pick it up with the full amount next week. I rang Mum, but she didn't sound as delighted as I expected. She said she wasn't well and Dad was never around so I sent one of my brothers round to check. She was fine. I wasn't, though. The cheque for the car bounced. I was down the bank, spitting blood at everybody's incompetence. The manager showed me the paying-in book – it was signed, but not stamped. There had been no payments at all. Crocodile tears from Mum and sulks from Dad. But that was it. I had tried to be a big man in the outside world – like you do when you're seventeen –

and I'd been publicly shafted by my own parents. I would never forgive them and from that day on saw them as little as possible.

Work on British Rail introduced me to a new class of people. I was a grafter and popular and got quick promotion, loving the thrill of riding the trains I had been fascinated by as a little kid. Soon I was on the Royal Train under a bloke called Jimmy Maylan. He knew Uncle George too – who didn't? – and was developing property here and there with the wizard of 21–23 Broadway.

It was now that I moved into a flat at Red Oaks, away from the cadging, shafting ways of my parents and in the orbit of Uncle George. No bailiffs called here, nobody hammering on the door screaming that they had been done over and asking where their fucking money was. When I was off shift I would often join George and Edith for a swift half at the Eagle before he buggered off home to Marjorie at Pedlar's Folly. Every Thursday, he and Edith would take a trip to Dallinghurst Drive, Leigh-on-Sea, to my auntie Kitty's house. She'd lay on champagne lunches for them, the works.

George and my dad continued to do business, each of them circling each other like prize fighters in the ring. Any proceeds that came George's way from a lorry hijack or country house burglary, my dad would move on via his network of fences. Needless to say, George didn't let Arthur out of his sight until he got paid. So I raked the gravel at Red Oaks and mowed the lawns, marvelling at George's double life. The various properties belonging to G. A. Stanley Enterprises were nearing completion now. The old school house at Hastings, sold in the name of Edith Simons, had now become six flats; one of them became the new home of Jimmy White, released on parole.

Confident that my income was clean, I'd take a girlfriend up West (funny that – in old-time criminal parlance, 'Going West' meant being hanged at Tyburn Tree) and we'd have tea at Fortnum's or the Savoy.

Looking back, it was obvious that George had an ulterior motive for getting me the railway job. I could pick up snippets of information for him exactly as Annie Oakley had done for the train robbery. 'Remember, Lee,' he would say, 'information is an expensive commodity.' It didn't matter what the product was – cash, of course, was preferable, despite the risk of notes being traced. But there were spices, spirits, meat, antiques, *anything* had a street value and George had firms lined up to offer their expertise in the acquisition of the same. At the other end of the process, of course, should Joe Law get lucky and collar somebody, good old Uncle George was there to dip his snout into the legal aid trough and come up smelling of roses again. When I saw, from time to time, the content of his safe at Lesser's, I nearly had a heart attack. My dad had wads of cash sometimes after a successful corner game but nothing like the amounts George had stashed away.

Occasionally I could do George a little favour in return for him getting me the railway job. I met a firm from west

London – I was eighteen by now and that was old enough to be accepted in gang circles – and they were a team of shoplifters, working the upmarket stores like Harrods and Selfridges. One of them slipped me a parcel of suede jackets and nice suits. I rang George. 'Pop over to the flat,' I said. 'I've got something you might like.' He was over the moon when he saw the clothes. They needed a bit of alteration of course and this is where Arthur Sturley, tailor, came in. 'Get your dad to do the work for me,' George said. 'I will square you up tomorrow night.'

I couldn't help smiling, imagining George in court, wearing clothes nicked from Harrods, defending the very men who had done the nicking in the first place. Poetic injustice or what? 'Like I always say, Lee,' I could hear him saying. 'Robbery without violence.'

Saturdays were when George set up most of his legal deals. Clients came with information – security vans, banks, payrolls, country houses, lorries. Anything hooky would be passed to my dad for fencing purposes. If a client had been arrested and no property had been recovered, that was fine – there would be a very big slice of the cake there for George. He would look after it, keep it safe. He specialised in villains who had little chance of getting off and was an expert at finding loopholes in the law. As to the payment, whatever the legal aid situation was, George would insist on ten grand, in cash, up front. Criminals could plead as much poverty as they liked in court, but it was no use doing that to Uncle George.

'Give it to me straight, son,' he would say, in language most of them understood. 'No bullshit.'

Back in April 1966, DS Jack Slipper found Jimmy White living in a flat at Littlestone, near New Romney in Kent. The man had been on the run for nearly two and a half years and he was glad it was all over. He had £2,250 (close to £40k today) at the time of his arrest and he told police there was another £4,800 in his caravan. George Stanley was round there like a rat up a pipe, cautioning Jimmy, for George's sake, of course, as well as his own, not to say another word. His trial only lasted one day, 16 June, and this in itself was a reminder that the world had moved on. The Great Train Robbery was already old hat and not yet the iconic crime it is today. The criminal world was rocked by the appalling revelations of child murder on Saddleworth Moor when Ian Brady and Myra Hindley were sentenced to life. People booed Bob Dylan at the Royal Albert Hall because he'd gone electric and an unmanned space ship landed on the moon.

There was little that George and the brief could do against the overwhelming evidence against Jimmy White. They advised him to plead guilty to robbery, but not conspiracy to rob. Mr Justice Nield gave him eighteen years, just over half what the others had got.

'They think it's all over,' Kenneth Wolstenholme said hysterically about the crowd invading the pitch two weeks later. 'It is now!' England had beaten Germany in the World

Cup and it was like VE night all over again. That summer, Buster Edwards gave himself up to DI Frank Williams in a pub near the Elephant and Castle, through a go-between. I've often wondered if that go-between was George Stanley because he certainly was quick off the mark to defend Buster at his subsequent hearing and trials. Incidentally, it doesn't say much for Edwards' intelligence when part of his statement read, 'I was never on that train and it's about time the truth was told. I have read that man [sic] Peter [sic] Fordham's book; it's full of childish lies.'

One part of the statement was right, however – 'Although people think I had a lot more [money] the truth is I didn't get very much.' And we all know why.

Buster's prints were everywhere and he was grilled at the Yard by Tommy Butler and Williams. It's not clear now whether George was present during this (there was no automatic right to a lawyer in those days and all sorts of rule-bending went on) but you can bet he had briefed Edwards on what to say. The florist-turned-train-robber stood his trial at Nottingham Assizes on 8 and 9 December. George had engaged Bernard Caulfield QC as his brief and the man's argument was that Edwards had been a virtual bystander to events. Freddie Foreman, who had got Uncle George on this one from the get-go was worried about the evidence stacked against Buster – 'I don't like it, George,' he said, 'I'm going to pull one of the jurors and try and get Buster a new trial.'

According to Freddie, George was shocked by this suggestion and said, 'You can't do that! That would be illegal – and
not only that, you'd go to prison.' If he said this at all, I'm
prepared to bet it was the other way round – Freddie's safety
first and the legality of it all second. George put his faith in
Caulfield.

The train driver Jack Mills looking shaky and unwell in
the witness box did the trick, however, and Edwards was
found guilty. The judge believed he was in on the job from
the start (as he was, having met the Ulsterman with Gordon
Goody) and he was sentenced to fifteen years.

Even though Charlie Wilson and Ronnie Biggs were on the
run, the only name in the original lineup that Tommy Butler
hadn't got yet was Bruce Reynolds. The man had moved back
to England in August 1968, with virtually no money left. He
was a pariah in the underworld and couldn't find work. The
end came on Friday 8 November when Tommy Butler turned
up at his rented house in Torquay. 'Hello, Bruce,' he said. 'It's
been a long time.'

Once again, George Stanley rode to Bruce's – and his own
– rescue, in a figurative sense. 'It's the easiest thing in the
world to steal money, Bruce,' he said to him in his holding
cell, 'and the most difficult thing to hang on to it.' I don't
know why Bruce didn't break his nose! He struck a deal with
Butler, with George's connivance – he would plead guilty as
long as his family and various people who had helped him
while on the run were left alone. At Aylesbury Crown Court,

Mr Justice Thompson sentenced him to twenty-five years. George had told him, in one of his glummer moments, that he might get thirty-five.

Outside the court, eager reporters asked Butler if this was the end of the train robbery story. 'No,' he said. 'Got to catch Biggs first.' And, he might have added, Freddie Foreman, Leslie Aldridge, Harry Smith and George Stanley.

But he didn't.

By this time I was chief steward on the Royal Train. We got a few perks – a few bottles of wine and miniature Scotches to take home. And in July 1969 I was on the special train that took Harold Wilson and 168 MPs on a jolly for Prince Charles' investiture as Prince of Wales at Caernarfon Castle. Perhaps 'jolly' is the wrong word for it. Plaid Cymru were setting off little bombs all over the place and security was sky high.

As we reached Caernarfon Station, I went through the motions. 'Have you had a comfortable journey, Prime Minister, and was the service suitable to your requirements?' (I even *sounded* like George Stanley!)

'Well done, steward,' he said and I asked him for a quick word. Wilson had the reputation of a people's man. He smoked a pipe (like any bloke over forty back then) and had gone to grammar school, so he was approachable, at least. I told him that my dad wrote to him on a regular basis (he wrote to Buckingham Palace too – I still have the replies) about this and that grievance. All right, so he was a convicted fraudster, but we're all equal in this great democracy of ours, aren't we? No? Never mind; read on. Wilson asked how Dad was and said he enjoyed reading his letters. 'There are no flies on him,' he said, lighting up his pipe.

'You're not kidding,' I said. 'His brother George is worse. He's a solicitor.'

'Where?'

'The East End,' I told him. 'Stratford, to be precise. He's been working on the Great Train Robbery case.'

'What a coincidence,' Wilson said. 'And you're working on the London Midland region; it's the same line, isn't it?'

'Yes, Prime Minister, but I'm not planning to rob it.'

Wilson laughed and shook my hand. 'You come from an interesting family,' he said.

He didn't know the half of it.

It was a couple of months before that that my heart almost stopped when two burly blokes from the Regional Crime Squad pulled me over. Ever since I started driving (legally, that is – I'd actually been doing it on and off since I was fourteen) I'd keep being stopped by the local fuzz in Southend, checking tyres, brake lights, asking questions. On this particular occasion, I was in a pub in Brentwood when two CID officers, DC Nice and DC Nasty, flashed their badges and sat down.

'Nothing to worry about, Lee.' Nice or Nasty, they use your Christian name, unsolicited, to put you at your ease, or patronise or both. 'We need a little chat. We're after your uncle, George Stanley. We know he was behind the train robbery and a lot else besides. We understand you keep getting stopped in your car.'

'That's right,' I said, my mind racing. 'Can't seem to get left alone.'

'We can do something to help you there,' the officer said. 'It's not you we want.'

Seeing that I was dithering, DC Nasty leaned towards me, all attitude. 'Alternatively,' he said, 'we can make it very hard for you.'

They told me they had had me watched for months and knew that I visited Uncle George more often than they – and I quote – 'had a shit'. I explained that George was more of a father to me than my actual dad. The reality – a love/hate relationship, I suppose – was too complicated and the last people I was going to open my soul to were the Old Bill. 'We know, Lee,' said DC Nice, nodding and all concerned. 'We know all about the school at Hastings and how Ronnie Biggs got out of the country.'

Nightmare. Regional Crime, like the Flying Squad, were very good at letting you think it was all over. They knew *everything* and all that was necessary was a signature on a dotted line. All the time, I could hear Uncle George's words pounding in my head. 'Give 'em zilch. And they'll get zilch.'

'Is this meeting official?' I asked them, some of George Stanley's awareness of the law kicking in.

'No,' said DC Nice. 'We'll leave this matter with you to think it over.'

I couldn't get out of that pub fast enough.

By this time I was living in Blenheim Close, Leigh-on-Sea and I nipped out the back way to make a call from the phone box in Fairfax Drive. I told Uncle George I had a problem – no, make that *we* had a problem. On the Monday, I was round to Edith's by 9.30 a.m. I hadn't seen a tail of any kind but I was paranoid by now. Edith got out the Benson and Hedges – George, with his TB, didn't approve of me smoking – and coffee. Then George came in. He said, 'Your Dad's had a visit, too – the Flying Squad.'

'What are we going to do?' I tried to sound like I wasn't shitting myself.

'Nothing. Sit tight.'

'Do what?'

'We'll give the Filth the runaround and your mum and dad will be looked after. If Joe Law had anything on me, I'd be under arrest by now. As it is, I haven't had so much as a glance from Mr Plod. Trust me, son; this is your Uncle George you're talking to.'

It took nerve, but we all held on as '69 became '70. William Boal, the only innocent train robber, died in prison that year. Lennie Field had been released in '67, John Wheater a year earlier. They had moved on, both to disappear into criminal folklore. But in the real world, the rest of us had work to do.

'I am building a number of chalets on the east coast, Lee,' Uncle George told me, airing his dirty laundry almost in public. 'I want you to keep an eye on things and arrange delivery of materials to the sites. You can get the stuff far cheaper than I can.'

What was this? Was I becoming indispensable to Mr Big? That was a scary notion.

CHAPTER 14
RONNIE, REGGIE AND GEORGE

A surprising amount of money was running through my hands on the railways by 1969. I would pay in the day's takings at the booking office at Euston Station and I noticed that the notes were counted but never checked – a golden opportunity to turn dirty money into snow white. Although it was now six years since the train robbery, George still had money to launder. I put it to him at Edith's shortly after man landed on the moon, so when he agreed to the plan, I said, 'Houston, we have lift-off.' He didn't get it, which is odd in such a bright bloke.

'You're way ahead of yourself, Lee. You always find an angle. I'm impressed.' I got a buzz from that, although George made it clear he needed ten times the amount to launder quickly.

I was now on a percentage from George and paying the notes directly in to British Rail by switching the takings from each train, so we no longer needed the Hellers, the Millbanks or Harry Isaacs. We had to be careful, of course. The Flying Squad were still sniffing around and if there was a hint of trouble, George would get a coded message to me by phone to meet him at the office. If it was sudden or unexpected, that meant a meet at the Eagle in Snaresbrook. George had a man inside the police and I didn't, at that time, know who he was.

'No panic, Lee,' George would say over his pint. 'We will just have to play a few games. And remember – we're untouchable.' It wasn't long after this that my dad phoned to say there was a parcel on offer – jewellery and porn. The asking price was £5,000 (not bad, considering the amount on offer) but I suggested he offer £3,000. In the end, he got the lot for £3,500, which I paid.

'I don't want the filth, Dad. You've got lots of perverts in Southend; you can move that on.' There must have been 3,000 porn mags stacked in his spare bedroom, catering for all sorts of tastes that would make your hair curl. I wasn't sure which way up some of the photos were supposed to be! But what I'd really bought this lot for were a couple of sheets of paper tucked inside one of the mags. It was a mailing list compiled by an old girl called Phoebe Young who ran a mail-order racket from Southend. This was dynamite. With a little bit of research, I found out that among those who were receiving regular deliveries in plain brown envelopes were barristers, taxmen, bank managers, policemen and politicians.

You have to understand that in the early Seventies stuff like this wasn't readily available. There was no internet, no

Naughty Channels on the telly, just Soho. 'Private' shops had yet to make an appearance on the high street and anyway, a pillar of society going into one of those, even with his collar turned up and his hat pulled down over his face, was asking for trouble. I told George about my little list and he was delighted – 'That should keep the police off our backs!' I moved the jewellery on via a railways oppo in Glasgow. In those days there was little in the way of joined-up thinking between Regional Crime Squads so no link with Scotland was ever made.

George had one of his little jobs planned at the time and I was part of it. Ron Leslie bought a second-hand lorry at an auction at Waltham Abbey and he passed it to my big brother Arthur. We had five tons of building materials to shift down at Hastings, in connection with George's rebuilding of the universe courtesy of the Postmaster General and several other faceless victims. However, the lorry would only hold 3½ tons. Thanks, Ron. Somehow we got up that bloody great hill out of Hastings, me at the wheel with a line of cars behind tooting like mad. *And* it was pissing down. In the back were tins of cash posing as tins of paint. By the time we got to Abridge, Essex the truck was belching smoke and steam was hissing out of the radiator. I saw a Noddy bike in my rear window and pulled over.

'Is there a problem, officer?'

I half expected him to say, 'Yes, you're one of the fucking Sturleys clearly up to no good and I'm going to lock you up and throw away the key.' But he didn't. He politely pointed out that the lorry was on its way to the knackers' yard and he'd like a look in the back. His torch shone on timbers and window frames, but he missed the paint tins completely.

'Are you delivering to the squire?' he asked. This was the local name for Uncle George and I must admit, it unnerved me a bit. Brother Arthur was alongside me in the cab shitting himself.

'That's right,' I smiled.

'Well, we'll get you some water for the radiator and I'll escort you to Red Oaks.'

'That's very kind of you, officer,' I said, my heart still firmly in my mouth.

'That's all right,' he said. 'Mr Stanley donates a lot of money to the police widows and orphans.'

He stopped short of telling me that George had a heart of gold – maybe because he thought I knew that already!

When we were driving again, Arthur let out his first breath for five minutes. 'I don't believe what just happened, Lee,' he muttered. 'You know and I know that you're the biggest villain I know.'

'If you treat people with respect,' I told him, 'they'll do anything for you.'

'You've changed,' he said.

'No,' I smiled. 'I've *learned.*'

As for the money in the paint tins, George got me to transfer it to the capacious boot of his 3.5-litre kingfisher-green Rover coupé and then it was off to Edith's.

*

By the early Seventies, the crime scene in London had changed. Read about that scene in the Sixties and you'll notice it was dominated by the Krays, Reggie and Ronnie, who I'd met for the first time outside the Grave Maurice in Whitechapel when I was eleven. That was where Superintendent Nipper Reed, who brought them down, first saw them too, but I bet they didn't buy him a lemonade and an arrowroot biscuit!

On one of my visits to see Dad in Pentonville with Mum, I told him all about the Krays, although obviously he knew most of it through the stir grapevine. After all, he had conned them out of £500 while on the run and the word was, you didn't mess with the twins. 'Those two mugs,' he laughed. 'They won't last long, son. You stand on me.' And whenever he said that he turned out to be right. He told me that George Cornell had been a good friend, a docker who passed various goods on that Dad had sold him. On 9 March 1966, Ronnie Kray, always the more deranged of the two, walked into the Blind Beggar, a pub just along the road from the Grave Maurice, and caught the eye of Cornell who was sitting at the bar. 'Look who's here,' Cornell said and dropped like a stone with Ronnie's bullet in his head. His mate Albie Woods then fired a couple of shots into the wall (the bullet holes are there to this day as part of gangland folklore) and the pair walked out.

Twenty years later, in one of the many books ghosted for the twins, Ronnie remembered, 'I took out my gun and held it towards his face ... I shot him in the forehead. He fell forward onto the bar ... That's all that happened. I felt fucking marvellous.' I bet he didn't feel quite so marvellous when Cornell's widow, Olive, went round to the Krays' and smashed all their windows.

What the many 'autobiographies' don't tell you is that Cornell gave the twins a rare – and deserved – hiding in the George pub, the only one with its eighteenth-century gabling still left from the old coaching days. I don't suppose any of them were admiring the architecture of the place when Cornell loosened two of Ronnie's teeth. The Blind Beggar was payback time and Cornell was one of a long list that mad Ronnie wanted to blow away. Dad was convinced, it was only a matter of time – 'They will take the law into their own hands and kill someone and get nicked.' Violence, he said, as he had said so often, achieves nothing. And the man who was doing time advised me to use my head.

The Krays have passed into legend now, the last of the hard men, but we couldn't see this in perspective at the time. I met Alfred Dean a few years later. He had been a professional wrestler who went by the name of Man Mountain. He certainly was a big bloke but by the time I knew him he was no longer a henchman for the Krays but a bedridden recluse living in Colliers Row, Romford. He bought all kinds of hooky gear and his family collected it for him. In his day, as well as being a minder like the Lambriano brothers, Teddy Machin, Freddie Foreman and Albert Donahue, he helped in the twins' long firm frauds.

I guess this was why my dad thought so little of the Krays. They were amateurs compared to him. A mate of mine – let's call him Peter – found out they had a lock-up in Hoxton full of silk handkerchiefs lifted by the bale from the docks. My mate got in there and nicked the lot. He was then stuck for what to do with them.

'Go south of the river,' I told him. 'Charlie and Eddie Richardson would be interested, especially when they know where they come from.' Peter did just that. The rivalry between the twins and the Richardsons, although it never quite escalated into total open warfare, was well known. There was a hefty drink in it for Peter when the Richardsons stopped laughing.

My dad's prophecy was fulfilled at dawn on 9 May 1968, when DS 'Nipper' Read arrested the Krays and most of the Firm. So barking had Ronnie become by this time that even the Firm feared they might be the next to disappear, just for looking at him funny one morning. People who had had collective amnesia suddenly remembered things, including the barmaid who had seen Ronnie kill George Cornell in the Blind Beggar.

The twins were loaded enough to approach any lawyer to defend them in their trial that began at the Old Bailey on 7 January 1969, but they sensibly opted for Messrs Lesser, specifically George Stanley. This time though, Uncle George turned the offer down. There was a nasty taste in the mouth when it came to the Krays and a sense that the world was tired of them. Lock them up and lose the key was the general consensus. George knew too many of the people involved, both in the Firm and outside it, and it was not one for him. So he took himself off to Rye Lane, Peckham, to a lawyer friend of his, Ralph Haeems, who he'd later work for.

'Fancy defending the Krays, Ralph?' he asked. 'For a fee, of course.'

Life quietened down on the criminal gang front after that. There were the Nashes – 'the wickedest brothers in England' as the *Sunday Pictorial* called them; the Dixons, ex-Kray men; and the Tibbs. Tit-for-tat violence was going on into the early Seventies and George Stanley had nothing to do with them.

He did have to do with others, however. Throughout the Seventies, as villains got out of nick – for example Jimmy White – they would contact George for help. George would be on the blower to me and I would ask them what they wanted – some nice bijou residence off the beaten track, for instance. I'd show them various properties, using every trick I'd seen my dad pull. George handled the conveyancing and fixed them up with dodgy mortgages. Estate agents? Who needs them?

Typically, it went like this – 'The flats in Southend are ready, George,' I would say to him one morning at the Broadway.

'Good,' he would say with a rare smile, 'I've got two clients lined up for them. I'll give them your number.'

'What? Are they out of jail already?'

'One is. The other one is getting out next week.'

The villains were indebted to George, with his heart of gold, but now they were on the usual treadmill – monthly mortgage payments, utility bills, life's little wrinkles. He knew they'd be back to work soon enough with a scam or a sawn-off, whatever. Not only could they provide him with valuable information, he could step in to defend them should Lady Luck desert them on the job.

One of the highest-profile people that George dealt with was George Ince, for a while Britain's Most Wanted. It was 1972 and we all groped around in darkness thanks to the miners' strikes. The IRA were on the warpath big time, especially since, at the end of January, thirteen people had been shot during a protesters v Army punch-up in Derry. It was the year of Watergate and a surprisingly bloody Olympics when Palestinian guerrillas hit the Olympic Village near Munich. It was Black September and Bloody Sunday, and a little provincial murder at the Barn Restaurant in Braintree got a bit lost in all that.

In the early hours of 5 November, two men broke into Sun Lido House in the grounds of the restaurant, at that time being refurbished. They had spent the day in nearby Chelmsford and had gone to see *The Italian Job*, an iconic heist movie with Michael Caine looking suspiciously like

Bruce Reynolds. The Barn had been bought by Bob and Muriel Patience ten years earlier, just as George Stanley was gearing up for the train robbery recruitment and twenty years after he and Billy Hill had pulled off the Eastcastle Street job. The restaurant, with its cabarets, live music and neon lights – 'Every night is party night' – had been packed that evening and the two burglars knew there'd be a fair wodge of cash in the safe.

Guests were still leaving the car park when Beverley, the Patiences' twenty-year-old daughter, and her mother crossed the tarmac to Sun Lido House. Inside, they were confronted with a man with a gun who told them to be quiet. He wrapped a velvet cushion around the muzzle to act as a silencer and Muriel tried to carry on a normal conversation to keep everybody calm. The gunman had cold blue eyes and spoke with a northern accent.

Bob Patience turned up at 2.15 a.m. to find a bizarre foursome – his terrified family and two increasingly rattled burglars. They demanded the keys to the safe. Bob Patience was a no-nonsense East Ender, built like a brick shithouse, and he offered to take the gunman across the road to the Barn where the cabaret artistes had yet to be paid for their night's work. 'Don't be a bloody fool, Bob,' the gunman said and, when he noticed Patience's reaction, said, cryptically, 'This is a family affair.' He then offered Patience a choice. 'Your wife or your daughter?' he asked.

Still thinking the man was bluffing, Patience made

no reply, so the gunman shot Muriel in the right temple, blood oozing over the carpet where she had fallen. Too late, Patience got the keys and opened the safe. The gunman took bank bags containing £900 (£11,100 today) in cash, ignoring jewellery that was there and not noticing a false compartment that held another £7,000 in notes (nearly £86,500). The gunman's oppo was helping a panicking Beverley staunch the blood from her mother's head.

'She'll be all right,' the gunman said. 'I've seen plenty of those in my time.'

Then they tied up father and daughter, face down on the floor and the gunman fired through a cushion into Beverley's back before doing the same to Bob Patience's head. The pair drove away in the car belonging to the Patiences' son, David, which was parked outside.

By the time of the Barn attack, sophisticated housebreaking had become quite a pattern. Van heists were still going on although there would never be another train robbery along the lines of 1963. Even so, this particular raid seemed so amateur, with so little taken, that police wondered whether it wasn't actually a vendetta attack on Bob Patience, loosely disguised as a robbery – 'This is a family affair.'

I was sitting in George Stanley's living room with Auntie Marjorie and it must have been Sunday 26 November. The nine o'clock news was on and Reggie Bosanquet was giving us the latest on the Barn Murder. Bob Patience was the luckiest bugger on earth – not that Reggie put it quite like that

– because he had moved his head a fraction as the gunman had pulled the trigger and he'd only been grazed. Muriel and Beverley had been rushed to hospital to undergo surgery, but Muriel had died on the 8th. Essex CID were leading a murder hunt. And the man they wanted to talk to was George Ince. That was one of the most surreal moments of my life. Not only did we know Ince but there was a knock on the door as we watched the telly. Marjorie opened it and there, shaken and quite probably stirred, was George Ince!

When he came into the lounge, he pointed to the screen with a silly look on his face. 'Look,' he said, as if none of us had noticed. 'That's me on the telly.' Nobody said George Ince wasn't quick on the uptake.

'Don't worry,' I said, pouring him a hefty Scotch. 'George will sort it out for you.' And we all looked at the Great Man to watch him go to work.

Ince was a Jack-the-Lad the Sturleys had known for years. He was born in Bow in 1937 just as Uncle George was starting his legal career. He was one of nine kids and his dad drove a dust cart. After school, he worked as a general labourer and did his National Service with the Royal Fusiliers. The positive side of George Ince was that he became a top-flight (no pun intended) pigeon fancier and his prize bird had won the Berwick to London race in 1966. He was quiet and polite, especially to women. That said, he had a temper and was light-fingered too, doing bird several times between 1957 and '61 for shop-breaking and fighting. He grew up in the East

End under the influence of the Krays and met Dolly, elder brother Charlie's wife, at various parties the twins threw. She would be important at his trial later. Uncle George of course knew Ince better than most of us because he had hired him as a foot soldier to carry out the Mountnessing silver bullion raid near Brentwood six months earlier. It wasn't just coincidence that made George Ince turn up at Pedlar's Folly and it wasn't just Uncle George's reputation that brought him there. As far as Ince was concerned, George was the man, an organiser, lawyer and trouble-shooter, all rolled into one. And of course, he had a heart of gold.

From gold back to silver. The Mountnessing silver bullion robbery involved the knocking over of a security van in Mountnessing in May. Some £60,000's-worth of silver (nearly three-quarters of a million pounds today) was taken and the Essex constabulary was anxious – over-anxious as it turned out – to get a conviction. George had got the necessary info from an insider from among his by now vast network of informants and picked four likely lads, including Ince, to carry the task out. I don't know who the insider was, but George and my dad had known another member of the team, Ronnie Molloy, since they were kids and the rest, as they say in that part of Essex, was 'istory.

But being suspected of a robbery was one thing. Being suspected of murder was something else. The death penalty had gone but Ince would be looking at life for the Barn job. A photofit of the killer in those pre-computerised days (it was made by placing face sections together to form a composite) appeared in the papers and on the TV. It looked nothing like George Ince – nor, as it turned out, like either of the men who were actually guilty. This wasn't too surprising. Remember what I said about the shock of witnessing a crime? A man shoots you, your mum, your dad and you have to remember what he looks like. Sounds easy, but it's not and young Beverley, escaping death by a fraction of an inch, got it wrong.

The underworld people that George and I knew didn't approve of this sort of crime. Guns were becoming more commonplace but the systematic murder and attempted murder of women was just not something that East End villains did. Somebody, however – and we never found out who – grassed up George Ince to the Yard's Serious Crimes Squad.

On Friday 10 November, Essex police showed Beverley and Bob Patience mugshots. One of them was Ince and, after much deliberation, Beverley picked him out as the gunman. Her dad picked two other blokes entirely. So there was a warrant out for George Ince and so he turned up on George's doorstep. And they talked tactics.

'I've got no fucking alibi, George, apart from [Charlie Kray's wife] Dolly, and nobody's going to believe her,' Ince said, 'but I had nothing to do with it. Shooters. You know that's not my style.'

George did. 'You'll have to give yourself up,' he said. 'Staying on the run solves nothing and makes you look guilty.'

The next morning, George rang the Braintree nick; George Ince would be giving himself up later that day. He met Ince at Theydon Bois underground station, as arranged, and together they drove to Epping police station, where George handed in a prepared statement as Ince gave himself up. It was midday by now and the suspect was taken to Braintree. There is a photograph of Ince, under the by now obligatory blanket, being escorted into the nick there. No sign of George, of course, but he wasn't far away.

I can't believe that he was still there that evening, though, when an illegal ID parade was set up, or he would have done something about it. Conducted by DCI James Gorham at 8.40 p.m. at Colchester nick, nine blokes were lined up for Beverley, Bob and David Patience to identify. The problem was that David had only seen the robbers briefly as they drove off in his car; Bob Patience pointed to the wrong bloke and only Beverley fingered Ince. Why was she so positive? Because she'd seen his photo already, shown to her by the police, and it was that that should have made the ID parade null and void. Incidentally, those nine blokes were in that line for nearly two hours.

George got Victor Durand QC as Ince's brief. It would be hard to find anybody better. He had defended Jack Spot back in the day and the Krays more recently. He had also handled the appeal of Roy James from the train robbery and defended the poor innocent bastards stitched up by Tanky Challenor who had planted bricks in their pockets.

The trial opened at Chelmsford Crown Court on Wednesday 2 May 1973. Milford Stevenson, who had handled the Kray trial, was on the Bench and John Leonard QC was prosecuting. George had made sure that Ince was nicely turned out, but he couldn't shut the bloke's family up. Eighty-year-old Mum, Minnie, sat near her boy and his five sisters were gobby in the gallery. George and Victor Durand were also horrified when Ince himself proved to have less decorum than was strictly good for him. He yelled at Bob Patience, 'Why don't you tell the truth? You know I wasn't the one that done it.' The lawyers made him apologise, but Durand tore into Patience over the shakiness of his identification.

The next day, Durand got out of Beverley that she had seen photos of Ince seventy-two hours before the ID parade. Ince was on his feet again, shouting the odds. This time the court adjourned and George and Victor Durand told Ince his fortune. 'For your own sake, Mr Ince, you must be quiet,' Durand boomed.

Uncle George was rather more *sotto voce*. 'For fuck's sake, George, do us all a favour!'

Ince apologised again. Over the weekend, his family sent a telegram to the Lord Chancellor, Lord Hailsham, complaining about the unfairness of the trial. That was a bit like pissing into the wind. They didn't come much more Establishment than Lord Hailsham.

George must have wanted to kick Ince into the middle of next week when the silly bugger threw out Victor Durand

and said he would defend himself. He then turned his back on the court, despite George's protestations, while the bizarre trial continued. Although Durand physically stayed in the courtroom, he was powerless to help, so there was no closing for the Defence, except for Ince interrupting the judge's summing-up sixteen times. What a plonker! The jury were hung – for which Ince shouted his thanks and a new trial started four days later.

By that time, George had had a few quiet words with Ince and Victor Durand was back. The judge was new, though – Mr Justice Eveleigh; Ince could live with that.

Of the many problems the Prosecution faced, the worst was that they had no forensic at all. The gunman and his accomplice at the Barn had worn gloves throughout, so there were no dabs. Saliva on the fag ends was inconclusive, so were fibres found on Ince's coat that seemed to have come from the Patiences' sofa; one of his sisters had exactly the same suite. Then there was the voice. The gunman had a northern accent; Ince was pure East End. Bob Patience explained this by saying that, in the ID parade, when everybody was asked to say 'I want the keys to the safe' Ince was disguising his voice. It was all pretty weak and Durand went for him, on the grounds that Patience had made no such claim in the first trial.

Durand made mincemeat of Beverley too, although in a typically gentlemanly way. When asked, in the ID parade, to pick out the gunman's Number Two, she chose a completely innocent bloke. Durand put Ince on the stand on Day Five, 18 May and the court heard his alibi. He had been at the home of a Mrs Grey and put her little girl to bed at 10 p.m. He then watched the telly with Mrs Grey until half past midnight, sixty miles away from the Barn Restaurant and the couple went to bed. The next morning, Ince left at about 10.45 a.m. and went back to his caravan at Seasalter, near Whitstable.

The problem for the Defence – and George and Durand were on tenterhooks about this – was the real identity of Dolly Grey. She was of course Doris Kray, Charlie's wife. She had changed her name by deed poll three years before after Charlie went away for a ten stretch and the twins got life. George had got a statement from Dolly exonerating Ince, but the Kray name stank in legal circles. Who would believe a word the woman said? John Leonard, for the Prosecution, wanted all this out in the open, but Durand intervened and the jury were sent out. The decision was made that the court should be told the woman had changed her name, but not from what. He savaged Dolly Grey on Monday 21 May, accusing her of lying from start to finish. 'I am a Catholic,' she sobbed to the court. 'I will not come here to lie.' Most accounts of the case will tell you that it was just a slip of the tongue when Leonard referred to the witness as Mrs Kray. George was not so sure.

Most of the closing speeches were about the problem of witness ID in stressful situations. It took the jury three hours to declare George Ince not guilty. There was pandemonium in court, the Defence congratulating each other on a job well done. It must have been a rare moment for Uncle George, defending an innocent man for once.

How do we know Ince was innocent? A chance bit of bravado from one petty crook to another in the Lake District led to the arrest of John Brook who owned a .32 Beretta which turned out to be the one used on the Patience family. There were three bullets missing from the clip. Police soon picked up Nicholas Johnson who freely confessed that he had been Number Two and felt ashamed, not only for the Barn murder, but for letting Ince take the rap. The trial of Brook and Johnson took place at Chelmsford in January and February 1974. Brook, clearly from the evidence a psychopath, got life; Johnson got ten years for manslaughter.

And that should have been that. Except that on 29 November 1973, before the Brook/Johnson trial started, George Ince, Ronnie Molloy, Frankie Sims and John Brett went down for the Mountnessing bullion raid and Uncle George couldn't get them out of it. The least George felt he could do was to get a fair deal for Ince, who had been well and truly shafted by the Essex police. I suppose that deep down, somewhere, George Stanley's heart of gold beat louder at certain times and this was one such occasion. He had set up the job in the first place and, without putting his own safety on the line obviously, he wanted to square things for his foot soldiers. Bob Patience and John Leonard QC wrote personally to Ince in prison apologising and several cozzers, including Detective Chief Superintendent Leonard White who led the case, got their knuckles rapped big time.

The issue was even raised, several times, in Parliament. In July 1977, Ian Mikardo, the MP for Bethnal Green and Bow, said, 'The Essex police were determined to get a conviction [in the Barn murder] by hook or by crook and they came very near to getting a conviction by crook.'

Ince had it tough inside. He had his face slashed in Long Lartin and tried to cut his own wrists. He got flu in his freezing cell and caught pneumonia. Moved to the Scrubs, they fed him large doses of Largactil that freaked him out. He turned into a zombie and writs were lodged on his behalf against the Home Office alleging negligent treatment.

If you like happy endings, George Ince was allowed out on 7 September 1977 to marry Dolly Grey, who had stood by him throughout. But the attempt to overthrow the Mountnessing conviction, again on ID evidence, failed and Ince wasn't paroled until 1980.

By that time I had established my own way in the criminal world. George was sixty-nine and should have retired, but you can't keep an old dog down. And George still had a couple more jobs in mind.

CHAPTER 15

TO THE END OF CRIME

Tuesday, 22 May 1979. Sunny Southend. The BBC called it the Cockney Costa del Sol, but it wasn't the same since they closed the Kursaal Amusement Park (incidentally, Helen Mirren, the future actress, used to operate rides there). Cinemas were closing down every week as Bingo took over. But it wasn't the slow, agonising death of a seaside town that dominated the headlines in the *Evening Echo* that day. It was something altogether more spectacular.

As a Security Express van pulled up outside Barclays Bank in the pedestrianised precinct along the high street at about half past nine in the morning, a man stepped up to it. He was wearing blue overalls but nobody was much looking at those. They were looking at the big, silver gun in his hand. Now, security blokes wear crash helmets and maybe a bullet-proof vest, but up close and personal, they aren't going to tangle with a bloke carrying an automatic and so it proved.

All this, of course, was in broad daylight with shoppers and passers-by shopping and passing by. The gunman barked at them, in what was obviously a disguised voice, 'Don't interfere and nobody'll get hurt.' And in case they'd missed the point or there was a have-a-go merchant among them, he fired at the pavement. The bullet ricocheted off the concrete, narrowly missing the foot of one of the security guards who had the sense to drop his bag containing £25,000 (£125,000 today). This was quickly in the gunman's hand and thrown into the back of a drag.

Terrified they might have been, but witnesses noted the getaway car. It was a white Granada with a black roof, registration number MXE 11K, and it had been revving up outside the Marley Tile shop. Then it was gone along Queen's Road. The bloke behind the wheel had a Zapata moustache but every other bloke you met in the Seventies had one of those, so not a great help, really.

The villains dumped the Granada in Whitefriars Crescent, Westcliff and hopped into another car. It's a ploy as old as the hills but it works and confuses the shit out of passers-by and the law.

What has the Barclays Security Express raid got to do with me? Well, quite a lot as it happens. Southend was my manor and I'd always had a lot of respect for that old mantra about not shitting on your own doorstep. I lived ten minutes away from the scene of the crime and was working on a building development very close to where the cars were swapped. Oh, and my Uncle George had planned the whole thing.

The Regional Crime Squad was all over this one like a

rash. There had been several similar raids over the previous months. In January, a six-man team had blasted a security van with shotguns at Battlebridge. They'd got £21,000 (£105,000). Four months before that, the same gang had hit a van in Hadleigh, this time snatching £106,000 (£578,000). Things went wrong in Basildon and the mob came away empty handed. And, would you believe, an hour and a half after the Southend job, another Security Express van was hit at Chingford, thirty miles away. Security Express must have thought that somebody out there didn't like them.

DCI Jim Dickinson of Southend CID appealed for witnesses to any and all of these raids. The press referred to the villains as the Chainsaw Gang and the Filth must have had their suspicions as to its makeup. One bloke they pulled over was a minor villain called Stanley Thompson. We hadn't quite got to PACE yet. That piece of legislation, whereby a suspect's rights are protected, wouldn't kick in for another five years, but the enlightened Plod at Southend asked Thompson if he wanted a solicitor.

'Yeah,' he said, right on cue. 'Get me George Stanley.'

Another person of interest (to use a modern, rather silly, phrase) was me. And I was hauled in. Now, I knew my way around police stations and I always heard George's advice buzzing in my head. 'Give 'em zilch and they've got zilch.' Over time, I've seen hard blokes go to pieces when they're in a jail cell. They can't handle all the claustrophobia, the chill, the smell.

DC Nasty sat opposite me in the interview room that looked like it had once been a public lavatory. 'I suppose you want George Stanley as your solicitor, like your friend Mr Thompson.'

'Oh, no, officer,' and I all but fluttered my eyelashes at him. 'I don't need a solicitor because I haven't done anything wrong.' Christ, if I'd been DC Nasty, I'd have splattered me all over the wall. Instead, he let fly with invective, as they call it in court – verbals. 'Like hell you haven't,' he said. 'You're in it up to your neck. We know all about you and your uncle and the houses all over the country. You've been under observation for eighteen months.'

So it was still going on. The shadowing, the watching. On the other hand, it could have been a bluff. 'I can assure you, officers' – I used the plural now to appeal psychologically to DC Nice, also sitting across the table from me – 'I am an honest, hard-working man struggling to bring up a family.'

Part of that sentence was true. I had met Gail at a disco back in 1972 and we'd married in '75. She knew – and knows – nothing of the darker side of my life and as far as my kids were concerned, I was already lavishing all the love on them I'd never got from my own mum and dad.

'Yeah, right.' DC Nasty wasn't falling for it. 'We've got a nice little cell for you, son. You're spending the night.'

'Thank God,' I smiled. 'I can have a kip. You don't know how exhausting the building trade can be.'

So I spent the night. The next day, released without charge, needless to say, I rang George from a phone box in Hockley. 'We need to talk,' I said. 'It's urgent.'

'OK, Lee. Same place, eight o'clock.'

The place was the Sixteen String Jack, a pub near Red Oaks named, appropriately enough, after Jack Rann, the eighteenth-century highwayman. Apparently the flash git used to wear eight ribbons around each knee when holding up coaches and when you're on foot with your hands in the air and this masked bloke is pointing a horse pistol at you, his knees are on a level with your eyes, so they stick in your memory. Along with the horse pistol, of course. We sat in the snug, just a nephew and his uncle out for a quiet drink, sipping single malt.

'Don't you think you should slow down a bit, George?' I said to him. 'It's like the fucking Wild West out there.' I knew that shotguns and automatics weren't George's style and with it all going off so close to home, it was getting a little hairy. I didn't say it at the time, but looking at him, here was a bloke knocking seventy, a time when most people are at home with the slippers on. Was he, maybe, just a little, beginning to lose it?

'Well,' he smiled. 'I have kept the Old Bill busy for some time. Maybe it is time to cool things down a bit.'

I thanked God for that, but there was something else on my mind. 'Robert Mark compiled a list of bent solicitors, George. And you're top of the list.'

George laughed. 'I know all that, Lee,' he said. 'It's sod all to worry about. Now, where were we?'

Robert Mark was a pain in the arse for criminals and criminal lawyers. He was made Commissioner of the Met in '72 and although he'd gone by the time George and I had our little chat in the Sixteen String, what he stood for – rooting out corruption – lived on. He'd been a carpet salesman before he joined the police and did a stint in the elite Phantom (GHQ Liaison) Regiment during the war, rubbing shoulders with people like the actor David Niven. He wrote a book – *In the Office of Constable* – the year before the Southend job in which he gave the excellent advice that the only way to extradite Ronnie Biggs from Brazil was to send Charmian over and Ronnie would be out of there like a rat up a pipe.

I don't know whether George Stanley's name was on Lord Goddard's bent lawyer list back in 1946 – after all, he was still relatively new back then – but I'm bloody sure it was on Robert Mark's in the Seventies. George Stanley doesn't exactly get a mention in Mark's book but he might as well. Lawyers, he says, have a duty to their client, but also to justice and the ethics of their profession (yeah, right!). They must not put forward a defence they know to be false. Even so, time after time, key witnesses disappear, old lags come out with impossibly difficult defences they have been coached to say by their solicitors. False alibis are dreamed up. Fingers are pointed at the police – you framed me, you stitched me up (and of course, in the case of George Ince, there's more than a grain of truth in that).

Mark wrote that some criminal lawyers do very well out of crime. Ongoing results and a lack of scruple draw the hopeless to their door. Most experienced detectives agree that criminal lawyers are more of a problem for society than the clients they represent.

In 1972, Mark was a new broom at the Yard and everybody from the biggest villain to the humblest grass knew that the place was long overdue for a bloody good spring clean. He set up A10, Scotland Yard's first Internal Affairs Department made up of uniformed blokes, and he was good with the press and systematically set about weeding out the corrupt cozzers among the plain-clothes men.

Times, of course, as Bob Dylan had told us in the Sixties, were a-changing and I have no doubt that if a Robert Mark had been on the scene at the time of Eastcastle Street and the Great Train Robbery, half the coppers working those cases would have had their collars felt. They were different times, of course, celebrated on the telly recently in *Life on Mars* in which Robert Glenister is every bent copper of the last hundred years rolled into one.

The focus of this corruption was in the West End, especially in the porn trade out of Soho. The Yard, by definition, has the finest collection of pornography in the world, but it was the various blind eyes and backhanders that Mark took exception to. He put DCI Bert Wickstead, a straight-as-a-die

East End copper, to manage operations and he leaned on a few rotten apples. And they didn't come much more rotten than Commander Kenneth Drury who ran the Flying Squad.

I liked Ken. He was a jolly, roly-poly sort of bloke on George's payroll. He usually appeared in the press with a fag in one hand and a pint in the other. And he didn't give a fuck. He was head of the 'firm within the firm' as the Flying Squad were known and was all that was wrong with it in Robert Mark's eyes. In our eyes, he was nearly all there was right about it. I remember passing him a bung from George in a buff envelope right outside that triangular sign endlessly turning outside the Yard. And I remember having a drink with him in some quiet watering place up West and he said, 'Trying to catch the Sturleys is like smothering your hand in grease and trying to catch an eel in a bucket.'

'That's why they called me Lee, Ken,' I told him. 'Eel backwards.'

He liked that.

But he didn't like it so much when it all came crashing down. In February 1972 the stupid bugger went on holiday to Cyprus. Nothing wrong with that; even a bent copper has to have time off. The thing was the holiday was paid for by the porn king James Humphreys who had gone on the selfsame holiday and met up with a few dodgy friends out there. The *People* got hold of it and splashed it all over the Sundays. Ken's story of course was that Humphreys was a snout and that he (Ken) was hoping to get some lowdown on

Ronnie Biggs – who of course was over 6,500 miles away at the time. He lost his job for that, but Ken was only the tip of the iceberg. Humphreys had kept records in a personal diary in which he named rather juicy names, apart from Ken Drury's. Commander Wallace Virgo, Head of CID, and DCS Bill Moody, head of the Dirty Squad, got a mention too. They all did time on corruption charges; almost an action replay of the trial of the detectives in 1877 that had led to the formation of the CID in the first place.

My most bizarre meeting with Ken Drury happened in '72, just as the shit was about to hit the fan. I had been out with some railway mates in the West End when the car we were driving hit the kerb and we got a punctured tyre. We were all over the limit but I could hold my drink better than the others. I changed the tyre and off we went. Then I realised we were being tailed by a blue Hillman Hunter, an unmarked police car I could recognise streets away. Sure enough, we were pulled over and breathalysed – a new scam then by the law to screw more money out of motorists – then we were off to Streatham nick in separate cells, which seemed a bit heavy for a drink-driving offence. After a while, I was taken to Scotland Yard, or at least that was where I was told I'd be going.

In fact we drove straight past the top cop shop to a little restaurant in Piccadilly and who should be sitting there but Ken Drury. We talked over old times, how we'd been introduced by Tommy Red Face Godfrey who was also involved passing bungs in all directions and he asked me what I was doing running around with amateurs – my mate had some rather nice silverware in the boot of his car that evening.

'There's a lot of interest being taken in you at the moment, Lee,' Ken said, 'and your Uncle George. But it's Ronnie Biggs I'm after. Any help you can give me there would be much appreciated. I'll be honest, I'm under a bit of a spotlight at the Yard at the moment and I could use the brownie points.'

I told him that after George had arranged Biggsy's vanishing act I had no idea where he was and couldn't help.

'This meeting is just a straightener,' he said, 'to warn you what's going on.'

'I appreciate your concern, Ken,' I said. 'I'll pass the word to George and Red Face and they'll square you up.'

'That'll be nice,' he said. 'See you soon, then,' and he buggered off.

'I'll pay for the drinks,' I said, as he disappeared. 'It's the least I can do.'

The least Ken Drury did was eight years. All that was partly down to us.

Throughout 1972, George was becoming increasingly worried about Drury, Virgo and Moody. They were becoming a liability just like the Krays had and George needed to put some distance between him and them. A lawyer from Lincoln's Inn, where George did most of his commissioning for court appearances, gave him the tip-off about Robert Mark's crusade and it was time to act. Over the years, Drury had kept George's name out of things – he was, of course, our man inside the Yard – but that was about to change. The Sturley clock is unfailing – it was time to move on.

A moment of truth arrived for me one Saturday in the summer of 1973. It was the summer of Watergate when Richard Nixon (talking of Promise Land) assured the world there'd be no 'whitewash at the White House'. I had a shopping list from Uncle George to buy up cheap properties in Leytonstone and Forest Gate and the Red Oaks properties were being turned into flats. I was checking the post that morning at 21–23 Broadway, sorting out files as usual, and George and my dad walked in. There was a tension, something in the atmosphere I couldn't quite put my finger on.

Dad said, 'Pop and make a cup of tea, son; George and I want a little chat.' I felt shut out, abandoned, almost. The man with the huge hands I'd barely known as a child was deep in whispered conversation with the man who had once bought me for £500. Neither of them took prisoners. One false move, one stroke pulled and you were out. There was no messing about and no second chances.

I brought in the tea. 'Have a seat, son,' Dad said.

'Your dad and I have been watching you over the years, Lee,' George said. 'We are impressed and we want you to progress.'

What followed was a list of do's and don't's. It was all about the importance of inside information, of keeping schtum, of picking up of unconsidered trifles in pubs, clubs, on street corners. The whole litany of crimes past was trotted out, and I wish to God I'd had a tape-recorder. There were a lot of people, from the Commissioner of the Met to the Postmaster General, to every journalist in and out of Fleet Street who would have given their right arms for what George told me now.

It started off with Dad. 'Remember the scrap iron, son?' he asked, the old charmer's smile creasing his face, 'and that poor bastard Roy Wiggins? And what about Monty Schwarz, eh?'

We all laughed. A mug is a mug and there was no room in any Sturley's heart for sympathy or remorse or regret. 'What you won't remember,' George said, 'is Eastcastle Street.'

'Before my time, George,' I agreed.

'Well, let me fill you in.' And it all came out – the stolen cars, the hiring of Billy Hill for a heist that had his name written all over it. He reeled it off like it was yesterday, so I missed the odd detail and never did find out who the 'GPO' man was who fixed the van alarm.

'But that was just the beginning.' George was in full flow. 'Let me tell you about Brucie and the crime of the century.' And the nitty gritty of the train robbery, the recruitment of Brian Field and McKenna the Ulsterman; it all came out. The one detail I didn't get from George that day was the identity of Biggsy's train driver. He'll always be the one that got away.

'I don't know if you remember those days, Lee,' George said. 'Those ladies that used to turn up here of a Saturday.'

'Vaguely,' I said, looking casual.

'Train robbers' wives.'

'Never!' I said, wondering how long I could con a conner. George laughed.

'You know bloody well who they were,' he said. 'Never let it be said that George Stanley doesn't look after his own.'

Some of it, of course, I knew already. Some of it I had gleaned from snippets of information, hurried conversations at home, here in these offices and at Edith's at Hermitage Court. If the Devil had cast his net at that moment, well, I don't have to paint you a picture.

'We'd like you to carry on when we're gone,' George said. 'Your grandfather would turn in his grave if you didn't follow in his footsteps.'

So that was it. In the eyes of the two greatest conmen of the twentieth century, I had arrived. I was *L'uomo Delinquente*, Criminal Man.

'Well,' George said. 'Now we've got that little matter sorted, shall we have a drink?'

'Too right,' my dad said.

'Make sure it's a large one, George,' was my advice.

So, here we are, six years later, and I'm still sitting in George's company, not in his office but at the Sixteen String Jack. He agreed then that the Southend job was a little too close for comfort. He had hired Thompson, Big Jim Moody, formerly a heavy for the Richardsons south of the river, and he intended to do the usual and defend them. But on this occasion, he passed the job to somebody else; a wise move, I thought.

I always got on well with Jim; he'd often call at Lessers' with George's cut or to get the next bit of vital info for a new job. If you look up Big Jim, say, on Wikipedia, it's got a photo of him as I remember him – square jaw, furrowed face, tattoos. Jim went down for armed robbery but escaped and got across to Gordon Goody's Green Isle. When he came back after several years, he didn't recognise the London he'd left behind. It was all drugs and gentrification and the old-time villains he'd grown up with had all but disappeared. He was shot dead in June 1993 in the Royal Hotel, Hackney. And no one was ever done for it.

'Anyway,' George said to me in the Sixteen String, 'my man in the security system tells me the new alarms and security cameras are in their infancy. Have a look at your mug on one of those screens and you'll look like a fucking Martian. At the moment, they can be bypassed, but we can't hang about, because the technology's bound to improve.' He came out with all the clichés about striking while the iron was hot and making hay while the sun shines.

'I've had a whisper from my man in the City,' he said, his eyes sparkling as they always did when there was money to be made. 'There are a couple of heists that can be pulled off and they'll need a bit of finance.'

Out of this tip-off came the Security Express job and Brinks-Mat. In April 1983 a gang of fifteen blokes wearing black smashed their way into the Security Express HQ (not them again!) in Shoreditch. As the staff arrived, they were effectively held at gunpoint and one of the guards had petrol poured over him. While one of the gang toyed dangerously with a lighter, one of the near-hysterical employees blabbed the combination of the safe, much to the relief of the petrol-soaked guard. It took the team five hours, but they netted nearly £6 million (£18.5 million today). Ronnie Knight, the husband of the *Carry On* star Barbara Windsor, gave himself up twelve years later and admitted handling £314,813 stolen from the Shoreditch job. An even bigger fish was Freddie Foreman, who was extradited from Spain in 1989 to face the music. Before the raid, Freddie had £75 in his bank account; after it, £360,000. All in all, only £2 million of the £6 million was ever recovered. As the judge at the trial of Terry Perkins and Johnny Knight for the robbery was to say, 'Other guilty men have not been caught.' He got that right – one of them was washing his dirty laundry in private at Pedlar's Folly.

Seven months after the Security Express, a gang hit Heathrow again. This time the takings, in gold ingots, were through the roof, making the train robbery look like pocket money.

Just as George had passed the necessary inside info to persons who shall remain nameless for the Security Express job, so he did for Brinks-Mat. There were similarities between the two raids – the petrol dousing and threat of immolation for instance – and there were curious re-echoes of earlier crimes too. The scene was not a hundred miles away from George's BOAC hit involving Buster Edwards, Gordon Goody and Roy James. The man who worked out the logistics was Brian Robinson, known as 'the Colonel' – a moniker Ronnie Kray liked to use for himself and the same self-image (take away a rank) that Bruce Reynolds had. There was, of course, an insider – security guard Anthony Black – but one who was daft enough to be there on the day. And there was even a bent solicitor, Michael Relton, up to his hocks in money laundering.

On 26 November 1983, a gang led by Mickey McAvoy used pass keys provided by Black to get into the Brinks-Mat warehouse on the Heathrow Airport trading estate. Guards were coshed, soaked in petrol, threatened with having their bollocks removed – all of it a million miles from the sort of thing Uncle George would have had in mind. Somewhere, George's info had been woefully short of the mark. He had expected up to £2 million, but here was a gleaming £26 million-worth of gold – the sort of stuff the young Freddie Foreman used to go weak at the knees over when he was a kid.

Naturally, the press had a field day with this one. It was another Great Train Robbery, more so in terms of cash taken. But McAvoy and Co. lacked the charisma of Brucie and the boys, and the inside man, the weak link, cracked almost at once. Robinson and McAvoy got twenty-five years each. But most of the gold was never found. Disposing of folding was a problem enough for George and his laundry business back in the Sixties but tons of high-purity gold was an alto-gether different task. Garth Chappell, managing director of a bullion company, got ten years. Another defendant, Brian Resner, got nine. Kenneth Noye, a glamorous heavy who had been acquitted of killing an undercover copper in the grounds of his home, got fourteen.

George had got his cut early on, as he had from the Security Express, in the form of some very expensive finder's fees – I remember picking up weekly cash payments from Edith's; £1,000 wrapped in Allied Irish Bank paper – and it was not, of course, in gold, so there was little chance of it all coming back to bite him in the arse. Inevitably, his interest, as he followed the press coverage of the case and listened to the legal tittle-tattle of his colleagues, was in the solicitor Michael Relton. He had an office in Verney Road, near the Old Kent Road, and he seemed cocksure and naive all at the same time. In fact if you could roll Brian Field and John Wheater into one, you'd end up with Michael Relton.

DS Tony Curtis (no relation) grilled the man and knew he had a rabbit in the headlights. Relton stalled and bluffed, but he looked guilty as hell. His car boot contained all the finan-cial details of the heist laundering business – the sort of details that never left Uncle George's safe. There were cash transactions and property deals going back over two years, all of which screamed to the Met and, later, the world, Yes, I'm the man you want. The police put him in a cell and he went to pieces. George must have chortled to himself later when it turned out that Relton had bought up the ex-Cheltenham Ladies' College and was busy turning it into flats exactly as he'd bought the old school in Hastings and had done the same – how history repeats itself!

In fact Relton could have been held up by Uncle George as an example of how *not* to be a bent solicitor. He was persuaded by his own counsel, in the summer of 1988, to plead not guilty. That meant his only defence was that the police had made everything up against him. Unfortunately, his statements were written in his own handwriting and signed by him, so the alleged crime of verballing was thrown out as pure bollocks. Relton got twelve years.

Despite various attempts over the years to trace it, most of the Brinks-Mat gold was never recovered. So next time you're out on the town or at a posh do, have a close look at the bling your fellow guests are flashing; it's probably from Brinks-Mat. On the other hand, you might own some yourself ...

Maurice Lesser retired from the legal rat race in 1982. In that year, George Stanley celebrated his seventy-first birthday. Did he slow down? Take the obvious opportunity to hang up his account books and take a well-earned retirement? Did he fuck. The whole world of the corner game and Promise Land was in his blood and he could no more give that up than breathing. Witness, the Case of the Missing Address Book.

George was still at Lesser's at the time and I'd gone to 21–23 Broadway on the Saturday after my birthday, which would make it October either 1980 or '81. Things weren't going well for Uncle. He'd had a row with Marjorie over Edith (one of many, as it turned out) but he was in a flat spin at the office. I offered him a soothing cup of tea.

'Fuck the tea, Lee,' he snapped. 'I've lost my little red book of contacts. Can you drive back to Red Oaks and check the garage and the driveway? I'll phone Edith.'

So off I went and sure enough, there it was, a little red book, not much bigger than Chairman Mao's but *so* much more valuable. It was lying on the gravel near the garage doors and obviously, with his brain still seething over the row with Marjorie, he'd dropped it. I used the phone in the village to tell him I'd got it and I've never heard a man so grateful in my life. When I got back to the Broadway, George was in full flight briefing a client and telling him how to shaft Prosecuting Counsel on the stand.

When he'd gone, George was gushing. 'Thank God, Lee, you saved the day. This book is the foundation of my whole business.'

I knew that because I'd taken a peek inside. There were the Hellers, Harry Isaacs, Tommy Red Face Godfrey, Electric Les Aldridge, people high and low who George had dealings with. There were addresses and phone numbers of bank managers, car dealers, finance companies, scrap merchants, solicitors, barristers, policemen. Nothing odd about that, you might think, except that I knew why this little list was worth millions to George. Every one of them was bent, on the take, susceptible, shall we say? They were George's network as we'd call it today, his contacts, his inside men. It was a Who's Who of the criminal fraternity whose names only appeared tangentially, if at all, in police files. If I've made one mistake in my life, it was when I didn't deny finding the book, or at least I should have photocopied the contents before handing it back. Not only was it the hard evidence that would have brought down George Stanley but, had I been of the black-mailing persuasion, I'd be a multi-millionaire today. Or dead and buried. A grateful George bunged me £50 from his safe.

The retirement of Maurice Lesser was a change of direction for Uncle George and for me too. He took his little book and crossed the river, to become Managing Clerk for Ralph Haeems. And when he went, I went with him. The new office in Peckham was the same – Spartan, no-nonsense furniture and a very large safe.

Haeems and George went way back. I liked Ralph. Like Maurice, he was a gent, always impeccably turned out and polite. Old school. Born in Bombay to Jewish parents, he was always a bit of an outsider on the legal circuit, that Old Boy network where, if you're not public school and Oxbridge, you're not quite one of us. Like George, he worked like Hell and knew his stuff. Like George, his reputation was passed by word of mouth among the criminal fraternity. George had given him the Krays in 1969 and he defended George Ince over the Mountnessing Raid, so that put him beyond the pale as far as polite society was concerned.

If you read Ralph's obituary (he died in 2005) you'll find he got to London in the Fifties with £4 in his pocket. He spent this on Scotch and fags. His first lodgings were in Mansell Street, Whitechapel, where he worked with Manny Fryde, a clerk to Sampson & Co near the Bailey. Sampson's defended Roy James and Charlie Wilson over the train robbery. When Fryde, who himself became a solicitor, retired, Ralph took over his role at Sampson's then set up in business for himself in 9 Blenheim Grove, Peckham. He was superstitious and the number nine was very important to him. By the time George joined him he had an office at 9 Temple Chambers in the heart of legal-land.

Ralph disapproved of long hair and enforced a rigid dress code in his offices. He would not let his people do anything he wouldn't and the *Guardian* obituary says, 'He commanded affection and loyalty; two of his managing clerks remained with him until well into their eighties.' One of them was Uncle George. In the early Eighties, the government issued a statement that cutbacks were necessary in the legal aid system because of a money shortfall. The rumour went round London that that was because George Stanley and Ralph Haeems had had it all!

*

If that day in George's old office when my dad and uncle had a word with me was a rite of passage, what happened outside Pedlar's Folly was another coming of age. It was the summer of 1992. George was eighty-one and still working and he'd bought some property at Westcliff; I moved into one flat with Gail and the kids. One morning he came to see how the work was going and said, 'Lee, I've made provision for you in my will.' I was touched and told him to stop talking rubbish. He was going to live forever. A few days later he sent me a letter telling me he'd bought the property out from under me and I had to get out. Sure enough, he posted the eviction notice. Gail and I moved out and she was worried. She told me not to do anything silly in regard to Uncle George. 'That's not good enough,' I told her and drove to Pedlar's Folly.

I parked beyond the cricket ground and shinned up the wall. George's garage was open, with a petrol can for his lawn mowers just inside. I poured the stuff liberally into the seat wells and boot of his unlocked Toyota Carina and threw in a match. By the time the fire engines were hurtling through the evening glow (caused by me) I was sitting outside a pub in Loughton, enjoying a Scotch.

George had spent his entire life, as had my dad, conning people and treating them like shit. But I should have been different; I was family. I'd been shafted by Mum and Dad all my life, but Uncle George was different. Here he was, talking about wills one moment and how I was the son he never had and the next, he was putting my young family on the street.

The next thing I knew, a local heavy turned up. I'd known this bloke for years and we discussed the problem, man to man. George had asked him to put the frighteners on me, but when I told him the score, he agreed with me. 'Carry on what you're doing,' he said.

It was showdown time. Like George and my dad, I am not a man of violence, but after all the years of loyalty I'd given my uncle, this kick in the teeth could not go unavenged. I borrowed a rat gun from a local farmer's wife I knew and went down to the OK Corral at Hermitage Court. It was a sawn-off and I must admit, not a typical farmer's wife's weapon! The stock and barrel had been shortened so that it could be used one-handed like a pistol.

George was walking up to Edith's door that morning and I kicked his arse before jamming both barrels up his nose. 'Listen,' I said to him. 'You fuck everyone you come into contact with, but you ain't fucking me.' I pushed him inside where a white-faced Edith just stood there like a ghost.

'Now, George,' I said. 'Tell Edith to get me £20k from the safe for the upset you've caused my wife and children.'

'This is daylight robbery,' George said, his hands still in the air like so many hijacks.

'Well, you'd know, George,' I told him. 'You've organised so many.'

In a way it was payback time not just for me but for everybody who had ever been shafted by George Stanley – and believe me, the list was long. What George had in me was a tiger by the tail. And on that day in the summer of '92, he let go. Edith passed me the bundles and I uncocked the gun.

'Any ideas, George,' I said before I left, 'and the bloke you paid to do me will be round here to earn £5,000 of this. Do we understand each other?'

We did. And nobody ever mentioned it again.

PAYBACK

Did I really need to torch George's garage and stick a shotgun up his nose? Maybe not, but you have to see it all in context. What I have tried to do in these pages is to paint a portrait of a master criminal, a man who was clever enough to get away with daylight robbery over and over again. His name is almost entirely missing from the annals of crime, which is evidence of his brilliance and also, I suppose, luck.

A lot of other stuff was going on for me which I haven't shared with you. Some of it is personal and most of it concerns my family. I don't want this to be a misery memoir, so I'll spare you the details. My brothers, John, Arthur and Victor, drank themselves to death long before their time and while I don't want to dwell on any of that, the waste of their lives took its toll on me too and was going on while George was slapping his eviction notice on my flat. Yes, I probably over-reacted, but I had my reasons.

Lennie was the saddest of all. He'd been in Runwell Hospital more or less ever since that terrible night in 1964 when Andy

Hempstead had gone for him with the coal hammer. I visited him every week until his death in 1998. Sometimes we'd laugh over old times. Other times he didn't know who I was and told me to fuck off. He was usually high as a kite on the medication they gave him and he died in my arms when his kidneys finally packed in.

My dad had gone three years earlier. Mum rang me on Christmas Eve to say he was in pain. He wore a support collar – ironic, that. He had a pain in the neck and he'd been a pain in mine for thirty-four years. Blood tests followed and he was diagnosed with cancer of the spine. The doctor told me he had days to live.

We were going through some boxes a couple of days later and he found a Bible. He threw it on the floor and said, 'Go and burn this, Lee. Jimmy Christ ain't going to help either of us.' When he went into hospital for the last time, the Sturley boys were around his bed. Nobody wanted to be there and the others kept buggering off for a drink. So I was on my own with him when the Deaconess of Chelmsford arrived. Dad was delirious now, slipping in and out of consciousness. He saw the large brass cross around the Deaconess's neck and said to her, 'There's something in that, isn't there?' 'Oh, yes,' she smiled. 'There is.' She didn't have to know he was referring to the gold and its street value. Was it the morphine? Or had Arthur Sturley at last come face to face with God? I was knackered, working every day and staying up nights with the old man, so I rubbed my tired eyes. Dad saw this and said, 'None of that, son.'

'Oh, no, Dad,' I said. 'You'll get no tears from me.'

By the time my brothers got back, he was dead.

I drove over to Mum's to break the bad news. 'Thank God for that,' she said. 'Perhaps now I can have peace.'

Uncle George came over and sat with us. I can remember him shaking his head. 'What a waste,' he said. 'Arthur was so talented. He's got through more money than I'll ever see.' He left £1,000 for the funeral and Mum's eyes lit up when she saw it. After he'd gone, she said, 'Half each, son?'

'You'll get no Bingo money from me,' I said. She didn't talk to me for eighteen months.

My brother John was hit with pneumonia over the August Bank Holiday in 1987. He'd been in the hooky antiques trade, leaving Lovejoy looking like an amateur. He was still dealing when he collapsed in a client's house. I got him back to Mum's and put him to bed. He had an empty vodka bottle in every pocket of his jacket and was unconscious by the time the ambulance arrived. By the time he reached Southend General he was dead. He was forty-five. Not one of his friends came to his funeral.

The next day I went to Mum's where John had been living. Virtually her first question was 'What have you done with the gear you picked up with Johnny?' She was talking about the antiques he'd been trying to collect from Hoddesdon on the day he collapsed. I told her it was in the lock-up.

'Well,' she said, 'when you sell it, I want his half.'

I couldn't believe what I was hearing. 'I tell you what,

Mum,' I said, barely able to control my temper. 'I will sell it and you can have the lot, all right?'

She then got all wistful. 'Why do you think John done this to himself? Arthur and Victor will follow in his footsteps; you mark my words.'

Suddenly there was no point in bottling everything up any more. Dad was dead and two of my brothers. I had my own family, my girls and my boy, and I wanted all this to go away.

'You're responsible,' I told her. 'You and Dad. I'd grow old listing the ways you two shafted your own children over the years. You didn't give us a chance. You know what Lennie said to me when I was a kid and too young to understand? He said "We've got rubbish parents, sonny boy. Get away from them as soon as you can." Well, it's a bit late maybe, but I'm taking that advice now.'

I threw her a bundle of notes I had in my pocket and walked out. I never spoke to her again. Mum died peacefully in her sleep in 1995. The good die young, they say. She was eighty-nine.

Before Arthur went, pretty well pickled in brandy, I made the mistake of mentioning to him that I was thinking of writing a book about George Stanley, the Mr Big of so many crime capers. Needless to say, George got to hear about it and asked for a meet at the Halfway House on the A127 near Brentwood. We hadn't seen each other since the rat gun incident and he didn't know whether I'd show up.

'Lee,' George said as I walked in, 'you're unarmed.'

'No, I'm not,' I laughed. 'Don't be silly. I've got this book. That's a sawn-off and a half, isn't it?'

George tried to act casual. 'Who's seen it?' he asked, like he was asking the time.

'Nobody,' I told him. 'Yet.'

'It's a shame we fell out, Lee,' George was buying. 'We had a good business relationship over the years.'

'Oh, we did, George,' I agreed. 'All one fucking way – yours.'

'Look, Lee,' he was grimly serious. 'This book can't come out. It will kill Marjorie. Like your wife, she knows nothing about any of this.'

I sipped my Scotch and let him stew.

'How much do you want not to write this while Marjorie is alive?'

I hadn't moved.

'Speak to me,' he said. 'How about five grand?'

'Give me ten,' I said, 'and I'll stall things.'

He took a sip and that reminded me. 'By the way,' I said, 'don't give Arthur any money. He just pisses it up the wall.'

'He's a nice bloke, Lee,' George said. 'I slipped him five grand the other day.'

'Well,' I said. 'That's another victim of George Stanley. You really don't give a fuck, do you?'

We met up regularly after that and each time I walked away with a cheque for my silence.

*

Edith, the love of George's life, died in 1995. George was heartbroken. He was a lost soul, having to spend all his time with Marjorie who he was growing to tolerate less and less. George was eighty-four now and had finally abandoned the law. He still had his contacts and a finger in a lot of pies but it could never be the same. The crime scene and technology had moved on and left George Stanley standing in the dust of drive-by shootings and drugs-related heists. It was a world he could barely understand.

'How do you do it, Lee?' he asked me one day at a hostelry where once old villains used to drink. 'You've lost most of your family, but you've still got this smile on your face. What keeps you going?'

'My kids,' I told him, 'and the knowledge that I'm going to write a book about you one day. And about Dad. And about me and how we all got away with what we did.'

He smiled. 'They were good times, Lee,' he said.

So many of them have gone now, like scenes fading in a film. George and I talked a lot about them in the last months of his life. And others have gone since. William Boal, the train robber who was not a robber, was the first to go, in prison in 1970, of a brain tumour. Roy James got out five years later and tried to return to the motor-racing circuit, but he broke his leg at Silverstone and it never really happened for him. In March 1994 he attacked his wife and father-in-law and went down for two years. Soon after his release he died of a heart attack, in August 1997. He was sixty-one. Big Jim Hussey, out in the same year as James, moved to Spain and ran a bar there. On his deathbed in November 2012 he apparently admitted that it was him who coshed Jack Mills, the train driver, who himself had died of leukaemia years earlier. Jack Mills' son didn't believe it and neither did anybody else. Brian Field, who tried so hard to be George Stanley but didn't have the talent, drove his Porsche head on into traffic in May 1979.

David Whitby, Mills' fireman on the Up Special night, died of a heart attack in January 1972. He was thirty-four. Buster Edwards, florist and train robber, hanged himself in a garage at Waterloo, near his flower stall, in November 1994. Tommy Butler, the grey fox who had put off his retirement to catch the train robbers, died of cancer two years before Whitby. His funeral was the Yard's version of an East End gangland one, with hundreds of coppers crammed into St Margaret's church, Westminster, to see him off. Charlie Wilson, sprung unceremoniously all those years ago from Winson Green, was shot dead by a hit man on a motorbike in April 1990 in his swimming pool in Marbella. Ronnie Biggs, the one who got away, came back to the UK in 2001 to serve out his time. A shambling wreck, unable to speak after several strokes, they wheeled him out to attend Bruce Reynolds' funeral at St Bartholomew's Church in the City. Freddie Foreman was there too, as was a small coterie of old-time villains. Biggs waved two fingers at the press, a prat to the end.

*

In May 2007 an elderly couple was making their steady way around the Meadows Shopping Centre in Chelmsford. The town has a long history – they hanged witches here in the sixteenth century – but, seen one twenty-first-century shopping centre, seen them all and the couple could have been anywhere. They were George Stanley, retired solicitors' clerk, of Pedlar's Folly, Red Oaks, Theydon Bois, and his wife Marjorie, knee high to a grasshopper. Suddenly, George staggered and fell, his face an ashy grey. Passers-by were on their mobiles in an instant and he was rushed to hospital. Here he had a massive stroke and died. He was ninety-seven. Authors Russell-Pavier and Richards have George Stanley dying in a car crash, but that was too spectacular for Uncle George. As it was, he wouldn't have liked all the fuss and attention, the flashing lights and wail of the ambulance; it would draw too much attention to him.

Marjorie rang me to break the news and she said something which I found strange at the time but which was probably right – 'Your teacher has died.'

Few people attended George's cremation the following week; he had outlived most of the people he knew. His ashes, like Edith's, were scattered as he wished; I saw to that. Somebody had suggested a sod off big stone, but that wasn't George's style. I saw to that. Ashes were the order of the day at George's passing. As soon as she had a moment to herself,

Marjorie burned all his papers, and any photos of him; everything up to and including that little red book. I don't think she was doing it to cover his tracks for him, now it was too late to matter. I think it was because he had led her such a life, one way or another, she just wanted to get rid of as much of George Stanley as she decently could. Whenever anyone is found guilty of a crime and he has a wife, the first thing the media says is 'she must have known'. Not Marjorie. She wrote to me later telling me what a ghastly life she had led with George and how that 'German Jew' (Edith) had ruined her life.

For anybody interested in the millions, in today's terms, that George Stanley made, I have a copy of his will. His executors were Peter Gerber, solicitor, of Feltons, March Wall, London and Robert Brewer, accountant, of Station Road, Chingford. Various Sturleys received sums of money including one who was put through law school and he hadn't forgotten his secretary, Joyce Nye. He gave £300,000 to Whipps Cross Hospital and of course there was a sum set aside for Marjorie. He had made this will in April 2003 and Maurice Lesser had signed it as a witness. Did I get a mention? Of course not. And the man who had made millions left less than £180,000. But all that was on paper. As he told Marjorie a few months before he died, 'If you're going to leave anybody any money, give it to them before you go. The taxman's not on my list of nearest and dearest.' And that's exactly what she did, giving it away like a woman with six arms. Freddie Foreman got a whack for his loyalty over the years. The *actual* value of George Stanley's estate was over £4 million which did not necessarily include various properties which he had sold seven or eight times over, without his name appearing on any dotted line. No, there's no paper trail. There's no hard evidence that George Stanley was richer than God for most of his life. And that's exactly how he planned it. Remember those words from the Post Office Investigation Branch back in 1963 – 'The actual part he was called upon to play is not known'? Bloody right. Not bad for a solicitor's clerk from the East End.

Did I follow in the footsteps of George Stanley and Arthur Sturley, two of the greatest conmen ever to come out of the East End? Did I follow a life of crime? That is another story ...

'You know all those stories about Mr Big ...' Gordon Goody said on a television programme in June 2001, and went on to deny that such a person ever existed.

'The original idea of a mail train robbery was thought out by a highly intelligent man who was (and still is) an uncrowned intellectual king of the underworld ... Technically, I suppose, he is in the clear.' So wrote Peta Fordham in *The Robbers' Tale* fifty years ago. And unwittingly, she knew the man very well.

The uncrowned intellectual king of the underworld. Not a bad epitaph and one that is all the more poignant because George Stanley never made any such claim. Unlike the Jack Spots and the Billy Hills, the Krays and the lesser fry who have come and gone, George Albert Stanley calmly made his criminal presence felt and left almost no trace behind. His invaluable advice to two generations of criminals saved many people from jug. His organisation of the Eastcastle Street job, the BOAC Heathrow heist, the Great Train Robbery, the Mountnessing bullion raid, Security Express and the vital information he passed on to the relevant parties for Brinks-Mat means that he was directly responsible for not one, but at least *three* crimes of the century. He laundered more money than most of us will see in a lifetime and he got away with it. They don't come much bigger than that.

And as for the book I promised I'd write one day, the one George Stanley paid me extremely well not to write … You've just read it.

ACKNOWLEDGEMENTS

My thanks to my agent Andrew Lownie and all the team at Ebury for their hard work on this project.

And to my kids – Emma, Kate, Amy and my son Jack – who have been my rock; never give up. Dad